Peak Oil, Climate Change, and the Limits to China's Economic Growth

T0303949

This book studies the limits imposed by the depletion of fossil fuels and the requirements of climate stabilization on economic growth with a focus on China. The book intends to examine the potentials of various energy resources, including oil, natural gas, coal, nuclear, wind, solar, and other renewables, as well as energy efficiency. Unlike many other books on the subject, this book intends to argue that, despite the large potentials of renewable energies and energy efficiency, economic growth eventually will have to be brought to an end as China and the world undertake the transition from fossil fuels to renewable energies.

China is at the center of global energy contradictions. Minqi Li argues that in one or two decades, economic, social, and environmental crises will converge in China, leading to the demise of China's existing social system. How China's crises can be resolved may determine not only China's but also the world's future.

This book will consider energy development in the broader context of economic and social changes, especially the historical dynamics of the capitalist world system. Historical lessons of capitalism and socialism will be discussed. The book will evaluate the implications of ecological limits to growth on the economic system and argue that the existing capitalist system is fundamentally incompatible with ecological sustainability.

Minqi Li is Associate Professor in the Department of Economics at the University of Utah, USA.

Routledge studies in ecological economics

Tables

Preface

In my earlier book, *The Rise of China and the Demise of the Capitalist World Economy* (Pluto Press and Monthly Review Press, 2009), I argued that the capitalist world system had entered into a structural crisis that could no longer be resolved within the system's own framework. Capitalism is a historical system that can function only under certain historical conditions. With the decline of the US hegemonic power, the rising challenges from the non-western working classes, and the approaching of global ecological collapse, the historical conditions required for capitalism can no longer be reproduced.

This book continues the earlier project by exploring the energy limits to economic growth. Being the world's largest energy consumer and the largest greenhouse gas emitter, China is at the center of the global energy contradictions. China's rapid economic growth has generated massive demands for coal, oil, and natural gas. China is set to overtake the United States to become the world's largest oil importer in a few years. On the other hand, world oil supply has struggled to keep pace with the demand.

How soon world oil production will peak remains controversial. Based on the currently available information, this book projects that world oil production will peak in the 2030s and total fossil fuel production will peak before the mid-twenty-first century. What is certain is that fossil fuels are nonrenewable resources and the consumption of fossil fuels generates greenhouse gas emissions that threaten to bring about global climate catastrophes. If future fossil fuel consumption turns out to be greater than is projected in this book, the future of humanity will be nothing but dire.

With total fossil fuel production peaking before the mid-twenty-first century, the cumulative carbon dioxide emissions over the century will be sufficient to bring about long-term global warming of between four and eight degrees Celsius, which may eventually lead to sea level rises of 75 meters, make much of the world uninhabitable, and cause a catastrophic decline in the global population.

Unfortunately, for all practical purposes, it is no longer possible to limit global warming to less than two degrees compared to the pre-industrial time, a safe limit recommended by climate scientists. The best the world can hope for is to limit global warming to no more than three to six degrees, and that can only be achieved if the global economy undergoes a transition to the end of growth as soon as possible.

Over the past five years, China has contributed to about four-fifths of the increase in global carbon dioxide emissions. Without a fundamental decarbonization of the Chinese economy, there will be virtually no chance of the world achieving reasonable climate stabilization that is consistent with the survival of human civilization. In this book, I argue that, in one or two decades, economic, social, and environmental crises will converge in China, leading to the demise of China's existing social system. How China's crises can be resolved will help to determine not only China's but also the world's future.

My own intellectual perspective derives primarily from Marx and the world system approach. From Karl Marx and Immanuel Wallerstein, I learned the concept of capitalism as a system based on "endless accumulation of capital." Capitalism is therefore fundamentally incompatible with the basic ecological requirement of "limits to growth."

I started paying attention to "peak oil" in 2003, when I was teaching political science at York University in Toronto. I drew inspiration from popular writers such as Richard Heinberg and James Kuntsler. Since 2006, I have taught economics at the University of Utah and written a number of academic papers on peak oil and climate change. In November 2011, I was invited to give a talk at the annual conference of the Association for the Study of Peak Oil and Gas (ASPO) in Washington, DC, where I met with Professor Kjell Aleklett and several other leading peak oil experts. For my current book, I benefitted from Professor Aleklett's recent research summarized in his book: *Peeking at Peak Oil* (Springer, 2012).

For years, I have paid close attention to Dr. James Hansen's works on climate change. I read several of his scientific papers as well as his book: *Storms of My Grandchildren: The Truth about the Coming Climate Catastrophe and Our Last Chance to Save Humanity* (Bloomsbury, 2010). From Dr. Hansen, I learned about the importance of "climate sensitivity" (the degree of global warming in response to doubling of atmospheric greenhouse gases) and deepened my understanding of many basic concepts in climate change.

This book relates peak oil and climate change to the Chinese economy. In addition to Marxist political economy, my economic thinking is influenced by the post-Keynesian tradition, especially the works by the late Hyman Minsky, who understood that the capitalist economic system was fundamentally unstable. I would go one step further to argue that a fundamentally unstable system cannot be stabilized. Moreover, a fundamentally unsustainable economic system cannot be made sustainable.

Since 2006, I have often benefitted from intellectual exchanges and professional support provided by my colleagues at the Economics Department of the University of Utah. In particular, I have drawn intellectual inspiration from Dr. Hans Ehrbar, who has as strong a commitment as I have (if not stronger) to the cause of ecological sustainability and socialism.

1   Peak oil, climate change, and China

Capitalism is a historically unique system driven by the pursuit of endless economic growth. In a modern capitalist society, periods of rapid economic growth are associated with expanding employment, rising living standards, declining social conflicts, and stable political systems. Periods of economic stagnation or decline are characterized by shrinking employment, falling living standards, growing social conflicts, and political instability. In the long run, capitalism cannot function and reproduce itself without growth. But can economic growth be sustained indefinitely? In fact, can humanity survive the consequences of infinite economic growth?

Modern economic growth, or systematic economic growth that brings about fundamental transformation to people's conditions of life in every one or two generations, was unknown to humanity until about two centuries ago. According to Angus Maddison (2010), who compiled the world's most authoritative data on historical economic statistics, world population grew slowly, from 230 million to 270 million, from AD 1 to 1000 (an increase of 40 million over 1,000 years). World population increased to 440 million by 1500 (an increase of 170 million over 500 years), to 1,040 million by 1820 (an increase of 600 million over 320 years), and to 6.1 billion by 2000 (an increase of five billion over 180 years). World economic output barely changed from AD 1 to 1000. It doubled from 1000 to 1500, tripled from 1500 to 1820, and increased by more than 50 times from 1820 to 2000.

The rapid expansion of world population and economic output over the past two centuries has been made possible by the massive growth of fossil fuel consumption. Without coal, there would have been no industrial revolution. Coal, oil, and natural gas have made possible the successive technological revolutions that have taken place since the nineteenth century.

But fossil fuels are nonrenewable resources and will eventually be depleted. Alternative energy resources exist in the form of nuclear and renewable energies (such as wind, solar, and biomass). But can the alternative energies replace fossil fuels on a sufficiently large scale to sustain the current and future global material consumption? Can the alternative energies keep expanding to sustain an ever-growing global economy? What are the economic and technological obstacles? Are the "renewable energies" also subject to the limits of resources and ecological constraints?

The consumption of fossil fuels results in the emission of carbon dioxide and other greenhouse gases. The accumulation of greenhouse gases in the atmosphere has led to rising global temperatures and threatens to bring about unprecedented ecological catastrophes. The survival of the global ecological system and the future of human civilization are at stake.

Climate stabilization, in a manner that is consistent with the preservation of civilization as we know it, requires drastic reductions of carbon dioxide emissions. However, historically, world economic growth has been closely linked to fossil fuel consumption and carbon dioxide emissions. Figure 1.1 shows the historical relationship between the world economic output and carbon dioxide emissions from fossil fuels burning from 1820 to 2012. Since 1820, world carbon dioxide emissions have increased by about 700 times.

Is it conceivable that, as the world economic output continues to skyrocket toward infinity, world carbon dioxide emissions would nevertheless manage a sharp U-turn, starting to decline soon and declining rapidly in the coming decades? Or will the required reductions of carbon dioxide emissions and fossil fuel consumption necessitate the end of economic growth, if not absolute contraction of the global economy?

The answers to these questions to a large extent depend on what will happen to China in the coming decades. In Figure 1.1, the growth of world carbon dioxide emissions accelerated in the early twenty-first century. The acceleration was due largely to China's rapid industrialization and the rise of China as a global economic power. It is safe to say that, without a fundamental decarbonization of the Chinese economy, there will be virtually no chance for humanity to achieve reasonable climate stabilization—that is, climate stabilization consistent with the preservation of civilization.

However, a decarbonization of the Chinese economy is likely to require not only major technical changes but also fundamental social and political transformations. This book contends that the requirements of climate stabilization and energy sustainability will impose insurmountable limits on both Chinese and global economic growth. Sooner or later, both China and the world will have to adapt to a steady-state economy or an economy consistent with zero economic growth. This book further argues that the current capitalist system is fundamentally incompatible with an economy based on zero economic growth. In this sense, an alternative social system

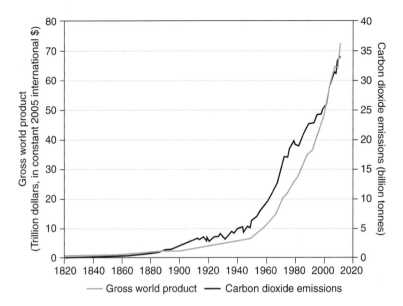

Figure 1.1 World economic output and carbon dioxide emissions from fossil fuels
burning (1820–2012) (sources: Gross world product in constant 1990
international dollars from 1820 to 1980 is from Maddison (2010), converted to gross world product in constant 2005 international dollars by
the author. Gross world product in constant 2005 international dollars
from 1980 to 2011 is from the World Bank (2013), updated to 2012
using world economic growth rates from International Monetary
Fund's *World Economic Outlook* (IMF 2013). Carbon dioxide emissions from fossil fuels burning from 1820 to 1965 are from EPI
(2012a). Carbon dioxide emissions from fossil fuels burning from 1965
to 2012 are from BP (2013)).

is not only possible but also inevitable, were human civilization to survive
the demise of capitalism.

Capitalism and accumulation of capital

Immanuel Wallerstein, the leading world system theorist, defined capitalism as a historical system based on "the endless accumulation of capital"
(Wallerstein 1974). Among many different definitions of capitalism, this is
probably the one that best captures the essential difference between capitalism and the previous historical systems.

For any human society to function and develop, material production has
to take place. Natural resources have to be exploited and transformed by

human labor into useful goods and services to meet certain human needs and desires. A society's total product is the total amount of goods and services produced over a certain period of time. Out of a society's total product, a portion has to be committed to the replacement of various means of production (such as raw materials, tools, and machines) used up during the production. Another portion has to be committed to the population's basic needs (what constitutes people's basic needs may vary depending on historical and societal conditions). If, after subtracting what is required to replace the means of production used up and to meet the population's basic needs, there are still some goods and services left, then the remaining part of the total product is known as the "surplus product." A society's basic character, to a large extent, depends on how the surplus product is produced, appropriated, and used.

Table 1.1 illustrates the relationship between a society's total product and its components.

For much of early human history, the levels of material production were barely sufficient to meet the population's subsistence. There was little or no surplus product. With the rise of agriculture, a sizeable surplus product began to be produced and early civilizations emerged in different parts of the world between 10,000 and 7,000 years ago.

Since the beginning of civilization, various human societies have been divided into different and often antagonistic social classes. In various pre-capitalist societies, the great majority of the population (such as peasants and slaves) did the basic productive work, producing the society's total product, but only received a portion that was barely sufficient for their subsistence. The surplus product was concentrated in the hands of a small group of elites (such as kings, aristocrats, feudal lords, and slave owners). It was used for the elites' luxury consumption, certain public functions (such as maintaining agricultural infrastructure and storage), and a variety of wasteful activities (such as military conquests and the building of imperial tombs).

In the pre-capitalist societies, the ruling elites were primarily interested in the "use values" of the surplus product. That is, they were principally concerned with the physical usefulness of the surplus product in order to meet certain needs or desires directly. Money existed and, in some

Table 1.1 A society's surplus product and total product

Society's Total Product
Surplus Product
Population's Basic Needs
Replacement of Means of Production Used Up

---

societies, monetary transactions were quite substantial (such as in the Roman Empire, the Arabic Empire, the Ottoman Empire, and China's Song Dynasty and Ming Dynasty). But, by and large, money and market relations did not dominate the pre-capitalist economies.

Because the pre-capitalist ruling elites were primarily interested in the surplus product's direct physical usefulness, the surplus product was almost entirely consumed. There was little left to be used for the expansion of production capacity or technological innovation. As a result, both the population and the economic output grew very slowly, if they grew at all.

Under capitalism, virtually all economic and social activities are dominated by market relations. Every good or service can be turned into a "commodity" or can be measured by a certain monetary value. The surplus product has been transformed into "surplus value." Unlike the pre-capitalist elites, the capitalists are primarily interested not in the surplus product's use values, but in the surplus value, more commonly known as "profit."

With the dominance of market relations, every capitalist has to engage in constant and intense competition against one another. Those who fail in competition will be bankrupt and cease to be capitalists. To prevail in the competition, every capitalist is compelled to use a large portion of his or her profit to make new investment—that is, to "accumulate capital"—in order to survive as a capitalist and to gain advantages against actual or potential competitors. Accumulation of capital leads to the expansion of production and the development of new technologies. As the capitalist economic relations become dominant, capital accumulation and economic growth become more or less self-sustained. Both the population and economic output start to "take off" and grow exponentially.

Thus, unlike the pre-capitalist societies, modern capitalism is inherently built to pursue economic growth on increasingly larger scales. As there is no inherent limit to the amount of monetary wealth any capitalist desires to have, and market competition compels all capitalists to accumulate increasingly larger amounts of capital, there is no limit to economic growth from within the system. In this sense, the capitalist system may be characterized as one that is based on the "endless accumulation of capital" or the pursuit of infinite economic growth.

But can economic growth really be infinite? Is infinite growth possible in a physically limited planet? This was the question raised by Meadows *et al.* (1972) in their classical book on *The Limits to Growth*.

The limits to growth

In the 1972 book, Meadows *et al.* used computer modeling to demonstrate that unlimited, exponential economic growth would eventually deplete the earth's resources and cause runaway ecological damages, eventually leading to economic and societal collapse.

In a recent study, Turner (2008) studied the historical data for world population, industrial production, services production, remaining non-renewable resources, and pollution from 1970 to 2000. Interestingly, Turner found that the observed data agreed well with the original "standard run" scenario presented in *The Limits to Growth*, a scenario which predicted global collapse by the mid-twenty-first century.

In June 2012, *Nature* magazine, one of the world's leading science journals, published a paper co-authored by 22 scientists. The scientists argued that, due to over-consumption, population growth, and environmental destruction, the earth is rapidly approaching a global tipping point beyond which the biosphere could experience swift and irreversible change, with catastrophic consequences for humanity and other species (Barnosky *et al.* 2012).

These studies raise important and urgent questions. Is the existing world system of capitalism compatible with the basic requirements of ecological sustainability and the long-term survival of human civilization? If not, can the system be reformed to meet these requirements? If not, can the system be replaced by a fundamentally different system? What will be the basic character of the new system? How long will it take for the systemic transition to take place? Does humanity still have time?

Peak oil: the beginning of the end?

How humanity responds to the current global crisis may determine the fate of the global ecological system and human civilization for centuries to come. But in the near future, it is the impending peak of world oil production that may impose the single greatest constraint on global economic growth.

Oil, or petroleum, is a naturally occurring flammable liquid consisting of hydrocarbons (a hydrocarbon is an organic compound consisting of hydrogen and carbon). It derived from ancient fossilized organic materials (such as zooplankton and algae). As many layers of the organic materials' remains settled to sea or lake bottoms, they were buried under sedimentary rock and underwent intense heat and pressure. If the temperature was high enough, the organic matter would be transformed into liquid or gaseous hydrocarbons, which became, respectively, oil or natural gas.

Most of the oil found today was formed during two geological eras: the Jurassic period of 169–144 million years ago and the Cretaceous period of 119–89 million years ago (Aleklett 2012: 25). Oil is in effect stored solar energy (the energy embodied in the organic matter derived from solar energy) that had taken millions of years to be formed and accumulated. However, over the past one and a half centuries, humanity has already extracted and consumed 170 billion tonnes of oil. By the mid-twenty-first century, the world will likely have consumed more than half of the ultimately recoverable oil resources.

Compared to other forms of energy, oil has some important advantages. It is liquid, and therefore can be easily stored in a tank or transported through pipes. It has high energy density. A kilogram of gasoline (a petroleum product) contains 46 megajoules of energy (one megajoule = 1,000,000 joules; a "joule" is a basic unit of energy in the international system of units and equals the "work" required to produce one watt of power for one second). By comparison, modern lithium-ion batteries can store only 0.5 megajoule of energy per kilogram. Thus, for a given amount of weight, a much greater amount of energy can be derived from oil than from many other forms of energy. Until recently, oil was relatively abundant and cheap (Heinberg 2011: 107, 160).

Because of these advantages, oil has played a central role in global economic expansion since the Second World War. In 1973, oil accounted for 48 percent of the world's total energy consumption. Today, oil continues to be the world's largest source of energy, accounting for about one-third of the world's total energy consumption (BP 2013). Oil plays an essential role in the world's transportation, chemical industries, and agriculture.

World oil production grew by 7.2 percent a year in the 1950s and 8.0 percent a year in the 1960s. However, the average annual growth rate of world oil production slowed down to 2.7 percent in the 1970s, 0.3 percent in the 1980s, 1.3 percent in the 1990s, and 1.1 percent from 2001 to 2012 (the growth rates are calculated from oil production data from BP 2013).

Figure 1.2 shows the long-term world oil supply curve, or the long-term relationship between the real oil prices (that is, oil prices corrected for inflation) and the world's total oil supply (including all liquid fuels). From 1950 to the early 1970s, world oil supply increased six-fold (from about 10 million barrels per day to near 60 million barrels per day), but the real oil prices remained cheap and stable. World real oil prices (in constant 2012 dollars) stayed around 15 dollars a barrel through the 1950s and declined toward 10 dollars a barrel by the end of the 1960s.

In 1974, the real oil price surged to over 50 dollars a barrel as a result of the Arabic countries' oil embargo. The real oil price surged again to more than 100 dollars a barrel after the Iranian Revolution in 1979.

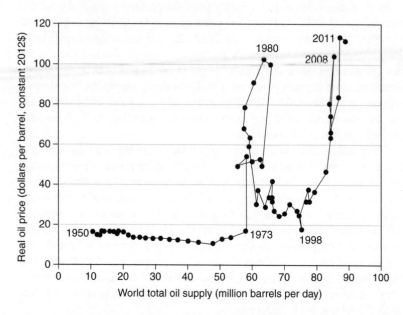

Figure 1.2 World oil long-term supply curve (1950–2012) (sources: World oil production from 1950 to 1964 is from Rutledge (2007). World oil production from 1965 to 1979 is from BP (2013). World total oil supply from 1980 to 2012 is from EIA (2013a). World real oil prices from 1950 to 2012 are from BP (2013)).

During the first half of the 1980s, the sluggish global economy reduced oil demand and the development of new oil fields increased supply. Real oil prices collapsed. From 1986 to 2003, as the world oil supply expanded steadily from 62 million barrels per day to 80 million barrels per day, real oil prices fluctuated around 30 dollars a barrel.

In 2004, the real oil price rose above 45 dollars a barrel for the first time since 1985. From 2004 to 2008, the real oil price rose by 57 dollars over four years. The oil price shock of 2008 was an important factor that contributed to the deepest global economic recession that had taken place since the Second World War. The real oil price fell back to 66 dollars a barrel in 2009 but surged again as the global economy recovered. By 2011, the real oil price reached 114 dollars a barrel, the highest level on record.

Unlike the oil price shocks in the 1970s, the oil price shock of 2008 and 2011 were not caused by geopolitical factors. Instead, the recent oil price shocks primarily reflected the inability of world oil supply to keep pace with world oil demand. From 2004 to 2011, world oil supply increased by only 5 percent. During the same period, the real oil price rose by 144 percent.

As the oil price surges to historical record levels, new and unconventional oil resources have been developed. Production from the US "shale oil" and the Canadian oil sands has risen rapidly. In the next few years, the shale oil boom may help to stabilize the world oil prices. But when the shale oil boom comes to an end, the global economy is likely to be hit by another round of oil price shocks.

Is the world approaching "peak oil," the moment when the world's total oil production reaches the maximum and starts to decline? If world oil production peaks in the near future, can alternative energy resources (such as natural gas, biofuels, and solar and wind electricity) and energy efficiency improvement help to offset the negative impact of "peak oil" on the global economy?

Or will "peak oil" turn out to be the beginning of the end of the "endless accumulation of capital"?

The rise of China

The dramatic rise of China as a new global economic power is among the most important global developments in the early twenty-first century. Figure 1.3 shows China's changing share in global economic output, energy consumption, carbon dioxide emissions, and oil consumption. In 2000, China accounted for 7 percent of the world's economic output, 10 percent of the world's energy consumption, 14 percent of the world's carbon dioxide emissions, and 6 percent of the world's oil consumption. By 2012, China's share of world total economic output, energy consumption, carbon dioxide emissions, and oil consumption had increased to 15 percent, 22 percent, 27 percent, and 11 percent, respectively. China is now the world's largest energy consumer, the largest greenhouse gas emitter, and the second largest oil consumer.

In recent years, China has accounted for most of the *growth* of global energy consumption and carbon dioxide emissions. Figure 1.4 shows China's share in the *growth* of world economic output, energy consumption, carbon dioxide emissions, and oil consumption over five-year periods from the period 1996–2000 to the period 2008–2012.

Back to the five-year period from 1996 to 2000, China accounted for 14 percent of world economic growth, 12 percent of energy consumption growth, 14 percent of carbon dioxide emissions growth, and 21 percent of oil consumption growth. Over the five-year period from 2008 to 2012, China's contribution to world economic growth rose to 42 percent. During the same period, China accounted for 72 percent of the world's energy

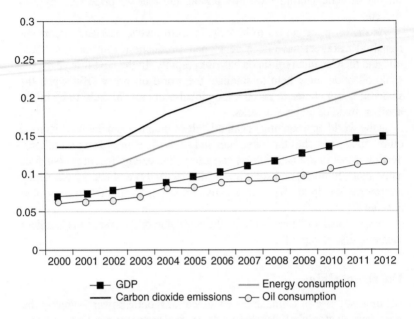

Figure 1.3 China and the global economy (China's share of the world total, 2000–2012) (sources: GDP in constant 2005 international dollars for China and the world is from the World Bank (2013). Energy consumption, carbon dioxide emissions, and oil consumption are from BP (2013)).

consumption growth, 82 percent of carbon dioxide emissions growth, and 75 percent of oil consumption growth.

Roughly speaking, China now accounts for about three-quarters of the world's total energy consumption growth and about four-fifths of the world's total emissions growth. This has taken place despite the Chinese government's pledges to reduce the Chinese economy's energy intensity and emissions intensity. China's huge contribution to global carbon dioxide emissions growth makes it plainly clear that no reasonable climate stabilization can be achieved without a fundamental decarbonization of the Chinese economy.

While China now accounts for the bulk of the global energy consumption growth, China's per capita consumption of energy and other resources remains a fraction of that in the advanced capitalist countries. In 2010, China's per capita GDP (measured by constant 2005 international dollars) was 16 percent of the US level and 25 percent of the South Korean level. China's per capita electricity consumption was 20 percent of the US level

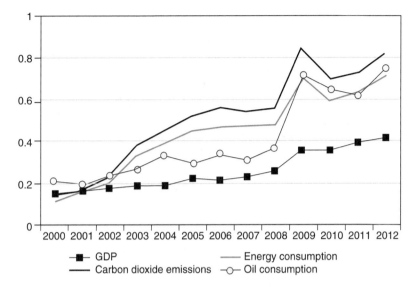

Figure 1.4 China and global economic growth: China's share of world total change over five-year periods (1996/2000–2008/2012) (sources: See Figure 1.3).

and 29 percent of the South Korean level. China's passenger cars per 1,000 people was only 8 percent of the US level and 13 percent of the South Korean level (World Bank 2013).

For many years, the Chinese economy has depended on the intense exploitation of a massive cheap labor force under sweatshop conditions to generate high capitalist profits and rapid pace of capital accumulation. But sooner or later, the Chinese workers will demand a set of basic economic and social rights and aspire to have the living standards now enjoyed by workers in the more advanced capitalist countries.

But does the world have the resources and environmental space to meet such aspirations? If Chinese capitalism fails to meet such aspirations, will the failure lead to intense social and geopolitical conflicts? Will the pressure on the world's resources and environmental space eventually lead to global ecological collapse? Or will the Chinese people and the people in the rest of the world have the collective wisdom to come to terms with the reality of "limits to growth"?

About this book

As late as the early nineteenth century, China was the world's largest economy. The rise of the West (Western Europe and North America) to global supremacy coincided with the dramatic decline of China from one of the centers of pre-capitalist civilization to a peripheral member of the capitalist world system. The history of modern China to a large extent can be understood as the successive attempts by different Chinese social groups to respond to the unprecedented historical challenge imposed by the capitalist world system. How to "catch up with the West" has been the ultimate question every modern Chinese political movement has to answer. Chapter 2 discusses more than one and a half centuries of historical interactions between China and the capitalist world system.

China's economic rise has greatly expanded the semi-peripheral layer of the capitalist world system and potentially could result in a major increase of global labor and resources costs. Whether the capitalist world system can afford the rise of China largely depends on if the world has the resources and environmental space to meet the rising energy demands from China and the rest of the world.

Chapter 3 gives an overview of the world's and China's energy consumption. The chapter explains how oil, natural gas, coal, and electricity play indispensable roles in the modern economy and prepares the readers with some basic concepts and definitions.

Chapter 4 considers the possibility that world oil production may reach its peak and start to decline in the near future. The chapter examines the oil production and consumption of Saudi Arabia, Russia, the United States, and China. The main oil exporters and importers may have to face irreconcilable conflicts by the 2030s and 2040s.

Chapter 5 examines the world's resources of oil, natural gas, coal, nuclear energy, and renewable energies. The world's total production of fossil fuels is likely to peak before the mid-twenty-first century. Neither the renewable energies nor energy efficiency can deliver infinite economic growth. The world economic growth rate will approach zero toward the end of the century. The chapter concludes by arguing that the capitalist economic system is fundamentally incompatible with a steady state of zero economic growth.

Chapter 6 makes projections of China's long-term energy consumption and economic growth. Despite optimistic assumptions of China's potential for renewable energies and energy efficiency, China's economic growth rate is projected to approach zero by around 2050.

China's capitalist accumulation has been based on the exploitation of a large cheap labor force and the rapid depletion of cheap and abundant energy resources. However, as the depletion of fossil fuels imposes an insurmountable limit to China's economic growth, the survival of Chinese capitalism will be in question. Chapter 7 argues that the combination of economic, social, and ecological contradictions will lead to a structural crisis that Chinese capitalism cannot overcome.

How China's economic, social, and environmental crisis can be resolved will determine not only China's but also the world's future. Without a fundamental decarbonization of the Chinese economy, there will be little chance for the world to achieve a reasonable climate stabilization that is consistent with the long-term survival of human civilization.

Chapter 8 examines the world's and China's carbon emission budgets required for alternative scenarios of climate stabilization. Scientists generally consider global warming of two degrees Celsius to be the safe limit, beyond which dangerous climate change may be unavoidable. However, for practical purposes, it is no longer possible to limit global warming to no more than two degrees. Only with a zero economic growth rate does the world have a chance of preventing the worst global ecological catastrophes.

Chapter 9 concludes the book by considering three possible scenarios for China's future in the twenty-first century: crisis and collapse; reform within capitalism; and transition to the end of growth. The chapter ends with a section on "Final reflection," which challenges the readers to consider whether there is any alternative to socialism if human civilization is to survive beyond the twenty-first century.

2 China and the capitalist world system

Figure 2.1 compares the long-term relative positions of China and Western Europe in the global economy from AD 1 to 2000.

For almost two millennia, China had consistently accounted for about one-quarter of global economic output. According to Maddison (2010), in the eleventh century (during China's Song Dynasty), China was the world's leading economy with the most advanced technologies and one of the world's highest per capita incomes.

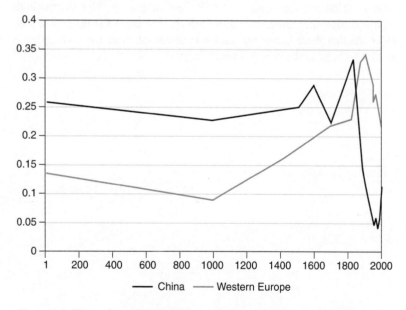

Figure 2.1 Share of world GDP (China and Western Europe, AD 1–2000) (sources: GDP for China, Western Europe and the world in constant 1990 international dollars from AD 1 to 2000 is from Maddison (2010)).

According to Maddison's estimate, Western Europe had overtaken China in terms of per capita income by 1500. But according to Arrighi *et al.* (2003: 260), if one compares Western Europe with China's economically advanced regions, China maintained the edge over Western Europe in terms of income, productivity, and technological sophistication as late as the eighteenth century.

During the early Roman Empire (*c.* AD 1), Western Europe accounted for about 14 percent of the global economy. After centuries of economic decline during the medieval era, Western Europe was reduced to 9 percent of the global economy by AD 1000. From 1000 to 1300, agricultural innovations led to substantial expansions of population, production, and trade in Western Europe. Although the European population fell by about one-third during the second half of the fourteenth century due to the Black Death, the European economy recovered in the fifteenth century (Hunt 2002: 16). The Western European share of the global economy rose to 18 percent by 1500, exceeding the Roman Empire level.

China's Ming Dynasty (1368–1644) collapsed in 1644. But economic expansion resumed under the Qing Dynasty (1644–1911), although, according to Maddison, China's economic growth during the eighteenth century was entirely absorbed by the growth of population. By 1820, China accounted for about one-third of the global economy, 50 percent larger than all the Western European countries combined. However, the economic fortunes of the two geographic areas were to be dramatically reversed over the following one and a half centuries.

By the early nineteenth century, the Europe-centered capitalist world system had taken shape and was on its rise to global supremacy. The European economic and political power peaked at the turn of the twentieth century. On the other hand, China suffered massive and sustained declines from the early nineteenth century to the mid-twentieth century and was reduced to one of the poorest countries in the world by 1950.

The rise of capitalism

The rise of the capitalist world system resulted from a set of more or less fortuitous historical conditions.

Almost all of the great pre-capitalist civilizations, such as the Roman Empire, the Arabic Empire, the Mughal Empire, and the Chinese dynasties, were centralized redistributive empires. The empires presided over vast land areas and controlled large populations. The centralized imperial bureaucracies collected the surplus product in the form of taxes and levies, to be used for the elites' luxury consumption and certain social functions.

As the bulk of the surplus product was consumed by the elites, little was left for capital accumulation and technological innovation. Capitalist activities did exist and some merchant capitalists made enormous fortunes through the highly risky long-distance trade. However, by and large, the capitalist activities accounted for only a small portion of the total economic output and the merchant capitalists had to depend on the imperial powers for protection.

The agriculture-based empires were often threatened by the invasion of nomadic peoples. From the third century to the sixth centuries, all the great empires on the Eurasian continent were destroyed by the nomadic attacks. In East Asia and the Middle East, centralized empires were later rebuilt. But in Western Europe, the Roman Empire was never restored (Stavrianos 1981: 46). Throughout the Middle Ages, Western Europe was divided between many feudal kingdoms and fiefs.

By the fourteenth and the fifteenth centuries, several national states (such as Spain, Portugal, France, England, Austria, and Prussia) of approximately equal size and power emerged in Western Europe. As the national states engaged in a permanent struggle for power in peace and war, they had to depend on the capitalist groups for financial support.

The competition between states for capital inflated the profits and power of the capitalist business communities. Moreover, to expand the potential financial resources, the European monarchs were motivated to directly undertake capitalist activities by sponsoring the high-profit, long-distance trade with Asia (Arrighi *et al.* 2003: 266–268).

The Ottoman conquest of Constantinople in 1453 forced the Europeans to look for alternate routes to Asia. Luckily for the Europeans, they "discovered" and conquered the Americas, a sparsely populated continent with abundant natural resources.

During the fourteenth and fifteenth centuries, Western Europe suffered from persistent and acute shortage of money as the European production of gold and silver stagnated but the rapid expansion of trade increased the demand for money. The massive imports of precious metals from the Americas eliminated the money shortage and led to the most long-lasting inflation in European history. During the "price revolution" in the sixteenth century, prices rose between 150 and 400 percent in different parts of Europe. Real wages and rents (that is, wages and rents measured by their real purchasing power) collapsed and an enormous amount of wealth was transferred from the rest of the society to the capitalist class (Hunt 2002: 18–19).

The capitalist dynamic was ready to take off in Western Europe.

Coal and capitalism

A political structure based on interstate competition was necessary for the rise of the capitalist world system, as it created a balance of power between the states and the capitalist groups that was favorable for capitalist accumulation.

Similar political structures that involved persistent competition between multiple states within one civilization had happened in earlier times. Examples included the classical Greek civilization (during the fifth and fourth centuries BC), China's "Spring and Autumn" and "War States" periods (from the eighth century to the third centuries BC), and Japan's Ashikaga period (from the fourteenth to the sixteenth centuries). However, before the rise of modern capitalism, interstate competition within one system eventually led to either the system's self-destruction or its conquest by a centralized empire.

All pre-capitalist civilizations were constrained by the availability of land, energy, and other resources. As the total amounts of available resources were limited, at best, interstate competition amounted to no more than a zero-sum game. More likely, conflicts between states would destroy existing resources and population, and declines of resources and population would lead to more intense conflicts. The vicious circle kept escalating until it was brought to an end by the system's demise.

In the medieval era, the European economy (like the rest of the world) relied upon traditional forms of renewable energy resources, such as wood, water, wind, and animal power. By the seventeenth century, the European economy already approached the ecological limits imposed by the traditional renewable energies. The rapid expansion of population and manufacturing led to the destruction of the European forest eco-system. Between AD 400 and 1600, the forest coverage as a ratio of the European land area was reduced from 95 percent to 20 percent (Heinberg 2003: 45–50).

Had there not been coal, the industrial revolution might never have happened and the emerging capitalist world system might have come to an end by the eighteenth century.

Coal, like oil, is a form of stored solar energy. It was converted from ancient plant matter through biological and geological processes over millions of years. The world's current coal resources were mostly formed during three geological eras: between 360 million and 290 million years ago, between 200 million and 65 million years ago, and between 65 million and two million years ago (Heinberg 2009: 18).

By the seventeenth century, coal was commonly used in Britain as the depletion of forests led to widespread wood shortage. But coal production was impeded by the frequent flooding of mines. In 1769, James Watt improved the design of steam engines, which were used for pumping water out of coal mines. The improvement of steam engines made possible the rapid expansion of coal production, and coal provided the fuel for the more extensive uses of steam power. By the beginning of the nineteenth century, steam engines were rapidly replacing water as the main source of power in the British industry.

Coal not only provided the fuel for the industrial revolution but also served as a key industrial input. In 1709, Abraham Darby developed a process to make coke from coal. The extensive use of coke in the smelting process led to transformations of the British metallurgical industry. The rapid increase of iron production made possible the widespread use of machines and the dramatic increase of labor productivity in the manufacturing industries (Hunt 2002: 41–45).

From 1800 to 1900, world coal production increased by almost 50 times, from 15 million tonnes to 700 million tonnes (Heinberg 2003: 53). Coal was the energy foundation of the industrial revolution. Coal, oil, and natural gas, or the fossil fuels, have been the energy foundations of all the technological revolutions that have taken place since the nineteenth century.

Fossil fuels are massive amounts of solar energy that were transformed, accumulated, and stored by nature over hundreds of millions of years. A large portion of these massive amounts of energy has been mined and consumed by humanity over just the past 200 years. The extraordinary squandering of nature's gifts has led to the belief that exponential economic growth has become a normal part of human civilization and can be sustained indefinitely.

The demise of the Chinese empire

In 1757, the British East India Company won the decisive Battle of Plassey against the forces of the Mughal Empire. In the following decades, the British consolidated its colonial rule in India. The conquest of India provided the rising British hegemony with huge demographic and financial resources.

India became "an English barrack in the Oriental Seas" (in the words of Lord Salisbury, the British Prime Minister in the late nineteenth century). The Indian soldiers were organized into a European-style colonial army and fought for British imperialism in a series of wars in Asia and Africa. The tributes collected from India allowed Britain to dramatically increase its government expenditures during the Napoleonic war and laid the foundation of British supremacy in the capital goods industries (Arrighi *et al.* 2003: 287–293).

The conquest of India and the completion of the industrial revolution (based on coal) allowed Britain to establish decisive military advantages over the declining Chinese empire.

Since the mid-seventeenth century, China had been ruled by the Manchurian Qing Dynasty. In the early nineteenth century, opium was virtually the only western commodity that could make a significant entry into the Chinese market. In 1839, the Chinese emperor banned the opium trade. The Chinese government confiscated and destroyed the smuggled opium. The British parliament denounced the Chinese government's action as "a grievous sin," "a wicked offence," and "an atrocious violation of justice" and sent an expeditionary force to enforce the British right to opium trade (Arrighi *et al.* 2003: 293).

The Opium War ended with China's defeat in 1842. China opened five ports to foreign trade and ceded Hong Kong to Britain. The defeat in the Opium War was followed by an escalation of China's internal social conflicts. From 1851 to 1864, the Qing Dynasty was almost overthrown by the massive Taiping peasant rebellion.

In response to the growing social crisis and the new challenges imposed by China's incorporation into the capitalist world system, sections of the ruling elites attempted to reverse the imperial decline by pursuing a program of military modernization (known as the "Westernization Movement").

But by the late nineteenth century, China had to confront not only the European powers but also the emerging Japanese imperialism. The Sino-Japanese War in 1894–1895 ended with China's decisive defeat. China ceded Taiwan to Japan and lost suzerainty over Korea.

By the early twentieth century, the enormous amounts of war reparations and debt payments had turned the Qing Dynasty into a tax collector for the foreign imperialist powers. Foreign armies were stationed near Beijing and foreign battleships sailed in the Yangzi River (Stavrianos 1981: 315–332).

After China's defeat in 1895, large sections of China's emerging intellectual class lost faith in the traditional social system and became influenced by modern western ideas.

In 1905, a new revolutionary organization (the predecessor of the Nationalist Party) led by Sun Zhongshan (Sun Yat-sen) was founded in Tokyo, Japan. The revolutionaries were determined to overthrow the Manchurian Qing Dynasty and make China a free democratic republic. However, coming mostly from overseas Chinese communities and wealthy families, Sun and his comrades had little connection with the peasants, which made up the great majority of the Chinese population.

In 1911, the Qing Dynasty collapsed and China became a republic. However, with neither financial resources nor military power, Sun

Zhongshan and the Nationalist Party were unable to take advantage of the situation. Political power fell into the hands of provincial warlords.

In 1924, the Soviet Union helped Sun Zhongshan to reorganize the Nationalist Party. The Soviet Union trained and armed the Nationalist Army. After Sun's death, Jiang Jieshi (Chiang Kai-shek) became the Commander in Chief of the Nationalist Army and led the "Northern Expedition" from 1926 to 1928 to expel the warlords in Northern China.

By 1928, China was nominally unified under the Nationalist Government. In reality, the Nationalist Government's effective control was limited to the provinces in the Yangzi valley. Its top leadership had close connections with foreign capital but had little interest in indigenous industrialization. At the provincial and local level, the Nationalist Government relied upon the traditional landlord class as its social base (Stavrianos 1981: 403–408).

When the full-scale Sino-Japanese War broke out in 1937, the Nationalist Army suffered numerous military catastrophes. China's most prosperous and densely populated provinces were lost to Japan within a year. In Nanjing (the Nationalist Government's capital) alone, about 300,000 civilians were massacred.

From 1840 to 1937, successive regimes of the Chinese ruling elites had failed to meet the unprecedented historical challenge imposed by the capitalist world system and reverse China's national decline. China was reduced to a peripheral member of the capitalist world system and one of the poorest countries in the world.

Core, periphery, and semi-periphery

By the late nineteenth century, the Europe-centered capitalist world system had become the first truly global system in human history. Within this global system, wealth and power was concentrated in the core states, consisting of Western Europe and a few countries where the European population had settled (the United States, Canada, Australia, and New Zealand). The combined population of Western Europe and the "Western Offshoots" (using the term used by Angus Maddison, the economic historian) was about 20 percent of the world total in 1900.

The great majority of the world population lived in Asia and Africa, accounting for about 63 percent of the world population in 1900 (or about 60 percent if Japan is excluded). At the beginning of the twentieth century, Asia and Africa consisted mostly of colonies and semi-colonies. Semi-colonies were countries such as China, which was nominally an independent state but in reality divided by imperialist powers into several spheres of influence. These colonies and semi-colonies constituted the periphery of the capitalist world system. Wealth was transferred from the periphery to the core through tributes, war reparations, debt payments, and unequal exchange.

The Latin American countries became independent in the early nineteenth century and a few East European countries became independent in the late nineteenth century. Latin America, Eastern Europe, and Russia specialized in raw material exports in the global capitalist market and lagged behind the core states in industrial and military capacities. These countries and Japan constituted the semi-periphery of the capitalist world system, with a combined population accounting for about 20 percent of the world total in 1900.

Figure 2.2 shows the long-term relative positions of the two historical core regions in the capitalist world system, measured by the ratios of their per capita GDP to the world average. Figures 2.3 and 2.4 compare the long-term relative positions of the historical semi-peripheral and peripheral regions in the capitalist world system.

In the early nineteenth century, Western Europe and Western Offshoots had a per capita income of about 180 percent of the world average. Most of the rest of the world had income levels around the world average. The

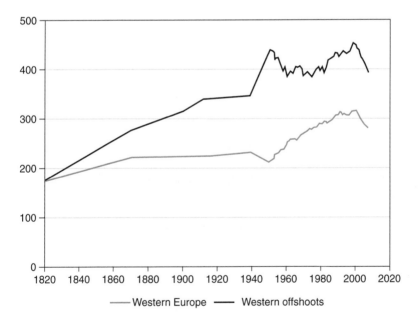

Figure 2.2 Index of per capita GDP (historical core, world average=100, 1820–2008) (sources: Per capita GDP in constant 1990 international dollars from 1820 to 2008 is from Maddison (2010)).

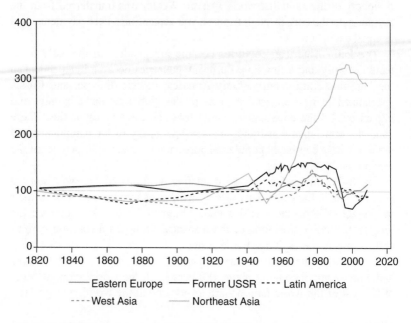

Figure 2.3 Index of per capita GDP (historical semi-periphery, world average = 100, 1820–2008) (sources: See Figure 2.2).

per capita GDP of China, India, Southeast Asia, and West Asia ranged between 80 and 90 percent of the world average ("Southeast Asia" includes Indonesia, the Philippines, Thailand, Burma, Malaysia, and Vietnam). The per capita GDP of Eastern Europe, the former USSR (the geographic area within the former Soviet Union), Latin America, and Northeast Asia deviated from the world average only by a few percentage points ("Northeast Asia" includes Japan, South Korea, and Taiwan). Only Africa lagged behind, with its per capita GDP at about 60 percent of the world average.

Over the nineteenth and twentieth centuries, there had been a long-term tendency for the gap between the West and the rest of the world to widen. By 1870, the Western European per capita GDP index rose to about 220 and the Western Offshoots per capita GDP index rose to about 280. The Western Offshoots (dominated by the United States) had become a class by itself, in effect becoming the core of the core. During the great global capitalist expansion after the Second World War, the western core states further increased their advantages relative to the rest of the world. By the end of the twentieth century, the Western Offshoots index peaked at about 460 and the Western European index peaked at about 320.

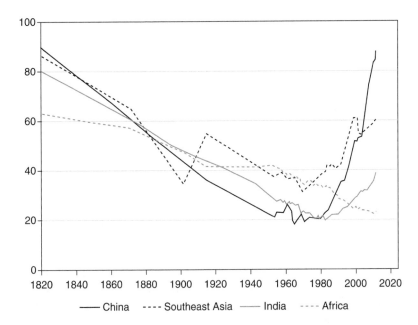

Figure 2.4 Index of per capita GDP (historical periphery, world average = 100, 1820–2008) (sources: See Figure 2.2).

The rise of the West was matched by the decline of the East. By 1870, the per capita GDP of China, India, Southeast Asia, and Africa converged to about 60 percent of the world average. The per capita GDP of Eastern Europe, the former USSR, Latin America, and West Asia ranged between 80 and 110 percent of the world average. Thus, by 1870, the capitalist world system was clearly divided into three structural positions: the core, the periphery, and the semi-periphery. The three structural positions remained mostly intact until the end of the twentieth century.

Northeast Asia was the only important exception. From 1870 to 1950, Northeast Asia was firmly in the semi-peripheral category as its per capita GDP index fluctuated between 80 and 130. After the Second World War, the US hegemony in East Asia created favorable geopolitical conditions for the rapid growth of the Japanese economy and, later, the East Asian "tigers" (South Korea, Taiwan, Singapore, and Hong Kong) (Arrighi *et al.* 2003: 300–308). By the early 1970s, the Northeast Asian index exceeded 200 and Japan became a member of the core. By the early twenty-first century, both South Korea and Taiwan had reached per capita GDP levels comparable to the core states.

The division of the capitalist world system into three structural positions has played indispensable roles for the system. The periphery specializes in highly competitive, low value-added activities. Through unequal exchange, much of the economic surplus produced in the periphery is transferred to the core. Unequal exchange takes place between the core and the periphery in the sense that the commodities exported by the periphery to the core typically embody a much larger content of labor, energy, and other resources than the commodities imported by the periphery from the core. From an ecological perspective, the periphery subsidizes the core with cheap labor and abundant natural resources.

The concentration of wealth in the core allows the core states to invest in the capital-intensive, high-risk "leading industries" that provide driving engines for the global capitalist economy.

The super profits reaped from the rest of the world allow the core states to buy social peace at home, securing the political loyalty of the domestic working classes by paying high wages and providing extensive social welfare programs. The world's best trained professional workers (such as managers, engineers, scientists, and university professors) and the most skilled production workers are concentrated in the core. Their political loyalty is essential not only for the core states but also for the entire capitalist world system.

The core specializes in monopolistic, high value-added activities. However, from time to time, due to technical change, rising labor costs, depletion of resources, and growing competition, the existing "leading industries" would lose their monopolistic advantages and suffer from declining profit rates. To restore the profit rate, the core states need to reallocate capital to new "leading industries" and the capital invested in the old industries needs to be relocated to other parts of the world system (Wallerstein 1979: 69–72).

The semi-periphery plays an indispensable role by serving as the geographic zone of capital relocation during times of major capitalist crisis. The Soviet Union, and to a lesser extent Eastern Europe and Latin America, were the major beneficiaries of the global capital relocation that took place in response to the major capitalist crisis in the first half of the twentieth century.

The Soviet Union laid its foundation of industrialization during the Great Depression. In 1931 and 1932, the Soviet imports accounted for 30–50 percent of the world's total exports of capital goods. Entire soviet industries were built with imported western capital goods and technologies (Deng 2002).

The Soviet Union, Eastern Europe, and Latin America enjoyed rapid economic growth from the 1950s to the 1970s. The Soviet per capita GDP index (relative to the world average; see Figure 2.3) surged from 109 in 1940 to 151 in 1976. However, the semi-periphery was hit particularly hard by the global capitalist crisis from the 1970s to the 1980s. The 1980s turned out to be the "lost decade" for all the semi-peripheral regions.

The twentieth-century "communism"

Nineteenth-century global capitalism rested upon British hegemonic power. From 1815 to 1914, Europe enjoyed "A Hundred Years' Peace" (in the words of Karl Polanyi, the great American sociologist), with the United Kingdom being the ultimate arbiter of the European balance of power.

Coal provided the material foundation for the expansion of the global capitalist economy in the nineteenth century. Global surplus value was maximized through intense exploitation of both the western industrial working classes and the peoples in the colonies and semi-colonies. However, the success of global capitalism in the nineteenth century eventually sowed the seeds of its own destruction.

As the global capitalist economy expanded, new industrial powers (such as Germany and the United States) emerged and undermined the British monopoly over the world manufacturing industries. By the late nineteenth century, Britain had lost the world industrial leadership. The decline of British hegemonic power paved the way for intense interstate conflicts, eventually leading to two world wars during the first half of the twentieth century.

With the completion of the industrial revolution, the industrial working class had become a powerful political and social force. By the late nineteenth century, socialist political parties and labor unions were formed throughout Europe. The western working classes demanded a growing range of economic, political, and social rights.

In the colonies and semi-colonies, indigenous capitalist classes (the "national bourgeoisies") and the new intellectual classes influenced by western ideas had emerged. Their political and economic interests were reflected by the demands for national independence and indigenous industrialization.

The industrial working classes in the West and the indigenous elites in the non-western world became the social foundations of the twentieth-century "anti-systemic movements": the social democratic movements (reflecting the interests and demands of the western industrial working classes), the national liberation movements (reflecting the interests and demands of the indigenous elites in the non-western world), and the communist movements.

In the early twentieth century, the communist movement emerged as a radical variant of the social democratic movement. According to the

Leninist analysis, in the monopoly capitalist era, the capitalist imperialist powers reaped super profits from the colonies and semi-colonies. The capitalist classes in the imperialist countries used the super profits to buy off a section of the working classes, who became the labor aristocracy. As the labor aristocracy took over the social democratic parties, the latter betrayed the proletarian revolution and degenerated into reformist parties (Lenin 1996[1916]).

The Leninist theory argued that, given the unbalanced capitalist development, the proletariat in a relatively backward country (such as Russia), which was "the weakest link in the imperialist chain," could lead the first successful socialist revolution, setting an example for the working classes in the more advanced capitalist countries.

In practice, the communist movement had evolved over the rest of the twentieth century into a radical form of the national liberation movement. In both Russia and China, the old ruling classes were completely unable to undertake basic capital accumulation and meet the challenges of the capitalist world system. After Russia's defeat in the Russo-Japanese War in 1905–1906, Russia was on the verge of declining from semi-periphery to periphery. From the mid-nineteenth century to the mid-twentieth century, successive regimes of the Chinese ruling elites had consistently failed to reverse China's long-term national decline. Only by mobilizing the great majority of the population (including both the industrial workers and the peasants) and replacing the entire old ruling classes with a new state structure could Russia and China start to undertake meaningful capital accumulation and "catch up with the West."

The fact that the communist revolutions were based on the broad mobilization of the great majority of the population had important implications for the post-revolutionary social structure. The survival of the communist state depended on the support of the general population. A de facto social contract was formed between the communist state and the general population. In the short run, the general population would make great sacrifices, in terms of material living standards and personal rights, in order to achieve rapid industrialization. In return, the communist state would provide a comprehensive package of social protection (including job security, basic healthcare, basic education, housing, and care for the children and the elderly). In the long run, the communist state promised that "socialism" would eventually evolve into "communism," which would be an egalitarian classless society based on high levels of development of "productive forces."

For much of the twentieth century, the strategy proved to be a great success. From the 1950s to the 1970s, the Soviet Union was the world's second largest economy and considered to be one of the two global super powers. The Eastern European socialist states also managed to improve their relative positions in the capitalist world system from 1950 to 1975 (see Figure 2.3). However, the very success of industrialization created a large industrial working class and an urban middle class consisting of professional workers. By the late 1960s and the 1970s, the working classes and the middle classes in the Soviet Union and Eastern Europe started to demand more political rights and aspired to have living standards similar to the western working classes.

The labor unrests forced the Soviet and Eastern European ruling classes to make concessions by accelerating the growth of mass consumption. But the Soviet Union and Eastern Europe could not match the western core countries in terms of technology and productivity. Moreover, the social protection package offered to the working classes as a part of the communist social contract in effect gave the workers greater control over the labor processes. Once the workers became disillusioned with the long-term communist promises, there was a tendency for the effort levels to decline. But given the social protection package, the state and the industrial managers had little leverage over the workers and were unable to force the workers to deliver higher effort levels (Cheng 2000).

Decades of rapid economic growth had depleted the cheap and easily available natural resources within the Soviet Union. Soviet oil production peaked in 1987 and coal production peaked in 1988. In 1987, the Soviet Union lost the title of the world's second largest economy to Japan, a title the Soviet Union had held since the 1930s. The Soviet Union and Eastern Europe were squeezed between high labor and resource costs and insufficient productivity levels.

In the 1970s, the Soviet Union and Eastern Europe attempted to accelerate economic growth by importing capital goods and technologies financed by the borrowing of foreign capital (Jia 1989). At first, the borrowing terms were favorable as the "petro-dollars" (the oil revenues deposited by the oil exporters in the western banks) flooded the international capital market. However, in 1979, the US Federal Reserve drastically raised the interest rate in response to the deepening economic crisis. The US interest rate hike triggered the debt crisis from Eastern Europe to Latin America and brought the postwar semi-peripheral economic progress to an end.

In the case of the Soviet Union and Eastern Europe, re-establishing favorable conditions of capital accumulation required the complete dismantling of the historical social contract established by the communist revolution. In Eastern Europe, drastic declines of living standards brought about by the neoliberal "shock therapy" (the economic program of rapid liberalization and privatization) turned the Eastern European countries into suppliers of cheap labor to Western Europe. Meanwhile, massive declines of domestic energy consumption made it possible for Russia to be transformed into an energy exporter.

China: from socialism to capitalism

The Chinese Communist Party came to power in 1949 as the result of a massive popular revolution that mobilized hundreds of millions of peasants and workers.

By eliminating the old ruling classes (the rural landlords, the foreign capital and their Chinese agents, and the "bureaucratic capitalists" associated with the Nationalist Government), the new communist state was able to concentrate the economic surplus in its own hands and use it for capital accumulation. In the early 1950s, productive investment as a share of China's national income rose to more than 20 percent compared to less than 5 percent in the pre-revolutionary years (Li 2009a: 27).

With the help of the Soviet Union, China achieved rapid economic growth and industrialization during the first five-year plan (1953–1957). By the late 1950s, China had been transformed into a socialist economy. The agricultural sector was reorganized under the collectively owned "people's communes." The industrial sector was dominated by state-owned enterprises. The state sector industrial workers were provided with a package of social protection known as the "iron rice bowl."

With the progress of industrialization, new privileged social classes (the new state bureaucrats and technocrats) emerged and expanded. The widening inequality between the new privileged classes and the general population led to growing social tensions.

In 1958, the Chinese Communist Party attempted to accelerate the pace of industrialization by launching the "Great Leap Forward" campaign. However, the combination of policy errors, natural disasters, and sabotages by sections of the privileged bureaucrats led to economic disasters from 1960 to 1962 (Li 2009a: 38–50).

Mao Zedong and his comrades attempted to reverse the tendency toward growing inequality and revive the revolutionary momentum by directly mobilizing the students and workers. The movement was known as the "Great Proletarian Cultural Revolution" (1966–1976). The privileged bureaucrats (or the "capitalist roaders who are in authority in the Party") fought back fiercely by inciting armed conflicts between different mass groups throughout the country. After Mao's death, the "capitalist roaders" staged a counter-revolutionary coup and arrested the Maoist leaders. By 1979, the capitalist roaders consolidated their political power (Li 2009a: 55–59).

By the 1980s, the basic problem for the Chinese economy was similar to the one that confronted the Soviet Union and Eastern Europe in the 1970s. The state-owned industries built in the 1950s were not competitive in the global capitalist market. Acceleration of economic growth would require massive imports of foreign capital goods and technologies. However, without a competitive industrial sector, any acceleration of economic growth would soon lead to rising trade deficits and a balance of payment crisis.

Unlike the Soviet Union and Eastern Europe, China had a large rural, cheap labor force that was readily available for capitalist exploitation. Throughout the 1980s, the new capitalist economic sector expanded rapidly based on the abundant supply of migrant workers from the rural areas. By the early 1990s, the domestic and foreign capitalist enterprises accounted for more than half of China's industrial output.

In 1992, the Fourteenth Congress of the Chinese Communist Party decided that the objective of economic reform was to build a "socialist market economy" in China. In the Chinese political context, it amounted to a commitment to the transition from socialism to capitalism. By the end of the 1990s, most of the state-owned enterprises were privatized and tens of millions of state sector workers were laid off.

In 2001, China became a member of the World Trade Organization. By then, China had been transformed into a capitalist economy based on cheap labor exploitation, ready to serve as the world's manufacturing export platform.

Long waves and crises

Since the nineteenth century, the global capitalist economy has gone through several long periods of rapid growth and relative stability followed by long periods of stagnation and crisis, a phenomenon known as the "long waves." Figure 2.5 shows the long-term growth performance of 13 western capitalist countries (Austria, Belgium, Denmark, France, Germany, Netherlands, Norway, Sweden, United Kingdom, Australia, New Zealand, Canada, and United States). The 13 countries have consistently been core capitalist countries since the late nineteenth century.

From 1893 to 1913, the western capitalism enjoyed a period of rising and relatively high growth rates. However, by the early twentieth century, the British hegemonic power was already in decline and the capitalist world system had to confront the rising challenges of the western industrial working classes and the non-western national liberation movements.

In the early twentieth century, the western capitalist economies were, by and large, free market capitalist economies with small government

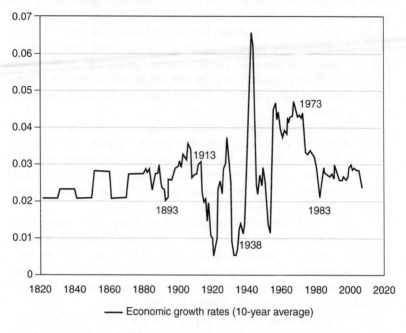

— Economic growth rates (10-year average)

Figure 2.5 Long-term economic growth rates (13 western countries, 1820–2008)
(sources: GDP for 13 western countries (Austria, Belgium, Denmark,
France, Germany, Netherlands, Norway, Sweden, United Kingdom,
Australia, New Zealand, Canada, and United States) from 1820 to 2008
is from Maddison (2010). For 1880–2008, the economic growth rates
are shown in 10-year moving averages. For the decades from the 1820s
to the 1870s, the average economic growth rate for each decade is
shown).

sectors. The free market capitalist economies were highly unstable and
suffered from frequent depressions.

From 1914 to 1945, global capitalism suffered a prolonged structural
crisis that included two world wars and the Great Depression in the 1930s.
From 1915 to 1923 and from 1932 to 1939, the trend economic growth
rates (measured by 10-year moving average economic growth rates) fell
below 2 percent.

After the victory in the Second World War, the United States consolidated its hegemonic power and led the restructuring of the capitalist world
system. In all the western capitalist economies, the government sector was
greatly expanded. In Western Europe and North America, total government expenditures as a share of GDP increased from 8–18 percent in 1913
to 30–45 percent in 1973 (Baker *et al.* 1998: 16).

Welfare state institutions were set up and expanded to accommodate the demands of the western industrial working classes. Institutionalized negotiations between big corporations and major unions allowed the working classes to share the benefits of productivity growth.

On the global stage, the Yalta agreement allowed the Soviet Union to have its own sphere of influence within which the Soviet Union and Eastern Europe pursued the socialist strategy of industrialization. The demands of the non-western national liberation movements were accommodated through decolonization and the western countries promised to help the newly independent countries to achieve "economic development" by providing investment and technology.

The global restructuring led to the unprecedented global economic boom from the mid-1950s to 1973. Trend economic growth rates for the western economies surged to more than 4 percent.

By the 1960s, the global economic boom had led to new transformations that started to undermine the boom's foundation. Western Europe and Japan were rapidly catching up with the United States and the competition from Europe and Japan undermined the US monopoly over the world industry. The US global hegemony was further undermined by the challenges from radical national liberation movements, especially in Indochina.

The long economic boom had depleted the rural surplus labor force in the core and some semi-peripheral countries. The bargaining power of the working classes in the core and the semi-periphery was strengthened. After the mid-1960s, the core capitalist countries suffered from sustained declines in profit rates and the Soviet Union and Eastern Europe suffered from declining economic growth rates.

Many years of rapid global economic growth led to massive increases in global energy demand. From 1950 to 1973, world oil consumption increased more than five-fold, with an average annual growth rate of 7.5 percent. By comparison, during the same period, world GDP grew at an average annual rate of 4.9 percent. The US oil production peaked in 1970 (the US had been the world's largest oil producer since the First World War). The dramatic increase in world oil consumption in combination with the peak of the US oil production increased the power of the semi-peripheral oil exporters. In 1973 and 1979, the global economy was hit by two major oil shocks that led to deep global recessions (Heinberg 2003: 69–74).

Thus, by the 1970s, global capitalism entered into another structural crisis, which was to last until the early 1990s, culminating in the disintegration of the Soviet Union. To re-establish favorable conditions of global capital accumulation, it was necessary to restore the global profit rate.

It would in turn require the destruction of the working class power in the core and the semi-periphery.

To accomplish these objectives, the global capitalist classes pursued a two-pronged strategy: neoliberalism and globalization. Neoliberal economic policies were carried out in both the core and the semi-periphery. In the core, monetarist macroeconomic policies led to persistent high unemployment that created a favorable environment for the big corporations to weaken and defeat the historically strong labor unions. In the semi-periphery, the International Monetary Fund and the World Bank took advantage of the debt crisis in the 1980s and imposed radical programs of privation and liberalization. "Structural Adjustments" and "Shock Therapies" destroyed the historical social contracts between the states and the working classes in the semi-periphery and helped to replenish the global supply of cheap labor force.

But it was the strategy of globalization that has played a decisive role in greatly expanding the size of the global cheap labor force and turning the global balance of power between labor and capital to the latter's advantage. Globalization, or the attempts to achieve free flows of goods, services, and capital throughout the global economy, provided the most favorable environment for global capital relocation. Many of the global manufacturing industries were relocated from the core and the historical semi-periphery to new production sites with lower labor costs.

China turned out to be the greatest beneficiary of the latest round of global capital relocation. From 1950 to 1980, China's per capita GDP fluctuated between 20 and 25 percent of the world average. China's per capita GDP index started to surge in the 1980s. By 2008, China's per capita GDP index rose to 88, placing China within the category of semi-periphery (see Figure 2.4). It was the first historical instance of a large geographic area moving from the periphery of the capitalist world system into the semi-periphery.

Historically, the great majority of the world population lived in the periphery. For the capitalist world system, the concentration of the great majority of the world population in the periphery helped to lower the labor costs and the levels of resource consumption. However, with the rise of China, the size of the semi-periphery has been greatly expanded.

In 2008, Western Europe, Western Offshoots, and Northeast Asia together accounted for about 14 percent of the world population. Eastern Europe, the former USSR, Latin America, West Asia, and China together accounted for 37 percent of the world population. The periphery now has less than 50 percent of the world population. Moreover, the economic trajectory of Southeast Asia and India, with a combined population of 25 percent of the world total, is diverging from the rest of the periphery. As

Southeast Asia and India approach the world average level of per capita GDP, the semi-periphery could be further expanded.

With the great expansion of the semi-periphery, the capitalist world system will have to accommodate a much larger population that demands higher living standards and higher levels of resource consumption. This could dramatically increase the global labor and resources costs, lower the global profit rate, and undermine the system's economic and political stability.

In the nineteenth century, the rise of global capitalism coincided with the decline of China. In the twenty-first century, will the rise of China herald the end of the capitalist world system?

The answer to this question largely depends on whether the remaining global resources and environmental space can afford the dramatic increase in energy demand brought about by the economic rise of China. This is the question the rest of the book will discuss.

3   Energy and the economy

In physics, "energy" is understood as the ability of a physical object to do "work" on some other object. Energy cannot be created or destroyed, but can be transformed. Every physical transformation that changes the position or condition of a physical object needs to "consume" energy or, strictly speaking, needs to involve some form of energy transformation.

There are four basic forms of energy: kinetic energy, gravitational energy, electrical energy, and nuclear energy. Thermal energy, or heat, is the kinetic energy associated with the rapid random motion of molecules. Molecules are combinations of atoms. At the atomic level, chemical energy can be considered a form of electrical energy, which can be released as the atomic electrons are rearranged. The energy contained in fossil fuels is a form of chemical energy. When a fuel is burned, the chemical energy it contains is converted into heat energy (Boyle 2004: 3–6).

The economy is the production, distribution, and consumption of goods and services that meet certain human needs or desires. All activities of production, distribution, and consumption involve some transformations of physical objects. This is true for not only industrial and agricultural activities but also services activities. Thus, energy consumption is required for all forms of economic activities.

In the modern global economy, energy is consumed either as fuels in liquid, gaseous, or solid forms or as electricity. Fuels are measured by the heat energy generated by burning. The basic international unit of heat energy is the joule, and of electrical energy is the kilowatt-hour. Given the importance of oil in the global economy, world energy consumption is commonly measured by tonnes of oil equivalent (TOE). A tonne of oil equivalent is defined as the heat energy generated by the burning of one tonne of crude oil, which equals 42 gigajoules or 42,000,000,000 joules.

Primary and final energy consumption

In 2012, the world's total primary energy consumption was 11.5 billion tonnes of oil equivalent. From 2000 to 2012, world primary energy consumption grew at an average annual rate of 2.5 percent.

In 2012, oil accounted for 35 percent of the world's primary energy consumption, natural gas accounted for 26 percent, coal accounted for 33 percent, nuclear electricity accounted for 2 percent, and renewable energies accounted for 4 percent (this book measures nuclear and renewable electricity by their electrical energy content rather than the "thermal equivalent"; see the Appendix to this chapter for further explanations).

Oil, natural gas, and coal often need to be processed and transformed before final uses (for example, oil needs to be processed into gasoline or diesel to be used for transportation). Coal, natural gas, and oil are also used to generate electricity. Fuels need to be transported and electricity needs to be transmitted to sites of final consumption. The methods of processing, transformation, transportation, and transmission consume energy and inevitably involve energy losses. Thus, the energy available for final consumption is smaller than the primary energy supply.

According to the International Energy Agency, the world's final energy consumption was 8.7 billion tonnes of oil equivalent in 2010 (IEA 2012a). Excluding traditional forms of renewable energy consumption (such as wood, vegetal waste, and animal waste), the world's final consumption of commercially produced energy was 7.3 billion tonnes, or 67 percent of the world's primary energy consumption in 2010. Of the world's commercial energy final consumption, oil (including biofuels) accounted for 50 percent, natural gas accounted for 18 percent, coal accounted for 11 percent, and electricity accounted for 21 percent.

Thus, liquid fuels currently account for about a half of the world's commercial energy final consumption and electricity accounts for one-fifth. Most renewable energies (such as hydro, wind, solar, tides, waves, and geothermal) are mainly used to generate electricity rather than to make liquid fuels. The inability to make liquid fuels may turn out to be a major obstacle that will limit the renewable energy expansion in the future.

China's energy consumption

In 2012, China's total primary energy consumption was 2.6 billion tonnes of oil equivalent, or 23 percent of the world total. Between 2000 and 2012, China's primary energy consumption grew at an average annual rate of 8.7 percent.

In 2012, coal accounted for 73 percent of China's primary energy consumption, oil accounted for 19 percent, natural gas accounted for 5 percent, nuclear electricity accounted for 0.3 percent, and renewable energies accounted for 3 percent.

Unlike the rest of the world, China's energy consumption is dominated by coal, the most carbon-intensive source of energy. China is now the world's largest energy consumer and China's energy consumption has been growing rapidly. Unless China's energy structure is fundamentally transformed and decarbonized, there is little chance for the global carbon dioxide emissions to be reduced at a sufficiently rapid pace to achieve reasonable climate stabilization.

In 2010, China's final energy consumption was 1.2 billion tonnes of oil equivalent, or 56 percent of China's primary energy consumption. Coal accounted for 34 percent of China's final energy consumption, oil accounted for 32 percent, natural gas accounted for 6 percent, and electricity accounted for 25 percent (calculated using data from the National Bureau of Statistics of China 2012).

China's relatively low ratio of final to primary energy consumption reflects the fact that coal dominates China's primary energy consumption and about 70 percent of China's primary coal consumption is used for electricity generation, heat generation, and coke-making. About two-thirds of the coal energy used for these purposes is lost in the process of transformation.

Oil

In 2012, the world's total oil consumption was 4.1 billion tonnes, or 89.8 million barrels per day (BP 2013, including 1.2 million barrels per day of biofuels). From 2000 to 2012, world oil consumption grew at an average annual rate of 1.2 percent.

The entire modern-world transportation is built around oil. In 2010, oil (including biofuels) accounted for 95 percent of the world's total transportation fuels (IEA 2012a). Oil is essential for modern agriculture, which depends on oil to provide fuels for agricultural machineries, to provide feedstock for the making of fertilizers, pesticides, and herbicides, for food processing and packaging, and for transportation. Oil is the essential input for petrochemical industries. Petrochemicals, such as ethylene, propylene, and butadiene, are basic building blocks used to make a variety of products, including disinfectants, solvents, antifreezes, coolants, lubricants, and various plastics (Heinberg 2006: 4–7).

In 2010, transportation accounted for 53 percent of the world's primary oil consumption, non-energy uses (oil used as a chemical feedstock) accounted for 15 percent, industry accounted for 8 percent, agriculture, services, and the residential sector accounted for 11 percent, electricity and heat generation accounted for 7 percent, other intermediate uses and losses accounted for 6 percent (IEA 2012a).

In 2012, China's oil consumption was 484 million tonnes, or 10.2 million barrels per day (BP 2013). From 2000 to 2012, China's oil consumption grew at an average annual rate of 6.6 percent.

In 2010, industry and construction accounted for 41 percent of China's primary oil consumption, transportation accounted for 34 percent, agriculture, services and the residential sector accounted for 18 percent, electricity and heat generation accounted for 2 percent, and other intermediate uses and losses accounted for 6 percent (calculated using data from the National Bureau of Statistics of China 2012).

Natural gas

In 2012, world natural gas consumption was 3.3 trillion cubic meters, or 3.0 billion tonnes of oil equivalent (BP 2013). From 2000 to 2012, world natural gas consumption grew at an average annual rate of 2.7 percent.

In North America and Western Europe, natural gas is widely used for heating and electricity generation. Gas turbines can be turned on or off quickly. Natural gas-fired electric power plants are best suited for meeting "peak-load" power demand, when demand for electricity surges within a short period of time. According to the International Energy Agency, natural gas accounted for 22 percent of the world's total electricity generation in 2010 (IEA 2012a).

Among the non-hydro renewable energies, wind and solar are the most important. Both are intermittent. Natural gas can be used in association with wind and solar. Natural gas-fired electricity would help to make up the shortfalls when electric supplies from wind and solar fail to meet the demand. In the future, if solar and wind account for a substantial portion of total electricity generation, large-scale back-up by natural gas may be indispensable.

Like oil, natural gas is used as a feedstock in the chemical industries. Natural gas is an essential input for the production of nitrogenous fertilizers (Heinberg 2006: 5).

In 2010, industry accounted for 17 percent of the world's primary natural gas consumption, non-energy uses accounted for 6 percent, transportation accounted for 3 percent, agriculture, services, and the residential sector accounted for 22 percent, electricity and heat generation accounted for 40 percent, and other intermediate uses and losses accounted for 11 percent (IEA 2012a).

Natural gas accounts for only about 5 percent of China's total energy consumption but China's natural gas consumption has been growing rapidly. In 2012, China's natural gas consumption reached 144 billion cubic meters, or 130 million tonnes of oil equivalent (BP 2013). From 2000 to 2012, China's natural gas consumption grew at an average annual rate of 15.9 percent.

In 2010, industry and construction accounted for 46 percent of China's primary natural gas consumption, transportation accounted for 10 percent, agriculture, services, and the residential sector accounted for 26 percent, and electricity and heat generation accounted for 18 percent (calculated using data from the National Bureau of Statistics of China 2012).

Coal

Coal dominated world energy production and consumption in the nineteenth century and the first half of the twentieth century. Under the current trend, coal will again become the world's largest source of energy in one or two decades.

In 2012, the world's total coal consumption was 3.7 billion tonnes of oil equivalent (BP 2013). From 2000 to 2012, world coal consumption grew at an average annual rate of 4 percent. Since 2000, coal has made a larger contribution than any other energy source to the world's energy consumption growth. From 2000 to 2012, coal accounted for 48 percent of the world's primary energy consumption growth.

Because coal is relatively abundant and cheap, coal-fired electric power plants are often used to meet "base-load" power demand, generating electricity at a constant rate to meet the consumers' continuous demand. According to the International Energy Agency, coal accounted for 41 percent of the world's total electricity generation in 2010 (IEA 2012a).

World steel production is dependent on coal. Coking coal is a vital input in the steel-making process. In 2010, about 720 million tonnes of coking coal was used for steel production (world steel production in 2010 was 1.4 billion tonnes) (World Coal Association 2012).

In 2010, industry accounted for 20 percent of the world's primary coal consumption, non-energy uses accounted for 1 percent, agriculture, services, and the residential sector accounted for 4 percent, electricity and heat generation accounted for 64 percent, and other intermediate uses and losses accounted for 11 percent (IEA 2012a).

In 2012, China's coal consumption reached 1.9 billion tonnes of oil equivalent, accounting for 50 percent of the world's total coal consumption (BP 2013). From 2000 to 2012, China's coal consumption grew at an average annual rate of 8.8 percent.

In 2010, industry and construction accounted for 37 percent of China's primary coal consumption, agriculture, services, and the residential sector accounted for 5 percent, electricity and heat generation accounted for 54 percent, and other intermediate uses and losses accounted for 3 percent (National Bureau of Statistics 2012).

Electricity

In 2012, the world's total electricity generation was 22,504 terawatt-hours (BP 2013). In terms of oil equivalent, 22,504 terawatt hours of electricity equals approximately 1.9 billion tonnes of oil equivalent (one million tonnes of oil equivalent = 11.63 terawatt-hours = 11.63 billion kilowatt-hours). Between 2000 and 2012, world electricity generation grew at an average annual rate of 3.2 percent.

Electricity is widely used in the industrial, commercial, and residential sectors. In 2010, industry accounted for 42 percent of the world's electricity consumption, transportation accounted for 2 percent, and agriculture, services, and the residential sector accounted for 57 percent (IEA 2012a). Electricity cannot be used to make liquid fuels. Nor can electricity be used as a feedstock in the chemical industries. Because of these limitations, electricity use is currently limited to about one-fifth of the world's final energy consumption.

In 2012, China's electricity generation reached 4,938 terawatt-hours, or 425 million tonnes of oil equivalent (BP 2013). China now accounts for 22 percent of the world's electricity generation. Between 2000 and 2012, China's electricity generation grew at an average annual rate of 11.4 percent.

In 2010, industry and construction accounted for 69 percent of China's total electricity consumption, transportation accounted for 2 percent, agriculture, services, and the residential sector accounted for 23 percent, and transmission and distribution losses accounted for 6 percent (calculated using data from the National Bureau of Statistics 2012).

Electricity generation: the world

Figure 3.1 shows the shares of different types of electricity in the world's total electricity generation from 1980 to 2010. Despite many talks of "green economy" by governments, environmental groups, and corporations, so far there has been little evidence of decarbonization in a sector where renewable energies can penetrate relatively easily.

Since the 1980s, the share of conventional thermal electricity (electricity generation from coal, natural gas, and oil) has stayed at around

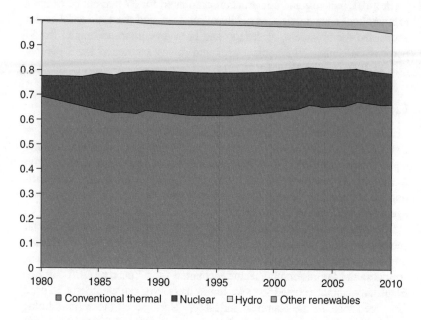

Figure 3.1 Share of world electricity generation (share of net generation, 1980–2010) (sources: Electricity net generation data from 1980 to 2010 are from EIA (2013a). Net electricity generation is defined as gross electricity generation less the power plants' own use of electricity).

two-thirds. The conventional thermal share fell from about 70 percent in 1980 to 62 percent in 1995, largely because of the nuclear electricity expansion in the 1980s. However, since then, the conventional thermal share has recovered. By 2010, the conventional thermal share stood at 67 percent.

The nuclear electricity share increased from 9 percent in 1980 to 18 percent in 1996. By 2010, it had fallen to 13 percent. Hydro accounted for 21 percent of the world's electricity generation in 1980. By 2011, the hydro share had fallen to 17 percent. The non-hydro renewable electricity share accounted for only 0.4 percent of the world's electricity generation in 1980. By 2010, its share had increased to 4 percent. In 2010, the share of total renewable electricity (including both hydro and non-hydro renewables) in the world's electricity generation was 20 percent, which was in fact not higher than in 1980 (when the total renewable electricity share was 22 percent).

From 2000 to 2010, the world's conventional thermal electricity generation grew at an average annual rate of 3.8 percent, nuclear electricity generation grew at an average annual rate of 0.7 percent, hydroelectricity generation grew at an average annual rate of 2.7 percent, and non-hydro renewable electricity generation grew at an average annual rate of 11.9 percent.

In 2010, wind accounted for 45 percent of the world's total non-hydro renewable electricity generation, biomass and waste accounted for 42 percent, geothermal accounted for 9 percent, and solar accounted for 4 percent. From 2000 to 2010, wind electricity grew at an average annual rate of 27.0 percent, solar electricity grew at an average annual rate of 33.9 percent, biomass electricity grew at an average annual rate of 7.0 percent, and geothermal electricity grew at an average annual rate of 2.5 percent.

Figure 3.2 shows the shares of different types of electricity in the world's electricity generating capacity. The electricity generating capacity tells the maximum rate at which a power plant can generate electricity. A generator with a capacity of one kilowatt can generate a maximum amount of electricity of one kilowatt-hour during one hour of operation. A large power plant with a capacity of one gigawatt or one million kilowatt can generate a maximum amount of electricity of one million kilowatt-hours during one hour of operation.

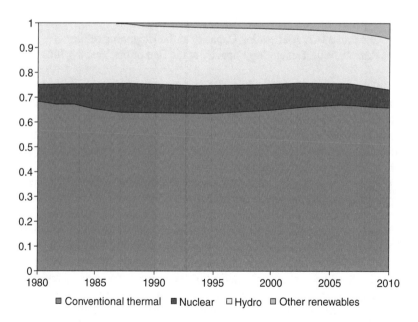

Figure 3.2 Share of world electricity generating capacity (share of generating capacity, 1980–2010) (source: Data for electricity generating capacity from 1980 to 2010 are from EIA (2013a)).

By the end of 2010, the world had a total electricity generating capacity of about 5,100 gigawatts, including 3,400 gigawatts of conventional thermal generating capacity, 380 gigawatts of nuclear generating capacity, 1,000 gigawatts of hydro generating capacity (including hydro pumped storage capacity), and 290 gigawatts of non-hydro renewable generating capacity.

In 2010, nuclear electricity accounted for 8 percent of the total generating capacity but 13 percent of the total electricity generation; the non-hydro renewable electricity accounted for 6 percent of the total generating capacity but only 4 percent of the total electricity generation. The differences between the nuclear electricity and the non-hydro renewable electricity reflect their different capacity utilization rates.

The concept of capacity utilization rate has important economic and technical implications. For example, nuclear power plants typically have a capacity utilization rate of about 80 percent and solar power plants typically have a capacity utilization rate of about 15 percent. Therefore, a nuclear power plant of one gigawatt can generate more than five times as much electricity as a solar power plant of one gigawatt.

A power plant's capacity utilization rate is calculated as follows:

Capacity Utilization Rate = Annual Electricity
Generation × 2 / (Generating Capacity at the Beginning of the
Year × 8,760 + Generating Capacity at the End of the Year × 8,760)

A full year has 8,760 hours (365 × 24 = 8,760). If a generator of one kilowatt capacity operates all year round, it would generate an annual electric output of 8,760 kilowatt-hours. Applying the numbers to the above formula, it would yield a capacity utilization rate of 100 percent. If the generator operates during half of the year, the formula would yield a capacity utilization rate of 50 percent.

Figure 3.3 shows the observed capacity utilization rates of different types of electricity based on the global electricity generation data. Since 1980, the conventional thermal utilization rates have fluctuated between 44 and 49 percent. The nuclear utilization rates increased steadily from 1980 to 2000 and have since then stayed around 80 percent. The hydro utilization rates have fluctuated just below 40 percent. The average non-hydro renewable utilization rates were about 60 percent in the early 1990s, when biomass and geothermal electricity accounted for more than 90 percent of the non-hydro renewable electricity. With the rapid growth of wind and solar electricity, the average utilization rate of non-hydro renewable electricity had fallen. By 2010, it fell to 32 percent.

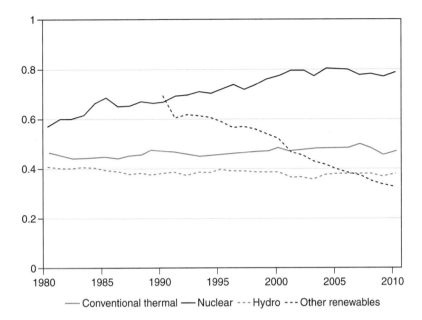

Figure 3.3 Capacity utilization rates (world electricity generation, 1980–2010) (sources: Calculated from data of electricity generation and generating capacity. Data from 1980 to 2010 are from EIA (2013a)).

Figure 3.4 shows the observed capacity utilization rates for different types of non-hydro renewable electricity. Figure 3.4 makes it clear that, in actual operation, the capacity utilization rates of wind and solar electricity are very low. In 2010, the world's average observed capacity utilization rate for wind electricity was 24 percent and for solar electricity was 13 percent.

Figure 3.5 shows the world's annual net installation of electricity generating capacity from 1985 to 2010 (net installation equals the electricity generating capacity at the end of the current year less the electricity generating capacity at the end of the previous year). Between 1980 and 2000, the world on average added about 70 gigawatts of electricity generating capacity a year. For the period 2001–2005, the average annual net installation surged to about 130 gigawatts. For the period 2006–2010, the average annual net installation increased further to about 190 gigawatts. China's construction boom contributed to much of the surge.

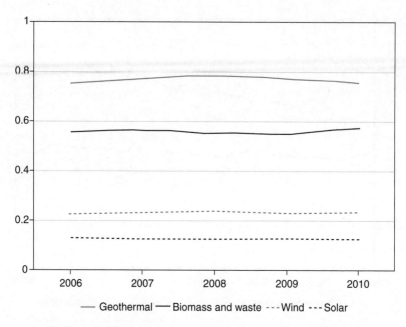

Figure 3.4 Capacity utilization rates (world non-hydro renewable electricity, 2006–2010) (sources: Calculated from data of electricity generation and generating capacity. Data for electricity generation and electricity generating capacity from 2006 to 2010 are from EIA (2013a)).

Electricity generation: China

In 2011, conventional thermal electricity accounted for 80 percent of China's total electricity generation, nuclear accounted for less than 2 percent, hydro accounted for 15 percent, and non-hydro renewables accounted for 2 percent (EIA 2013a).

From 2000 to 2011, China's conventional thermal electricity generation grew at an average annual rate of 11.9 percent, nuclear electricity generation grew at an average annual rate of 16.2 percent, hydroelectricity generation grew at an average annual rate of 10.9 percent, and non-hydro renewable electricity generation grew at an average annual rate of 38.5 percent.

By the end of 2010, China's total installed electricity generating capacity stood at about 990 gigawatts, including 710 gigawatts of conventional thermal electricity, 11 gigawatts of nuclear electricity, 230 gigawatts of hydroelectricity, and 36 gigawatts of non-hydro renewable electricity (EIA 2013a).

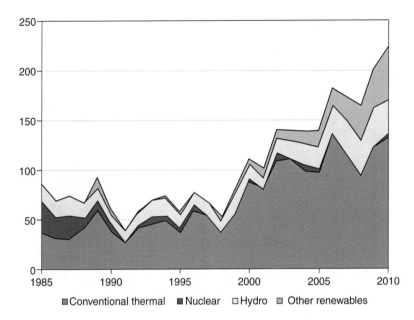

Figure 3.5 Net installations of electricity generating capacity (world, 1985–2010, gigawatts) (sources: Calculated using data of electricity generating capacity from 1984 to 2010 (EIA 2013a)).

The US currently has an installed electricity generating capacity of about 1,050 gigawatts. Given China's rates of construction, China will soon overtake the US to have the world's largest electric power sector.

Figure 3.6 shows China's net installations of electricity generating capacity from 1985 to 2010. Between 2005 and 2010, China on average added about 93 gigawatts of electricity generating capacity a year, accounting for about a half of the world's total net installations.

GDP and energy efficiency

Economic output is usually measured by gross domestic product, or GDP. GDP is defined as the market value of all final goods and services produced within a country during a specified period of time. GDP does not include the "intermediate goods," that is, the goods that are used in the production of other goods, such as raw materials. However, GDP is "gross" and does include depreciation of fixed capital. GDP measures current economic activities. Resale of used goods and transactions of financial assets are not included in the GDP.

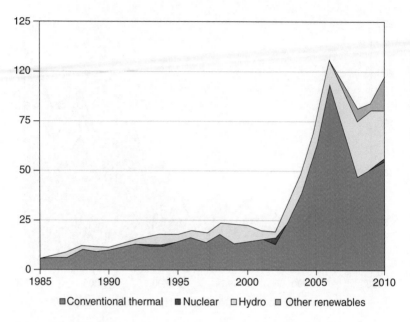

Figure 3.6 Net installations of electricity generating capacity (China, 1985–2010, gigawatts) (sources: See Figure 3.5).

People often point out that GDP is a poor measure of quality of life. GDP does not include useful activities that are not measured by market values (like household production). GDP fails to take into account "externalities," such as pollution and resource depletion. GDP does not consider the social costs of unemployment and inequality. GDP treats certain social costs, like the building of prisons due to rising crimes or increases in healthcare spending due to poor health, as "goods and services."

An implicit assumption of many critics of GDP is that GDP should be a measure of people's quality of life or living standards. However, the purpose of capitalist economic activities is not to advance the population's long-term well-being, but to make profit and accumulate capital (although sometimes higher living standards can be a byproduct of capital accumulation). GDP would be a fairly reasonable measure if it were regarded primarily as a measure of capital accumulation rather than of people's quality of life.

To arrive at the measure of GDP, different goods and services need to be added up using prices. GDP measured by the "current prices," or the prices of the current year, is called "nominal GDP." To measure the economic growth rates, nominal GDP needs to be corrected for inflation. GDP corrected for inflation is known as the "real GDP," which is usually measured by "constant prices" in a selected base year.

If the economic growth rate and the inflation rate is small (in single digits), the following approximate formula may be used to calculate the relationship between the economic growth rate, the inflation rate, and the nominal GDP growth rate:

Economic Growth Rate ≈ Nominal GDP Growth Rate – Inflation Rate

To arrive at the world GDP, different countries' GDP need to be added up. One convenient approach is to add different countries' GDP by using the market exchange rates between their currencies. But the market exchange rates often do not correctly reflect the true purchasing power of each currency in its own domestic market. Currently, the main international institutions, such as the International Monetary Fund and the World Bank, usually use the measure of "purchasing power parity" to compare different countries' GDP and to calculate the world GDP. The purchasing power parity approach compares different currencies by measuring how many goods and services a currency can buy in its own domestic market.

An economy's energy efficiency is measured by the ratio of GDP over the primary energy consumption:

Energy Efficiency = GDP / Primary Energy Consumption

The level of energy efficiency depends on several factors. First of all, it depends on how much of the primary energy consumption is transformed into energy available for final consumption. Second, it depends on how the final energy consumption is distributed between different economic sectors. Third, it depends on how efficient each economic sector uses the final energy to generate economic output.

In international comparison, a country's energy efficiency is also affected by its position in the global division of labor (whether or not a country specializes in energy-intensive industries) and the country's geographic position (for example, countries located in high latitudes need to consume more energy for heating).

Figure 3.7 shows the energy efficiency levels of the world's four largest economies as well as the world's average energy efficiency from 1980 to 2012. Germany and Japan have the world's highest energy efficiencies. In 2012, Germany's energy efficiency reached the level of 10,200 dollars per tonne of oil equivalent (in constant 2005 international dollars). Japan's energy efficiency was about 8,700 dollars per tonne of oil equivalent, the US energy

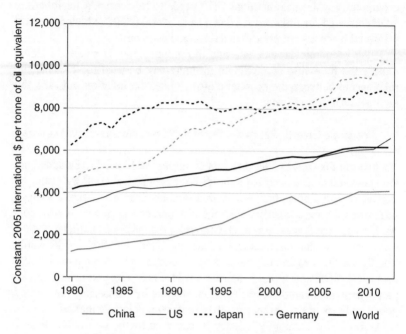

Figure 3.7 Energy efficiency (selected countries, 1980–2012, $/TOE) (sources: Calculated from each country's GDP and primary energy consumption. Energy data are from BP (2013). GDP in constant 2005 international dollars is from the World Bank (2013)).

efficiency was about 6,700 dollars per tonne of oil equivalent, and China's energy efficiency was about 4,200 dollars per tonne of oil equivalent.

In the era of neoliberal globalization, many energy-intensive industries have been relocated from the core of the capitalist world system to the periphery and semi-periphery. Much of the energy consumed by the periphery and semi-periphery is used for the production of goods to be consumed by the core countries. A more genuine measure of a country's energy consumption should include the energy embodied in the goods imported from the rest of the world and exclude the energy embodied in the goods exported to the rest of the world.

I make a rough estimate of the energy embodied in each country's exports and imports by assuming that the "energy intensity" (that is, energy consumption per dollar of economic output) of a country's exports is the same as the energy intensity of the country's GDP and the energy intensity of a country's imports is the same as the energy intensity of the rest of the world's GDP.

Figure 3.8 shows the energy efficiency levels of the world's four largest economies adjusted for the "trade effects," that is, correcting each country's energy consumption by including energy embodied in imports and excluding energy embodied in exports. Based on the adjusted measure, in 2011, Germany had an energy efficiency of 8,200 dollars per tonne of oil equivalent, 20 percent lower than the unadjusted level. Japan had an adjusted energy efficiency of about 8,500 dollar per tonne of oil equivalent, 5 percent lower than the unadjusted level. The US had an adjusted energy efficiency of about 6,000 dollars per tonne of oil equivalent, 7 percent lower than the unadjusted level. China had an adjusted energy efficiency of about 4,900 dollars per tonne of oil equivalent, 17 percent higher than the unadjusted level.

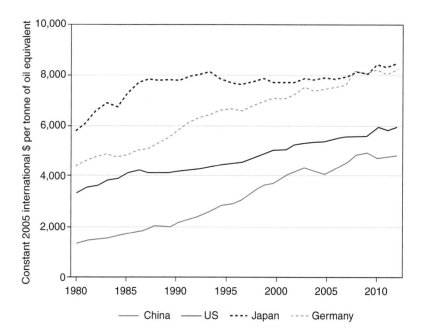

Figure 3.8 Energy efficiency adjusted for trade effects (selected countries, 1980–2011, $/TOE) (sources: Energy efficiency levels are adjusted for energy embodied in exports and imports. Energy data are from BP (2013). GDP, exports, and imports data are from the World Bank (2013)).

Concluding remarks of the chapter

Global economic growth depends on the expansion of energy consumption.

Currently, fossil fuels account for about 94 percent of the world's total energy consumption. Nuclear and renewable energies account for 6 percent. Fossil fuels are nonrenewable resources and the consumption of fossil fuels results in greenhouse gas emissions threatening to bring about global ecological catastrophes.

Eventually, the global economy will have to be fundamentally transformed and future human civilization will have to be based on renewable energies. The question is at what rate the renewable energies can be sustainably utilized and whether the future global economy based on renewable energies can keep pursuing infinite economic growth as the global capitalist system has done for centuries.

Nuclear energy and most renewable energies are mainly used to generate electricity rather than to make liquid fuels. Oil currently accounts for about one-third of the world's primary energy consumption and one-half of the final energy consumption. Oil is essential for transportation, modern agriculture, and chemical industries.

Current evidence suggests that world oil production may peak in the near future. If world oil production does peak and start to decline, will "peak oil" bring global economic growth or China's economic growth to an end? Or will the negative impact be offset by the development of alternative energies and rising energy efficiency?

The next three chapters will consider these questions.

Appendix: alternative energy measurements

According to the International Energy Agency (IEA), the world's total primary energy supply was 12,717 million tonnes of oil equivalent in 2010 (IEA 2012a). According to the BP *Statistical Review of World Energy*, the world's total primary energy consumption was 11,943 million tonnes of oil equivalent in 2010 (BP 2013). According to this book's measurement, the world's total primary energy consumption was 10,966 million tonnes of oil equivalent in 2010.

The different measurements result from differences in statistical coverage and different approaches in converting nuclear and renewable electricity into heat energy. The IEA definition of total primary energy supply includes not only the commercially produced energy but also the estimated energy consumption derived from various traditional forms of biomass consumption, such as wood, wood waste, crop residuals, animal materials, and animal waste. The BP definition of total primary energy consumption includes only the commercially produced energy.

BP measures nuclear and renewable electricity by their "thermal equivalent" and assumes a conversion efficiency of 38 percent. That is, nuclear or renewable electricity is not measured by its electrical energy content. Instead, it is measured by how much heat energy it would take if the same amount of electricity were generated from fossil fuels. With the assumption of 38 percent conversion efficiency, the thermal equivalent equals the actual electrical energy content divided by 0.38. The implied conversion ratio between heat energy (in terms of oil equivalent) and electricity is as follows:

one million tonnes of oil equivalent = 4.4194 terawatt-hours =
4.4194 billion kilowatt-hours = 4.4194 trillion watt-hours.

The IEA measures nuclear electricity by its thermal equivalent and assumes a conversion efficiency of 33 percent. For geothermal electricity, the IEA assumes a conversion efficiency of 10 percent. However, the IEA measures hydro, wind, solar, and other renewable electricity by their electrical energy content.

In this book, energy production or consumption is defined as the production or consumption of commercially produced energy. Various traditional forms of biomass consumption are not included.

The measurement of thermal equivalent depends on the assumed conversion efficiency. With the development of technology, the conversion efficiency between the fossil fuels consumed and the electricity generated changes constantly. The future thermal equivalents will be different from the present and the past ones. This book studies long-term developments of energy production and consumption. To have a constant ratio between oil equivalent and electricity that can be applied to all time periods and to avoid the difficulty of having to make assumptions about historical and future thermal equivalents, this book measures nuclear and renewable electricity by their electrical energy content. When electricity is measured directly by its energy content, one million tonnes of oil equivalent = 11.63 terawatt-hours = 11.63 billion kilowatt-hours = 11.63 trillion watt-hours.

4   Peak oil

According to BP (2013), in 2012, the world's total production of crude oil and natural gas liquids was 4.1 billion tonnes. Crude oil is what is commonly known as "oil" or petroleum, the liquid hydrocarbons extracted from oil fields. Natural gas liquid is a liquid byproduct of natural gas production.

Oil production is commonly stated in terms of barrels. On average, one tonne of crude oil equals 7.3 barrels. Therefore, one million barrels of daily crude oil production corresponds to 50 million tonnes of annual production. The conversion ratio applies to crude oil only and varies across oil fields. Natural gas liquids have less energy content than crude oil for the same volume. On average, a barrel of natural gas liquids has the same energy content as 0.7 barrels of crude oil (Aleklett 2012: 116). According to BP (2013), in 2012, the world's total production of crude oil and natural gas liquids was 86.1 million barrels per day.

According to the US Energy Information Administration (EIA), in 2012, the world's total oil supply (including all liquid fuels) was 89.1 million barrels per day. The EIA's "total oil supply" includes 75.6 million barrels of crude oil, 8.9 million barrels of natural gas liquids, 2.3 million barrels of other liquids, and 2.4 million barrels of refinery reprocessing gains (EIA 2013a). Other liquids include biofuels and liquid fuels made from coal and natural gas. Refinery reprocessing gains refer to the increase in volume resulting from the processing of crude oil into petroleum products.

For the rest of the chapter, "oil production" refers to the total production of crude oil and natural gas liquids. The term "total liquid fuels production" refers to the total production of crude oil, natural gas liquids, other liquids, and refinery reprocessing gains. The term "oil consumption" is used in the same sense as the term "total liquid fuels consumption," including the consumption of oil and other liquid fuels.

Oil and economic growth

Figure 4.1 shows the historical relationship between the world economic growth rate and the annual change in oil consumption from 1981 to 2012 and the linear trend. The annual change in oil consumption equals the current year's oil consumption less the previous year's oil consumption.

A simple linear regression between the annual change in oil consumption and the world economic growth rate for the period 1981–2012 yields the following results:

$$\text{Change in Oil Consumption} = -0.890 + 0.542 \text{ Economic Growth Rate}$$

That is, with zero economic growth rate, there is an autonomous tendency for world oil consumption to fall by about 890,000 barrels per day a year. Other things being equal, if the world economic growth rate rises by 1 percentage point, oil consumption tends to rise by about 540,000 barrels per day. If oil consumption does not change, the implied world economic growth rate is 1.6 percent.

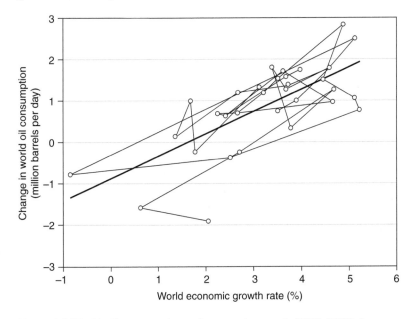

Figure 4.1 World oil consumption and economic growth (1981–2012) (sources: World oil consumption for 1980–2012 is from BP (2013). The BP definition of "oil consumption" includes the consumption of crude oil, natural gas liquids, and other liquid fuels. GDP in constant 2005 international dollars for 1980–2011 is from the World Bank (2013), updated to 2012 using data from IMF (2013)).

The results from this simple linear regression suggest that, if world oil production does peak and start to decline, the world economic growth rate may fall below 1.6 percent. Historically, world economic growth rates fell below 2 percent a year only during periods of major crisis and instability (see Figure 2.4). Thus, global capitalism may suffer from persistent economic and political instability in the post-"peak oil" era.

China's oil consumption has undergone exponential growth. It is more appropriate to use China's oil consumption growth rate (rather than the annual change) compared with China's economic growth rate. Figure 4.2 shows the historical relationship between China's economic growth rate and the oil consumption growth rate from 1981 to 2012 and the linear trend. The oil consumption growth rate equals the ratio of the annual change in oil consumption over the previous year's oil consumption.

A simple linear regression between China's oil consumption growth rate and the economic growth rate for the period 1981–2012 yields the following results:

Oil Consumption Growth Rate = 0.508 + 0.537 Economic Growth Rate

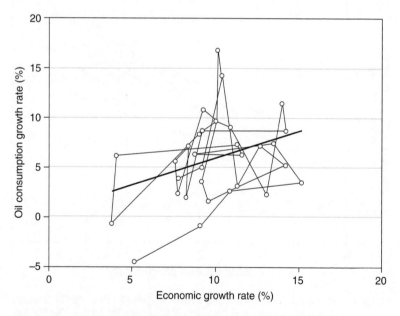

Figure 4.2 China's oil consumption and economic growth (1981–2012) (sources: China's oil consumption for 1980–2012 is from BP (2013). GDP in constant 2005 international dollars for 1980–2011 is from the World Bank (2013), updated to 2012 using data from IMF (2013)).

Other things being equal, if China's economic growth rate rises by 1 percentage point, the oil consumption growth rate tends to rise by 0.54 percentage points.

National oil production peaks

Since oil is a nonrenewable resource, it is obvious that oil production cannot keep growing forever. At some point, oil production from a field, a region, or a country, and eventually from the entire world, will reach the maximum level and decline thereafter. The question is not whether peak oil will happen but when it will happen.

More than half of the world's oil production comes from the "giant fields" (a giant oil field is defined as one with original oil reserves greater than 500 million barrels). The world's giant oil field discovery rates peaked in the 1960s and have declined since then. As of 2009, of the world's 20 largest oil fields, 16 had passed the peak (Hirsch *et al.* 2009: 45–46).

In 1956, American geologist M. King Hubbert made the famous prediction that US oil production would peak between 1965 and 1971 (Aleklett 2012: 7–11). In fact, US oil production peaked in 1970. In 2012, US oil production stood at 74 percent of its peak level.

Table 4.1 shows the world's 20 largest oil producers in 2012. The 20 countries together accounted for 85 percent of the world's total oil production in 2012. Of the 20 countries, 14 produced in 2012 at levels less than the observed peak. Six countries (United States, Iran, Mexico, Venezuela, Norway, and the United Kingdom) produced at levels that were at least 20 percent less than the peak.

Iran's oil production has been affected by geopolitical risks that may persist for years. Venezuela has large heavy oil deposits that may be developed in the future. US oil production has risen rapidly since 2008, largely due to the growth of "shale oil" production. But the US may never regain the peak production level recorded in 1970. Production in Mexico, Norway, and the United Kingdom is likely to have permanently passed the peak.

Hubbert linearization

In 1982, M. King Hubbert summarized his method of predicting oil production peak in a published paper (Hubbert 1982). Hubbert assumed that a country's oil production would follow the pattern of a bell-like logistic curve. According to the Hubbert model, in the early stage of a country's oil development, oil production rises with accelerating rates. At some

Table 4.1 The world's 20 largest oil producers, 2012

	Observed peak year	Peak production (million tonnes)	2012 production (million tonnes)	2012 production as % of peak
Saudi Arabia	2012	547.0	547.0	100
Russian Federation	1987	569.5	526.2	92
United States	1970	533.5	394.9	74
China	2012	207.5	207.5	100
Canada	2012	182.6	182.6	100
Iran	1974	303.2	174.9	58
United Arab Emirates	2012	154.1	154.1	100
Kuwait	1972	167.3	152.5	91
Iraq	1979	171.6	152.4	89
Mexico	2004	190	143.9	76
Venezuela	1970	197.2	139.7	71
Nigeria	2005	122.1	116.2	95
Brazil	2011	114.2	112.2	98
Norway	2001	162.5	87.5	54
Angola	2008	93.1	86.9	93
Qatar	2012	83.3	83.3	100
Kazakhstan	2011	82.4	81.3	99
Algeria	2007	86.5	73.0	84
Colombia	2012	49.9	49.9	100
United Kingdom	1999	137.4	45.0	33

Source: BP (2013).

point, oil production growth slows down. The oil production peak is likely to happen when about half of the ultimately recoverable oil resources have been exploited.

In the Hubbert model, the parameters used to project future oil production are derived from a procedure known as the "Hubbert linearization." Let "P_t" be the current oil production of year "t" and "Q_t" be the cumulative oil production up to year "t" (the sum of the current year's and all the previous years' production). "P_t/Q_t" is the ratio of the current production to the cumulative production or the cumulative production growth rate. As the cumulative production (Q_t) rises, "P_t/Q_t" tends to fall and, at some point, a downward sloping linear relationship can be observed between "P_t/Q_t" and "Q_t." The linear relationship helps to predict the ultimately recoverable amount of oil.

This can be illustrated with the following formula:

$$P_t/Q_t = a - b\,(Q_t)$$

The formula represents the linear relationship between the cumulative production growth rate and the cumulative oil production. Note that, when the cumulative production growth rate (P_t/Q_t) falls to zero, it suggests that all the recoverable oil resources have been exploited. Thus, the cumulative production up to the point where $P_t/Q_t=0$ would represent the ultimately recoverable amount of oil. It can be easily derived that the ratio "a/b" tells the ultimately recoverable amount of oil implied by the linear relationship.

Figure 4.3 shows the evolution of the world's cumulative oil production from 1951 to 2012. Applying the Hubbert linearization technique to the period 1993 to 2012, the linear relationship indicates the ultimately recoverable amount of oil to be 386 billion tonnes. The regression R-square is 0.971—that is, the linear relationship statistically explains 97 percent of the observed variations of the cumulative production growth rates.

The Hubbert model suggests that the world oil production peak should happen when half of the ultimately recoverable amount has been produced. It follows that world peak oil should happen when the world's cumulative oil production exceeds 193 billion tonnes.

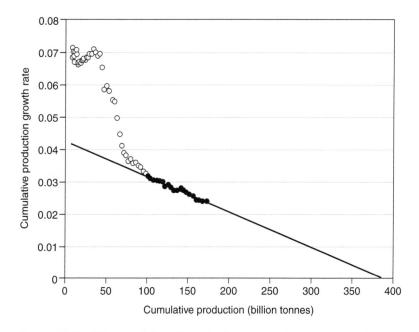

Figure 4.3 World's cumulative oil production (1951–2012) (sources: Historical world oil production before 1965 is from Rutledge (2007). World oil production from 1965 to 2012 is from BP (2013)).

The world's cumulative oil production by 2012 was 172 billion tonnes. The world currently produces about four billion tonnes of oil a year. Simple arithmetic suggests that the world's cumulative oil production will exceed 193 billion tonnes by 2018. Thus, according to this exercise of Hubbert linearization, world oil production should peak in 2018 and decline thereafter.

The Hubbert linearization is easy to understand and apply. It relies exclusively on historical production data and reflects the historical evolution of technical, economic, and geological conditions. But it cannot predict possible future changes in technologies and economic conditions. Hubbert linearization cannot be properly applied if the downward linear relationship between the cumulative production and its growth rate has not yet been formed and stabilized. Because of these limitations, results of Hubbert linearization need to be interpreted cautiously and compared with estimates based on other research methods.

For more detailed explanations of the Hubbert linearization and its applications, see the Appendix.

Oil megaproject analysis

It typically takes 6–10 years after initial planning for a large oil project to start significant oil production (Hirsch *et al.* 2009: 62). By examining the currently planned oil projects, it is possible to establish the likely world oil production levels in the near future.

The Wikipedia "Oil Megaprojects" page reports the world's new additions of crude oil and natural gas liquids capacity from 2003 to 2020, including all projects that proposed to have a production capacity greater than 20,000 barrels per day (Wikipedia 2013).

From 2002 to 2011, the world's cumulative additions of oil production capacity were 34.6 million barrels per day. During the same period, the world's observed oil production capacity (the sum of crude oil production, natural gas liquids production, and the OPEC surplus crude oil production capacity; "OPEC" stands for the Organization of the Petroleum Exporting Countries; data are from EIA 2013a and 2013b) increased from 79.5 million barrels per day to 85.7 million barrels per day, with a total net increase of 6.2 million barrels per day. Thus, the world's observed total depletion of oil production capacity from 2002 to 2011 amounted to 28.4 million barrels per day, with an average annual depletion of 3.2 million barrels per day.

The world's average annual oil production from 2002 to 2010 was 79.7 million barrels per day. Thus, the observed average annual depletion rate (the ratio of oil production capacity depletion relative to the previous year's oil production) was 4 percent. This is in line with the oil capacity depletion rates reported by other studies. According to Skrebowski (2008), the International Energy Agency and the Cambridge Energy Research Associates reported depletion rates between 4 and 4.5 percent. The world's current oil production is about 85 million barrels per day (crude oil and natural liquids). With a 4 percent depletion rate, the world needs to add at least 3.4 million barrels per day of new production capacity every year just to keep the oil production level constant. To put this number in perspective, it requires the world to add the equivalent of a new "Saudi Arabia" (in terms of oil production capacity) every three years.

In June 2012, the Harvard Kennedy School of Government published a highly optimistic report on the world's future oil supply: *Oil: The Next Revolution* (Maugeri 2012). According to Maugeri, the US shale oil production boom is bringing about a paradigm shift. Beyond 2015, new oil production projects will advance significantly. The world could face a significant overproduction of oil, leading to lower oil prices. Maugeri (2012: 6) summarized his argument as follows: "Oil is not in short supply. From a purely physical point of view, there are huge volumes of conventional and unconventional oils still to be developed, with no 'peak oil' in sight."

According to Maugeri, the total additional production from all possible new oil projects from 2011 to 2020 amounts to 49 million barrels per day. After taking into account various "risk factors," the more realistic estimate of the additional production that could materialize by 2020 is 29 million barrels per day.

In the report, Maugeri explained that he had assumed that the global average oil capacity depletion rate would be 2–3 percent (Maugeri 2012: 20). However, Maugeri claimed that the world oil production capacity would increase by 18 million barrels per day between 2011 and 2020. The implied cumulative oil capacity depletion from 2011 to 2020 is only 11 million barrels per day, with an average annual depletion of 1.2 million barrels per day (Hamilton 2012). Relative to the current world oil production of 85 million barrels per day, the implied depletion rate is only 1.4 percent. This is substantially less than the observed world average depletion rate of about 4 percent.

If the world needs to compensate for at least 3.4 million barrels per day of depleted capacity every year, then from 2011 to 2020 the cumulative depletion will amount to 30.6 million barrels per day. Given the more realistic total addition of 29 million barrels per day suggested by Maugeri, the net change in world oil production capacity between 2011 and 2020 turns out to be a net reduction of one million barrels per day.

The world oil supply curve

Figure 4.4 shows the observed "world oil supply curve," or the relationship between the monthly real oil prices and the world's monthly total supply of liquid fuels. Real oil prices are oil prices corrected for inflation.

Before 2004, the observed oil supply curve was nearly flat. From January 1994 to December 2003, on average, it took an increase in real oil price by 0.9 dollar per barrel to bring about one million barrels per day of additional oil supply. Since 2004, the observed oil supply curve has steepened sharply. From January 2004 to December 2012, on average, it took an increase in real oil price by 9.8 dollars per barrel to bring about 1 million barrels per day of additional oil supply. That is, the observed slope of the oil supply curve has increased 10-fold.

Two factors have contributed to the steepening of the world oil supply curve. As the conventional oil supply struggles to keep pace with the rising oil demand, the world has to rely upon the more expensive unconventional oil resources to meet incremental oil demand. It takes an incremental cost

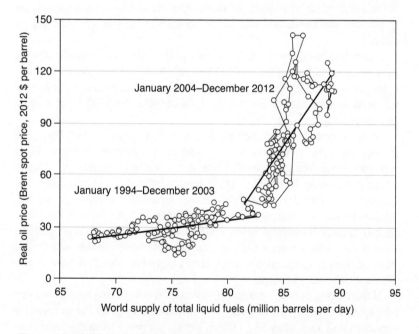

Figure 4.4 World liquid fuels production and oil prices (1994–2012, monthly) (sources: World monthly production of liquid fuels and monthly average Brent spot prices of oil are from EIA (2013a). Real oil prices in constant 2012 dollars are derived by deflating the nominal oil prices by the US consumer price index).

of 60–80 dollars a barrel for the Brazilian deep-water oil fields and 70–90 dollars a barrel for the Canadian oil sands to be developed. On the other hand, in response to the growing political instability in the Middle East region, the Middle East OPEC governments have increased military, security, and social expenditures and need higher oil prices to balance their fiscal budgets. Saudi Arabia now needs an oil price around 100 dollars a barrel to keep its budget balanced (Skrebowski 2011; APIC 2012). Saudi Arabia is the world's largest oil producer and exporter. Saudi Arabia usually keeps a surplus crude oil production capacity of 1.5–2 million barrels per day. It is the world's only "swing producer" that can increase or decrease oil production by a significant amount within a short period of time in response to changing world oil demand. Through its own production swings and its impact on other OPEC countries, Saudi Arabia has a greater impact on the world oil price than any other country in the world.

Saudi Arabia

In 2012, Saudi Arabia produced 11.5 million barrels of crude oil and natural liquids per day (corresponding to an annual production of 547 million tonnes; currently, one million barrels of daily oil production in Saudi Arabia corresponds to about 47 million tonnes of annual production), accounting for 13 percent of world oil production (BP 2013). According to the *OPEC Annual Statistical Bulletin 2012*, in 2011, Saudi Arabia exported 7.2 million barrels per day of crude oil, accounting for 19 percent of the world's total crude oil exports (OPEC 2012a).

Saudi Arabia has discovered about 700 billion barrels or 95 billion tonnes of oil resources ("original oil in place") (Aleklett 2012: 171–173). Up to 2012, Saudi Arabia's cumulative oil production was about 139 billion barrels or 19 billion tonnes (cumulative production up to 1965 is from OPEC 1999 and production from 1965 to 2012 is from BP 2013). Saudi Arabia's official proved oil reserves are 266 billion barrels, or 36.5 billion tonnes (BP 2013). The sum of the cumulative production and the proved reserves equals 405 billion barrels, or 55 billion tonnes. This implies a recovery ratio (the ratio of estimated recoverable resources to original resources) of 58 percent.

Given the current technology, the world on average recovers about 40 percent of the original oil in place (Ban 2012). The Uppsala Global Energy Systems research group in Sweden is one of the world's leading centers of peak oil study. Given Saudi Arabia's geological conditions (the Saudi oil reservoirs are limestone reservoirs that normally have high recovery ratios) and the Saudi Aramco's management practices (the Saudi national oil company intentionally keeps production rates from individual fields low in order to achieve high recovery ratios), the Uppsala research group believed that it was possible for Saudi Arabia to achieve a near 60 percent recovery ratio (Aleklett 2012: 172, 183).

Figure 4.5 shows the results of a Hubbert linearization exercise. The exercise does a linear regression between Saudi Arabia's cumulative oil production and its growth rate from 1982 to 2012. The linear relationship indicates Saudi Arabia's ultimately recoverable oil resources to be 58 billion tonnes, implying a recovery ratio of 61 percent relative to the original oil in place. This is consistent with the Uppsala research group's estimate.

Using the estimated parameters from the Hubbert linearization exercise, Saudi Arabia's oil production is projected to peak in 2029, with a peak production level of 13.4 million barrels per day (or an annual production of 632 million tonnes). Similarly, the Uppsala research group estimated that Saudi Arabia would be able to sustain a production rate of 12 million barrels per day from now to 2029 (Aleklett 2012: 182–184).

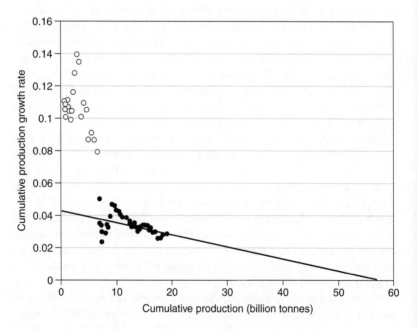

Figure 4.5 Saudi Arabia's cumulative oil production (1950–2012) (sources: Saudi Arabia's cumulative and annual oil production from 1950 to 1965 is from OPEC (1999). Oil production from 1965 to 2012 is from BP (2013)).

Saudi Arabia is the world's sixth largest oil consumer, after the United States, China, Japan, India, and the Russian Federation (BP 2013). From 2000 to 2012, Saudi Arabia's oil consumption grew at an average annual rate of 5.3 percent. In 2011, Saudi Arabia's population grew at an annual rate of 2.3 percent and per capita oil consumption reached 36.9 barrels a year (the population data are from World Bank 2013). By comparison, in 2011, the US per capita oil consumption was 22.2 barrels a year.

Figure 4.6 compares Saudi Arabia's oil production and consumption from 2000 to 2050 in terms of barrels per day (Saudi Arabia's total oil production is about the same as the total liquid fuels production). The projected production from 2013 to 2050 is based on the parameters estimated by the Hubbert linearization exercise shown in Figure 4.5. Saudi Arabia's oil consumption is assumed to grow by 2 percent a year from 2012 to 2050 (assuming that the population grows by 2 percent a year and the per capita oil consumption stays constant). Compared to Saudi Arabia's recent oil consumption growth rates, the assumed oil consumption growth may prove to be too conservative.

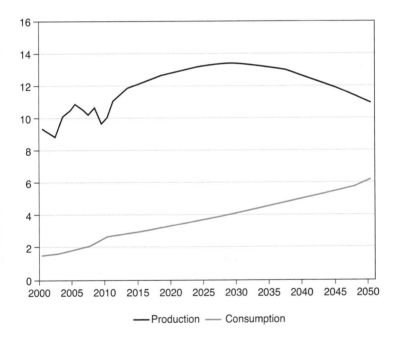

Figure 4.6 Saudi Arabia's oil production and consumption (million barrels per day, 2000–2050) (sources: Saudi Arabia's oil production and consumption from 2000 to 2012 are from BP (2013). For projections from 2013 to 2050, see text).

The "net oil exports" are defined as the difference between oil production and oil consumption. In 2012, Saudi Arabia's net oil exports were 8.6 million barrels per day. Saudi Arabia's net oil exports are projected to peak in 2023 at 9.6 million barrels per day.

Russia

Russia is the world's second largest oil producer and exporter. In 2012, Russia produced 10.6 million barrels per day of crude oil and natural gas liquids (corresponding to an annual production of 526 million tonnes; currently, one million barrels of daily oil production in Russia corresponds to about 49 million tonnes of annual production), accounting for less than 13 percent of the world's oil production (BP 2013). According to the *OPEC Annual Statistical Bulletin 2012*, in 2011, Russia exported 5.8 million barrels per day of crude oil, accounting for 15 percent of the world's total crude oil exports (OPEC 2012a).

Up to 2012, Russia's cumulative oil production was 162 billion barrels, or 22 billion tonnes (Russia's cumulative oil production from 1900 to 2010 was 155 billion barrels; see Aleklett 2012: 196). According to BP (2013), Russia's proved oil reserves at the end of 2012 were 87 billion barrels, or 12 billion tonnes. But Russia possesses many unexplored areas and production in already developed areas may be further increased with new technology (Aleklett 2012: 196, 200).

Figure 4.7 shows the evolution of Russia's cumulative oil production from 1960 to 2012. Russia's cumulative oil production growth rates (the ratios of current production to cumulative production) fell sharply during the Soviet era. After the post-Soviet collapse, it appears that a new downward linear trend has emerged since 2004. The linear trend from 2004 to 2012 indicates the ultimately recoverable oil resources to be about 70 billion tonnes, or about 510 billion barrels, more than twice as large as the sum of the current cumulative production and proved reserves. As the linear trend includes only nine years, the estimated ultimately recoverable resources could prove to be too optimistic (though the regression R-square is high, with a value of 0.935).

Assuming that Russia's ultimately recoverable oil will be 70 billion tonnes, Russia's oil production is projected to peak in 2035, with a production level of 12.4 million barrels per day or an annual production of 607 million tonnes.

In the 1980s, the former Soviet Union was the world's second largest oil consumer. In 1987, the former Soviet oil consumption peaked at 8.5 million barrels per day. Russia accounted for about 60 percent of the former Soviet oil consumption. In 1987, Russia's oil consumption was 5.1

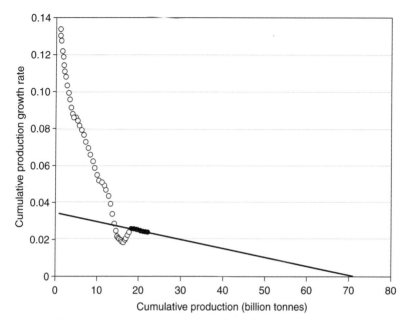

Figure 4.7 Russia's cumulative oil production (1960–2012) (sources: Russian oil production from 1985 to 2012 is from BP (2013). Historical oil production data from 1960 to 1984 are from OPEC (2012b). Russia's cumulative oil production up to 1960 is estimated to be one billion tonnes).

million barrels per day. After the disintegration of the Soviet Union, Russia's oil consumption collapsed. In 1998, Russia's oil consumption fell to the lowest level in the post-Soviet era, 2.5 million barrels per day. Since then, Russian oil consumption has recovered. From 2002 to 2012, Russian oil consumption grew at an average annual rate of 2.2 percent, reaching 3.2 million barrels per day by 2012 (BP 2013).

Figure 4.8 shows Russia's oil production and consumption from 2000 to 2050 (Russia's total oil production is about the same as the total liquid fuels production). Russia's oil consumption is assumed to grow by 2 percent a year from 2013 to 2050. In 2012, Russia's net oil exports were 7.5 million barrels per days. Russia's net oil exports are projected to rise to 7.9 million barrels per day by 2023 and decline thereafter.

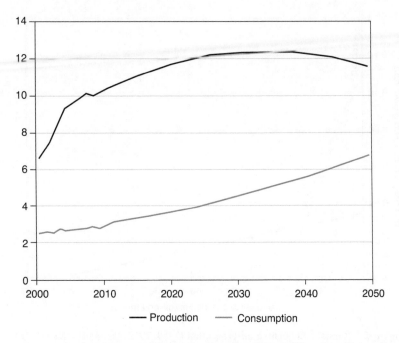

Figure 4.8 Russia's oil production and consumption (million barrels per day, 2000–2050) (sources: Russia's oil production and consumption from 2000 to 2012 are from BP (2013). For projections from 2013 to 2050, see text).

United States

The US is the world's third largest oil producer. In 2012, the US produced 8.9 million barrels per day of crude oil and natural gas liquids (corresponding to an annual production of 395 million tonnes; currently, one million barrels of daily oil production in the US corresponds to about 44 million tonnes of annual production), accounting for 10 percent of the world's total oil production (BP 2013).

US oil production peaked in 1970 with a production level of 11.3 million barrels per day (an annual production of 534 million tonnes). In 1977, Prudhoe Bay in Alaska came into production. Prudhoe Bay is the largest oil field ever discovered in the US (Aleklett 2012: 195). US oil production resumed growth after 1975 and reached the second peak in 1985 with a production level of 10.6 million barrels per day (an annual production of 499 million tonnes). From 1986 to 2008, US oil production fell steadily for more than two decades. By 2008, US oil production fell to the lowest level since 1950, with a production level of 6.8 million barrels per day (an annual production of 302 million tonnes). Between 2008 and 2012, US oil production grew by 2.1 million barrels per day. Most of the growth came from increases in the tight oil production and the natural gas liquids production. Tight oil is also known as "shale oil" (not to be confused with "oil shale," to be explained in the next chapter). It refers to the oil trapped in rocks with low permeability. Traditionally, it was too expensive to be developed.

In recent years, US oil companies have used new technologies, known as hydraulic fracturing and horizontal drilling (methods that were first developed for the production of shale gas) in shale oil production. These new technologies, in combination with high oil prices, have made it economically profitable to extract the shale oil resources (Aleklett 2012: 109–111; Kuntsler 2012: 165–172). The US Energy Information Administration estimates that the US has 58 billion barrels (7.9 billion tonnes) of technically recoverable shale oil resources (EIA 2013c). But it is not clear what proportion of the technically recoverable shale oil resources will prove to be economically recoverable.

Figure 4.9 shows the historical evolution of the US's cumulative oil production from 1950 to 2012. Between 1975 (when the cumulative production growth rate fell just below 3 percent) and 2008, the cumulative production growth rates followed a downward linear trend. However, since 2009, the cumulative production growth rates have tended to rise. When the cumulative production growth rates tend to rise, conventional Hubbert linearization cannot be properly applied. Alternative methods are needed to estimate the US's ultimately recoverable oil resources.

Figure 4.10 shows an alternative method to apply the Hubbert linearization technique. It shows the historical evolution of the US's observed recoverable oil resources in comparison with their growth rates. The observed recoverable oil resources are defined as the sum of the cumulative oil production and the proved oil reserves. The growth rate is defined as the ratio of the annual change in the observed recoverable resources over the current year's observed recoverable resources.

In 2012, the US's observed recoverable oil resources were 36 billion tonnes. A regression using the historical data from 1960 to 2012 results in a downward linear trend. Where the linear trend meets the horizontal axis, it indicates the US's ultimately recoverable oil resources to be 44 billion tonnes. The US's cumulative oil production up to 2012 was about 31 billion tonnes. Thus, the US's remaining recoverable oil resources are about 13 billion tonnes.

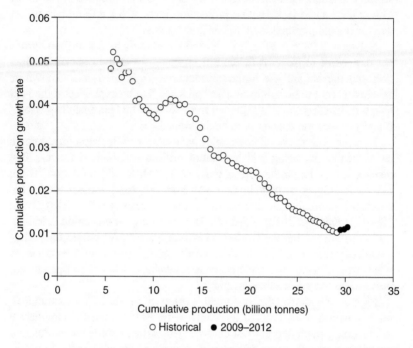

Figure 4.9 The US's cumulative oil production (1950–2012) (sources: US historical oil production up to 1965 is from Rutledge (2007). US oil production from 1965 to 2012 is from BP (2013)).

The underlying methodology used in Figure 4.10 is essentially the same
as the Hubbert linearization, except that in this case it is applied to the
observed recoverable resources instead of cumulative production. The
observed recoverable oil resources in a given year are determined by two
factors: the cumulative oil discoveries in the past and the estimated proportion of the discovered oil resources that can be recovered. By applying
the Hubbert linearization to the observed recoverable resources, it helps to
capture not only the historical trend of oil discoveries but also the historical trend of reserves growth. Reserves growth refers to the upward adjustment of oil reserves as technological development allows a greater
proportion of the original oil resources to be recovered (Aleklett 2012:
49–50).

The US Energy Information Administration (EIA) projects that US oil
production (crude oil and natural gas liquids) will peak again in 2019, with
a production level of 10.6 million barrels per day (an annual production of
468 million tonnes) (EIA 2013d). After 2020, EIA projects that US oil

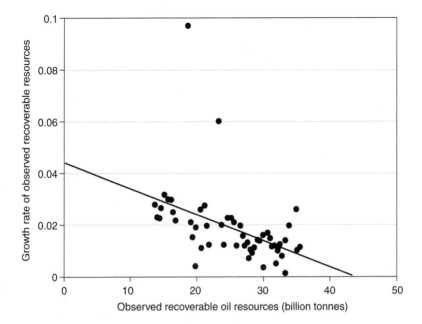

Figure 4.10 The US's observed recoverable oil resources (1960–2012) (sources: Observed recoverable oil resources are defined as the sum of the cumulative oil production and the proved oil reserves. US historical oil production up to 1965 is from Rutledge (2007). The US proved oil reserves from 1960 to 1979 are from OPEC (2012b). US oil production from 1965 to 2012 and the proved oil reserves from 1980 to 2012 are from BP (2013)).

production will decline slowly and plateau at about nine million barrels per day (an annual production of about 400 million tonnes) by 2040.

If one takes EIA's projection literally, the US's cumulative oil production from 2013 to 2040 will amount to 12 billion tonnes, leaving the US with only one billion tonnes in remaining recoverable oil resources by 2040.

In 2012, the ratio between the US's annual oil production and the remaining recoverable oil resources was about 3 percent. Based on the EIA projection, by 2025, US oil production will be about 440 million tonnes, the US's remaining recoverable resources will decline to 7.4 billion tonnes, and the ratio of annual production to remaining recoverable resources will rise to about 6 percent.

Experience from other oil production areas suggests that, as the ratio of annual production to remaining recoverable resources rises to about 6 percent, the ratio is likely to stabilize or decline (Aleklett 2012: 86–93). If this is not the case and the ratio keeps rising, the remaining recoverable resources will be depleted at an accelerating pace.

I use the EIA's projection of US oil production from 2013 to 2025 but assume that, after 2025, US oil production will decline at an annual rate of 6 percent. US oil production is projected to decline to 3.9 million barrels per day by 2040 and 2.1 million barrels per day by 2050.

According to the EIA (2013a), US total liquid fuels production in 2012 was 11.1 million barrels per day, including 6.5 million barrels per day of crude oil, 2.4 million barrels per day of natural gas liquids, 1.1 million barrels per day of biofuels and other liquids, and 1.1 million barrels per day of refinery reprocessing gains. I use the EIA's projections for US biofuels production and the refinery reprocessing gains for 2013–2040. Beyond 2040, I assume that US biofuels production will stay at two million barrels per day and refinery reprocessing gains will stay at 1 million barrels per day. The US total liquid fuels production is projected to peak in 2019 at 13.2 million barrels per day and decline to 5.1 million barrels per day by 2050.

The US is the world's largest oil consumer and importer. According to BP (2013), in 2012, the US consumed 18.6 million barrels per day of oil (an annual consumption of 820 million tonnes), accounting for 20 percent of the world's total oil consumption. In 2011, the US imported 8.9 million barrels per day of crude oil, accounting for 23 percent of the world's total crude oil imports (OPEC 2012a).

Figure 4.11 shows US liquid fuels production and consumption from 2000 to 2050. US liquid fuels consumption from 2013 to 2040 is based on the EIA projection (EIA 2013d). For 2041–2050, US liquid fuels consumption is assumed to stay constant at 19 million barrels per day.

US net oil imports (defined as the difference between the liquid fuels consumption and production, ignoring changes in inventories) peaked at 12.5 million barrels per day in 2005. The net oil imports are projected to fall to 6.7 million barrels per day by 2019 but grow again thereafter. By 2050, US net oil imports are projected to rise to 13.9 million barrels per day.

China

In China, significant oil production began with the discovery of Daqing in 1959. Daqing is one of the world's largest oil fields, with ultimately recoverable resources of 24 billion barrels (3.3 billion tonnes) (Aleklett 2012: 209).

In 2012, China produced 4.2 million barrels per day of crude oil (corresponding to an annual production of 208 million tonnes; currently, one

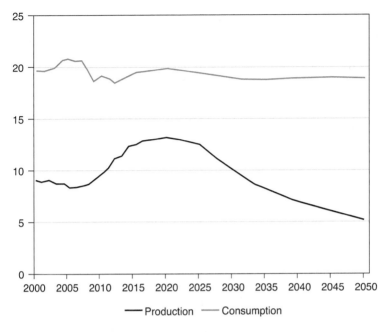

Figure 4.11 The US's liquid fuels production and consumption (million barrels per day, 2000–2050) (sources: US liquid fuels production and consumption from 2000 to 2012 are from EIA (2013a). For projections from 2013 to 2050, see text).

million barrels of daily oil production in China corresponds to about 50 million tonnes of annual production). China does not produce natural gas liquids. China is the world's fourth largest oil producer, accounting for 5 percent of the world's total oil production (BP 2013).

Figure 4.12 shows the evolution of China's cumulative oil production from 1965 to 2012. The linear trend from 2003 to 2012 indicates China's ultimately recoverable oil resources to be 16.5 billion tonnes.

The Uppsala research group collaborated with the China University of Petroleum in Beijing to conduct research on China's oil resources. Oil production from Daqing peaked in 1999. Production from nine of China's largest oil fields, which accounted for two-thirds of China's oil production in 2007, was expected to fall by 56 percent from 2007 to 2035. The Uppsala research group estimated that China's ultimately recoverable oil resources would be between 90 and 100 billion barrels (or between 12.3 and 13.7 billion tonnes) (Aleklett 2012: 208–211).

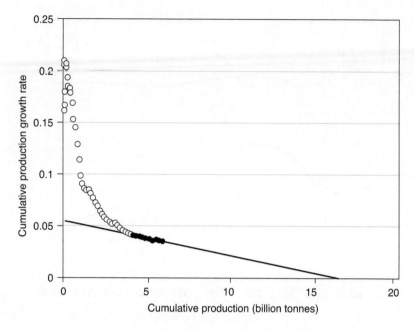

Figure 4.12 China's cumulative oil production (1965–2012) (sources: China's cumulative oil production from 1949 to 1965 is from the National Bureau of Statistics of China (1985). China's oil production from 1965 to 2012 is from BP (2013)).

Assuming that China's ultimately recoverable oil resources will be 16.5 billion tonnes, China's oil production is projected to peak in 2023, with a production level of 4.5 million barrels per day or an annual production of 225 million tonnes.

According to the EIA (2013a), China's total liquid fuels production in 2012 was 4.4 million barrels per day, including 4.1 million barrels per day of crude oil, 46,000 barrels per day of biofuels and other liquids, and 240,000 barrels per day of refinery reprocessing gains. I assume that China's biofuels production will stay at 50,000 barrels per day for the period 2013–2050. China's refinery reprocessing gains are assumed to grow by 4 percent a year from 2012 to 2020 and by 2 percent a year from 2020 to 2050. China's total liquid fuels production is projected to peak in 2024 at 4.9 million barrels per day and decline to 3.4 million barrels per day by 2050.

China is the world's second largest oil consumer and importer. In 2012, China consumed 10.2 million barrels per day of oil (an annual consumption of 462 million tonnes), accounting for 12 percent of the world's total oil consumption (BP 2013). In 2011, China imported 5.1 million barrels per day of crude oil, accounting for 13 percent of the world's total crude oil imports (OPEC 2012a).

Figure 4.13 shows China's liquid fuels production and consumption from 2000 to 2050. From 2000 to 2012, China's liquid fuels consumption grew at an average annual rate of 6.5 percent. For this section's projections, I assume that China's liquid fuels consumption will grow by 4 percent a year from 2012 to 2020 and by 2 percent a year from 2020 to 2050.

In 2012, China's net oil imports reached 5.8 million barrels per day. Under the projected trends, China's net oil imports will rise to 9.2 million barrels per day by 2020, 12.3 million barrels per day by 2030, 16.6 million barrels per day by 2040, and 22.0 million barrels per day by 2050. China is expected to overtake the US to become the world's largest net oil importer by 2016.

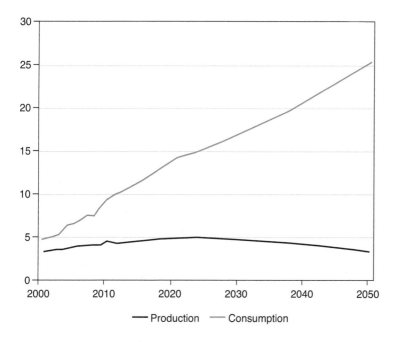

Figure 4.13 China's liquid fuels production and consumption (million barrels per day, 2000–2015) (sources: China's liquid fuels production and consumption from 2000 to 2012 are from EIA (2013a). For projections from 2013 to 2050, see text).

Acceptable and affordable oil prices

The previous sections evaluated the possible future trajectories of oil production and consumption for the world's four largest oil producers. Saudi Arabia and Russia are the world's two largest oil exporters. The US and China are the world's two largest oil consumers and importers. The four countries together will have a dominant influence on the global oil market in the coming decades.

The main oil exporters rely upon the oil exports revenue to finance most of their government budgets and to sustain economic growth. For the oil exporters, there are a set of minimum acceptable oil prices that are required for them to meet various national objectives.

In recent years, Saudi Arabia has dramatically increased military and social spending in response to the growing regional instability. A study by the Arab Petroleum Investment Corporation found that, in 2012, Saudi Arabia needed an oil price around 100 dollars per barrel to balance the budget (APIC 2012). Given Saudi Arabia's population and net oil exports in 2012, an oil price of 100 dollars per barrel translates into per capita oil exports revenue of about 12,200 dollars.

In the future, the primary challenge for Saudi Arabia is to meet the rising economic and political aspirations from a young and rapidly growing population. I assume that, from 2013 to 2050, Saudi Arabia needs to sustain the per capita oil exports revenue at the constant level of 10,000 dollars (in constant 2012 dollars). Saudi Arabia's population is assumed to grow by 2 percent a year from 2012 to 2050.

This assumption may prove to be too conservative. Given the growing geopolitical challenges in the Middle East region, Saudi Arabia may need to have rising per capita oil exports revenues in the future in order to achieve domestic and regional political stability. If the actual oil prices fall below Saudi Arabia's minimum acceptable oil prices, it could result in major political instabilities in Saudi Arabia and the surrounding countries. The political instabilities will in turn cause oil supply disruptions.

For Russia, the overwhelming national objective is to regain the big power status the Soviet Union once enjoyed. Failure to meet this national expectation could lead to general frustration of the population and potentially destabilize the current political regime (Rodionov 2012).

To achieve this national objective, it is necessary for Russia to maintain rapid economic growth. A 4 percent growth rate is probably the minimum Russia needs to have in order to match the performance of other large "emerging market" economies (such as China, India, and Brazil) and keep its big power aspiration alive.

In 2011, oil exports revenue reached 16.2 percent of Russia's GDP. I assume that the Russian economy will grow at an annual rate of 4 percent from 2012 to 2050 and oil exports revenue needs to account for at least 10 percent of Russia's GDP (implying a minimum acceptable oil price of 73 dollars per barrel in 2013).

For the oil importers, the main concern is to keep the oil price sufficiently low so that the oil spending does not become an unbearable burden on the importing country's economy. In US economic history, oil imports spending as a share of GDP exceeded 2.5 percent only in 1979–1980 and in 2008. In both cases, the US economy suffered from deep recessions. The experience suggests that the US economy probably cannot afford oil imports spending greater than 2.5 percent of GDP.

I assume that the US economy will keep growing at 2.5 percent a year from 2012 to 2050 and the maximum limit for US oil imports spending is 2.5 percent of GDP. The US affordable oil prices are then calculated based on the maximum US oil imports spending and the projected US oil imports.

Before 1993, China was a net oil exporter. Since then large trade surpluses have allowed China to pay for its oil imports. The recent oil price shocks have had limited impacts on the Chinese economy. In 2011, oil imports spending reached 3 percent of China's GDP as the Chinese economy managed to grow by 9.3 percent.

However, it seems unlikely that the Chinese economy can survive a 70 percent increase of the oil price from its current level. If the oil imports spending surges to 5 percent of China's GDP, the Chinese economy will most likely suffer from a recession.

I assume that the Chinese economy will grow by 8 percent a year from 2012 to 2020 and by 4 percent a year from 2020 to 2050. The maximum limit for China's oil imports spending is assumed to be 5 percent of GDP. The assumptions and China's projected oil imports are used to calculate China's affordable oil prices.

Figure 4.14 compares Saudi Arabia's and Russia's acceptable oil prices with the US's and China's affordable oil prices. The actual world oil prices (based on the Brent spot prices) from 2000 to 2012 are also shown. All prices shown in Figure 4.14 are stated in constant 2012 dollars per barrel.

Russia's and Saudi Arabia's acceptable oil prices will exceed the US's affordable oil prices by the late 2030s. The oil exporters' acceptable oil prices will exceed China's affordable oil prices by the 2040s.

Thus, by the 2030s and 2040s, the main oil exporters and importers will find themselves trapped in irreconcilable conflicts. Either the oil importers will have to accept much slower economic growth rates and possibly economic declines, or the oil exporters will have to give up some of their main national objectives. If the failures to meet national objectives lead to

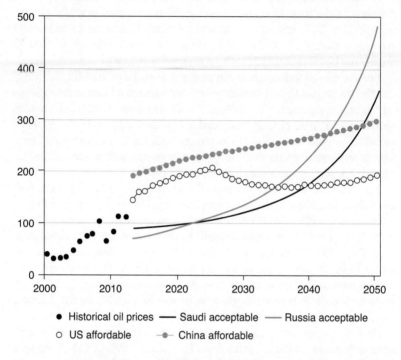

Figure 4.14 Acceptable vs. affordable oil prices (real oil prices, constant 2012 dollars per barrel, 2000–2050) (sources: Real oil prices from 2000 to 2012 are from BP (2013). For projections from 2013 to 2050, see text).

political instabilities for the oil exporters, the world oil supply could be further undermined.

These projections assume that the world's major economies will be able to maintain "normal" economic growth in the coming decades. However, the depletion of crucial natural resources and impending global ecological catastrophes suggest that the global economy will not stay on a path of "normal" economic growth. Instead, both the global economy and the Chinese economy will have to confront insurmountable limits to growth.

Appendix: estimating resources potentials with Hubbert linearization

"Hubbert linearization" is a common technique used to predict the ultimately recoverable amount of a nonrenewable resource. The basic assumption of Hubbert linearization is that the annual production trajectory of a nonrenewable resource can be described by a logistic equation. The annual production initially grows at an accelerating rate. Beyond a certain inflection point, the growth slows down. The annual production reaches the peak when about half of the ultimately recoverable amount has been produced. After the peak, the annual production initially declines at an accelerating pace. But the decline slows down as the resource approaches complete depletion.

As the production level approaches the peak, a linear relationship is likely to be formed between the growth rate of the cumulative production (that is, the ratio of the current annual production over the cumulative production from all previous years) and the cumulative production. The horizontal intercept of the linear function would indicate the ultimately recoverable amount. This can be described by the following equation:

$$P_t / Q_t = a - a \, (Q_t / Q_u) \tag{1}$$

Where Q_t represents the cumulative amount that has been produced up to year "t," P_t is the current annual production in year "t" or the growth of the cumulative production, "a" is the intrinsic growth rate that determines how rapidly Q_t grows or how rapidly the ultimately recoverable amount is depleted, and Q_u stands for the ultimately recoverable amount of the resource. Estimating equation (1) through linear regression would allow one to determine the value of "a" and "Q_u."

The peak year of the annual production can be determined by the following equation:

$$Q_t = Q_u / \{1 + \exp [-(t - t_m)]\} \tag{2}$$

Where "t" is the current year and "t_m" is the peak year (Korpela 2005).

Hubbert linearization delivers reasonably reliable results when the annual production approaches the peak or has passed the peak. The model allows one to use the latest available data to continuously update the estimated coefficients.

Equations (1) and (2) allow one to estimate the ultimately recoverable amount of a resource and its peak production year. But Hubbert linearization may also be used to project the future production trajectory if the ultimately recoverable amount is already known or can be otherwise estimated. If the ultimately recoverable amount of a resource is already known, "a" can be estimated by regressing (P_t / Q_t) on $(1 - Q_t / Q_u)$, imposing the constant term to be zero.

Hubbert linearization is usually used to analyze the production trajectory of nonrenewable resources. But, with some re-interpretations, it can also be used to analyze the renewable resources or energy efficiency.

If a renewable resource or energy efficiency is subject to a certain ultimate physical limit, one would expect that the annual production of the renewable resource or the annual level of energy efficiency would at first grow at an accelerating pace. Beyond a certain point (when about half of the ultimate physical potential is realized), the growth would slow down. The annual production or the annual level of efficiency would keep growing at an increasingly slower rate until the ultimate physical potential is realized.

When equations (1) and (2) are applied to a renewable resource or energy efficiency, Q_t would represent the annual production of a renewable resource or the annual level of energy efficiency, P_t would stand for the annual increase of the renewable resource production or the annual increase of energy efficiency, "a" remains the intrinsic growth rate that determines how rapidly Q_t grows or how rapidly the ultimate physical potential is realized, Q_u would stand for the ultimate physical potential, and "t_m" would stand for the "half potential" year (the year when half of the ultimate physical potential is realized).

5 Peak energy and the limits to global economic growth

Fossil fuels (coal, oil, and natural gas) currently account for 94 percent of the world's total energy supply (with nuclear and renewable electricity measured by electrical energy content rather than thermal equivalent; see Chapter 3). But fossil fuels are nonrenewable resources. As this chapter will argue, the world's total fossil fuels production is likely to peak before the mid-twenty-first century. With the coming decline of fossil fuels, can nuclear and renewable energies replace fossil fuels to sustain global economic growth through the twenty-first century and beyond?

Nuclear electricity generation uses uranium, which is a nonrenewable resource. Moreover, the development of nuclear energy has been undermined by safety, security, and pollution issues. At best, nuclear energy may achieve no more than sluggish growth from now to the end of the century.

With the exception of geothermal energy, all renewable energies derive from solar energy. The theoretical amount of solar energy is enormous. But in practice, only a very small fraction of the solar energy can be productively harvested. The production of renewable energies is limited by the availability of land and nonrenewable mineral resources. Most renewable energies are best used to generate electricity rather than to make liquid fuels. This may prove to be a major obstacle to the expansion of renewable energies.

Beyond the twenty-first century, the world will have to rely upon renewable energies to meet all or almost all of the global energy demand. The global economic output will be determined by the total amount of renewable energies that can be sustainably utilized and the level of energy efficiency. To the extent that neither the production of renewable energies nor the level of energy efficiency can grow indefinitely, there is an ultimate and insurmountable limit to global economic growth. Eventually, the global economy will have to settle at a steady state—that is, a global economy with zero economic growth.

The capitalist economic system is inherently built to pursue endless economic growth. Historically, when global economic growth rates fell below a certain level, the capitalist system tended to suffer from major crises and instabilities. Toward the end of this chapter, I will argue that capitalism cannot be viable with zero or negative economic growth.

Oil

Chapter 4 considers the possibility that world oil production may peak in the near future. A Hubbert linearization exercise using world historical oil production data finds that world oil production may peak before 2020. However, Hubbert linearization exercises applied to Saudi Arabia and Russia find that production from the world's two largest oil producers will not peak until around 2030–2035.

The world's total conventional oil resources are estimated to be about six trillion barrels or 820 billion tonnes (Aleklett 2012: 106; Ban 2012). Currently, the world's average recovery ratio of conventional oil fields (the ratio of estimated recoverable oil to original oil resources) is about 40 percent (Ban 2012). With a 40 percent recovery ratio, the world's recoverable conventional oil resources are about 330 billion tonnes.

In 2000, the US Geological Survey conducted a comprehensive study of the world's conventional oil and natural gas resources. According to the US Geological Survey, the world's technically recoverable conventional resources of crude oil and natural gas liquids amounted to 3.3 trillion barrels, or 460 billion tonnes of oil equivalent (USGS 2000).

The Venezuelan heavy oil has higher gravity than water and is considered to be "extra heavy" in comparison with conventional oil. Bitumen is the heaviest naturally occurring hydrocarbon, existing in solid or nearly solid form. Canada has large bitumen deposits that are known as "oil sands" or "tar sands."

The heavy oil resources from Venezuela's Orinoco Belt are estimated to be 1.3 trillion barrels, of which 220 billion barrels are currently considered to be reserves. Canada's oil sands resources amount to two trillion barrels, of which 170 billion barrels are currently considered to be reserves (Aleklett 2012: 99–100, 106–108; BP 2013). The total reserves from the Venezuelan heavy oil and Canadian oil sands add up to about 400 billion barrels, or 65 billion tonnes (for heavy oil and bitumen, one tonne equals about 6.2 barrels).

The world's oil shale resources are estimated to be 3.5 trillion barrels, most of which are concentrated in the US. Oil shale is not the same thing as "shale oil." "Shale oil" is also known as "tight oil," referring to oil trapped in rocks with low permeability and can be extracted using techniques of horizontal drilling and hydraulic fracturing.

Oil shale is the source rock of conventional oil and contains kerogen. Kerogen was formed from ancient organic matter. If oil shale is buried sufficiently deep (between 800 and 5,000 meters in depth) and the temperature and pressure are high enough, kerogen would be transformed into oil. But at shallower depths, kerogen stays in the solid form. To make oil from oil shale, it has to be mined and heated to turn the kerogen contained in the oil shale into synthetic oil.

Currently, there is little commercial production of oil from oil shales. The mining of oil shales requires massive amounts of water, electricity, and infrastructure investment. The potential environmental damages related to oil shale development might exceed the economic benefits. The production from oil shales is likely to remain insignificant in the future (Aleklett 2012: 108–109; Kuntsler 2012: 165–172).

The world's cumulative oil production up to 2012 was about 170 billion tonnes and the proved oil reserves were about 240 billion tonnes (BP 2013). Thus, the world's currently observed recoverable oil resources are about 410 billion tonnes. Figure 5.1 shows the evolution of the world's observed recoverable oil resources from 1961 to 2012 in comparison with their growth rates. The downward linear trend indicates the world's ultimately recoverable oil resources to be about 550 billion tonnes.

Assuming that the world's ultimately recoverable oil resources will be 550 billion tonnes, world oil production (crude oil and natural gas liquids only) is projected to peak in 2035 with a production level of 4.8 billion tonnes. Figure 5.2 shows the historical and projected world oil production from 1950 to 2100.

In terms of barrels, the world production of crude oil and natural gas liquids is projected to grow from 86 million barrels per day in 2012 to 101 million barrels per day in 2035.

Natural gas

The US Geological Survey estimated that the world's technically recoverable conventional natural gas resources were 15,400 trillion cubic feet, or 385 billion tonnes of oil equivalent (USGS 2000).

According to the International Energy Agency, the world's remaining technically recoverable conventional natural gas resources are estimated to be 420 trillion cubic meters. The world's remaining technically recoverable unconventional natural gas resources are estimated to be about 330 trillion cubic meters (including 204 trillion cubic meters of shale gas, 76 trillion cubic meters of tight gas, and 47 trillion cubic meters of coalbed methane) (IEA 2012b: 18). The remaining conventional and unconventional natural gas resources add up to 750 trillion cubic meters.

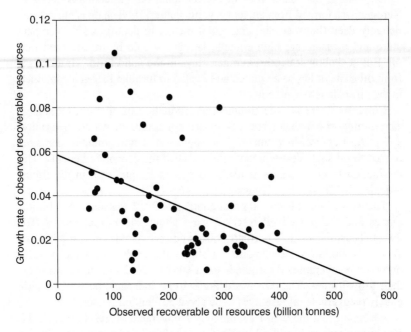

Figure 5.1 The world's observed recoverable oil resources (1961–2012) (sources: Observed recoverable oil resources are defined as the sum of the cumulative oil production and the proved oil reserves. Historical world oil production before 1965 is from Rutledge (2007). The world proved oil reserves from 1960 to 1979 are from OPEC (2012b). World oil production from 1965 to 2012 and the proved oil reserves from 1980 to 2012 are from BP (2013). Oil reserves are converted from barrels to tonnes at the ratio of 7.3 barrels=1 tonne).

One trillion cubic meters of natural gas equals about 0.9 billion tonnes of oil equivalent; 750 trillion cubic meters of natural gas resources correspond to about 675 billion tonnes of oil equivalent. Only a portion of the technically recoverable natural gas resources will prove to be economically recoverable and the development of unconventional natural gas resources may be curbed by environmental concerns (IEA 2012b: 18–41).

In addition to the above conventional and unconventional natural gas resources, about 1,800 trillion cubic meters of natural gas (about 1,600 billion tonnes of oil equivalent) may be contained in aquifers and methane hydrates (BGR 2012: 15). But it is not clear if the resources can ever be commercially exploited. Some countries are currently pushing ahead with ambitious projects to exploit their domestic methane hydrate deposits. But no technological breakthrough has been reported (BGR 2012: 22–23).

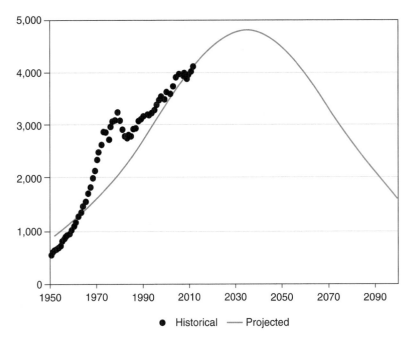

Figure 5.2 World oil production (historical and projected, million tonnes, 1950–2100) (sources: Historical world oil production before 1965 is from Rutledge (2007). World oil production from 1965 to 2012 is from BP (2013). For projections from 1950 to 2100, see text).

Methane is a powerful greenhouse gas. Its warming potential is 20 times stronger than carbon dioxide over a century. Destabilization of the world's methane hydrate deposits will lead to runaway global warming with catastrophic consequences (Embleton 2008).

In an earlier study, French geologist Jean Laherrere estimated that the world's ultimately recoverable conventional and unconventional natural gas resources would be about 12,000 trillion cubic feet or about 300 billion tonnes of oil equivalent (Laherrere 2008).

Aleklett (2012: 243–247) estimated that the world's cumulative production of conventional and unconventional natural gas by 2100 would be about 2.5 trillion barrels of oil equivalent or about 340 billion tonnes of oil equivalent.

The world's cumulative natural gas production up to 2012 was about 90 billion tonnes of oil equivalent (based on the historical natural gas production data from Rutledge 2007 and BP 2013). In 2012, the world's proved natural gas reserves were about 190 trillion cubic meters, or 170 billion tonnes of oil equivalent (BP 2013). Thus, the world's currently observed recoverable natural gas resources are about 260 billion tonnes of oil equivalent.

Figure 5.3 shows the evolution of the world's observed recoverable natural gas resources from 1961 to 2012 in comparison with their growth rates. The linear trend indicates the world's ultimately recoverable natural gas resources to be about 340 billion tonnes of oil equivalent. This is similar to Laherrere's and Aleklett's estimate.

Assuming that the world's ultimately recoverable natural resources will be 340 billion tonnes of oil equivalent, world natural gas production is

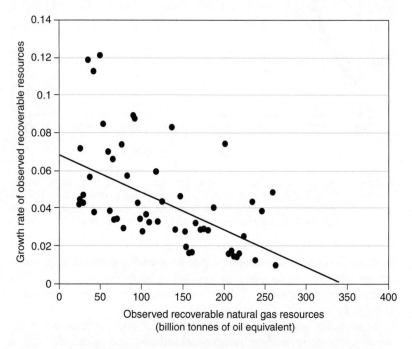

Figure 5.3 The world's observed recoverable natural gas resources (1961–2012) (sources: Observed recoverable natural gas resources are defined as the sum of the cumulative natural gas production and the natural gas reserves. World cumulative natural gas production up to 1960 is estimated to be 10 billion tonnes of oil equivalent (Rutledge 2007). World natural gas production from 1960 to 1969 and proved natural gas reserves from 1960 to 1979 are from OEPC (2012b). World natural gas production from 1970 to 2012 and the proved natural gas reserves from 1980 to 2012 are from BP (2013). The proved natural gas reserves from OPEC are multiplied by 0.85 to make them compatible with the reserves reported by BP).

projected to peak in 2034, with a production level of 3.8 billion tonnes of oil equivalent. Figure 5.4 shows the historical and projected world natural gas production from 1960 to 2100.

Coal

Coal mining destroys landscapes and is dangerous for the miners. China is the world's largest coal producer and thousands of Chinese coal miners die from accidents every year.

Coal is the dirtiest of fossil fuels. Coal burning emits sulfur dioxide, which causes acid rain. Very fine coal dust may enter into human lungs and cause respiratory damage, heart disease, or cancer. In China, which accounts for one-half of the world's total coal consumption, acid rain falls affect about one-third of the territory. About one-third of China's urban population breathes heavily polluted air (Heinberg 2009: 6–10).

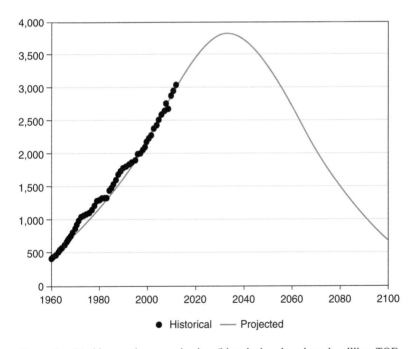

Figure 5.4 World natural gas production (historical and projected, million TOE, 1960–2100) (sources: World natural gas production from 1960 to 1969 is from OEPC (2012b). World natural gas production from 1970 to 2012 is from BP (2013). For projections from 1960 to 2100, see text. "TOE" stands for "tonnes of oil equivalent").

For a given amount of energy, coal consumption results in more carbon dioxide emissions than oil or natural gas. One tonne of oil emits 3.07 tonnes of carbon dioxide, one tonne of oil equivalent of natural gas emits 2.35 tonnes of carbon dioxide, and one tonne of oil equivalent of coal emits 3.96 tonnes of carbon dioxide (BP 2013).

Coal resources have a wide range of energy intensity and quality, varying from the high-quality anthracite with an energy content of 30 megajoules per kilogram to lignite and sub-bituminous coals with energy contents ranging from six to 25 megajoules per kilogram. Most coals are bituminous coals with energy contents between 19 and 29 megajoules per kilogram (Heinberg 2009: 20). By comparison, the average energy content of crude oil is about 42 megajoules per kilogram.

In 2012, the world produced 7.9 billion tonnes of coal, which equaled 3.9 billion tonnes of oil equivalent (BP 2013). Given the currently observed average coal quality, one tonne of coal equals 0.49 tonne of oil equivalent.

The world's coal resources are very large, estimated to be 17 trillion tonnes (BGR 2012: 15). But given technical, economic, and environmental considerations, only a small fraction of the coal resources will eventually be recovered.

According to BP (2013), at the end of 2012, the world's total "proved reserves" of coal were 860 billion tonnes. Based on the historical coal production data from Rutledge (2011) and BP (2013), the world's cumulative coal production up to 2012 was 330 billion tonnes. Thus, the world's current observed recoverable coal resources are about 1.2 trillion tonnes.

Figure 5.5 shows the world's observed recoverable coal resources from 1974 to 2012. Since 1992, the world's observed recoverable coal resources have stayed around 1.25 trillion tonnes.

Assuming that the world's ultimately recoverable coal resources will be 1.25 trillion tonnes, world coal production is projected to peak in 2044 with a production level of 10.1 billion tonnes. Figure 5.6 shows historical and projected world coal production from 1900 to 2100.

Nuclear electricity

World consumption of nuclear electricity reached an all-time high of 2,807 terawatt-hours in 2006. By 2012, it declined to 2,477 terawatt-hours (BP 2013). As of January 2013, the world's nuclear electricity generating capacity stood at 374 gigawatts (WNA 2013a).

Currently, 65 gigawatts of nuclear power plants are under construction. If all nuclear power plants currently being constructed become operational within five years, 65 gigawatts of new nuclear power plants will begin to

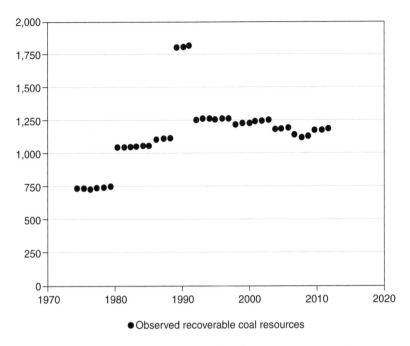

 Observed recoverable coal resources

Figure 5.5 The world's observed recoverable coal resources (billion tonnes, 1974–2012) (sources: Observed recoverable coal resources are the sum of cumulative coal production and proved coal reserves. Historical world coal production up to 1980 is from Rutledge (2011). World coal production from 1981 to 2012 is from BP (2013). World coal proved reserves in 1974, 1980, 1986, 1992, 1995, 1998, 2001, 2004, 2007, 2008, and 2010 are from the World Energy Council, cited in Rutledge (2011). World coal proved reserves in 2011 and 2012 are from BP (2013)).

contribute to world electricity generation between 2013 and 2017. On the other hand, about 10 gigawatts of existing nuclear power plants will retire every year (assuming an average power plant lifetime of about 40 years). Thus, by 2017, the world's total nuclear electricity generating capacity may increase to 389 gigawatts.

In addition, 184 gigawatts of nuclear power plants are currently being planned and 360 gigawatts have been proposed (WNA 2012a).

The current nuclear technology is based on nuclear fission reactions (obtaining energy liberated by fission of atoms). Uranium is the basic raw material for nuclear fission reactions. In 2012, the world's total uranium requirements from nuclear power plants were about 68,000 tonnes. World uranium production was about 55,000 tonnes. The difference was made up

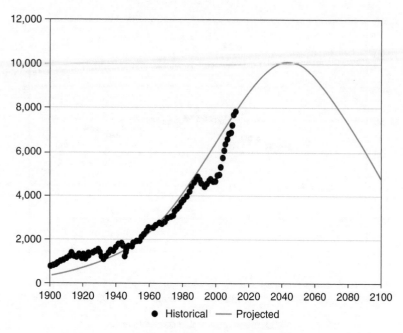

Figure 5.6 World coal production (historical and projected, million tonnes, 1900–2100) (sources: Historical world coal production before 1981 is from Rutledge (2011). World coal production from 1981 to 2012 is from BP (2013). For projections from 1900 to 2100, see text).

with the "secondary sources" (supplies from civilian and military uranium stockpiles).

If all of the currently planned and proposed nuclear power plants become operational before 2030, the world will have about 800 gigawatts of nuclear electricity generating capacity operating by 2030. The total uranium requirements will have to rise to about 150,000 tonnes, or almost three times the world's current uranium production. The insufficient supply of uranium alone will force many of the currently planned or proposed nuclear power plants to be abandoned.

The world's cumulative uranium production up to 2011 was 2.6 million tonnes. As of 2011, the world's total identified uranium resources were 7.1 million tonnes at a production cost up to 260 dollar per kilogram. In addition, there were 10.4 million tonnes of undiscovered conventional uranium resources (NEA 2012: 9–10).

Unconventional uranium resources associated with phosphates, nonferrous ores, shales, and granites are estimated to be 10–22 million tonnes

(WEC 2010: 202–242). Theoretically, there could be up to four billion tonnes of uranium resources in the world's sea water. But the concentration of uranium in the sea water is only 0.003 ppm (0.003 parts per million or three parts in every billion molecules). Leeuwen (2007) pointed out that, for the unconventional uranium resources, the energy required to extract and process the uranium would be greater than the energy that could be produced.

I assume that the world's ultimately recoverable uranium resources will be 20 million tonnes (roughly equaling the sum of the world's cumulative uranium production, the currently identified uranium resources, and the undiscovered conventional uranium resources). Figure 5.7 shows the historical and projected world uranium production and nuclear electricity consumption. World uranium production is projected to peak in 2090, with a production level of 121,000 tonnes. World nuclear electricity consumption is assumed to grow in proportion with uranium production. By the end

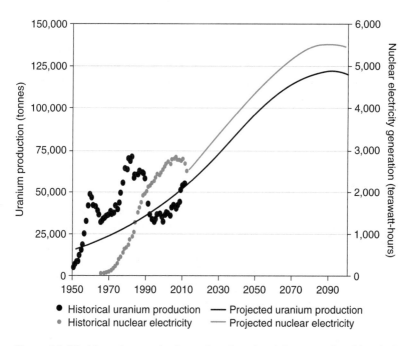

Figure 5.7 World uranium production and nuclear electricity generation (historical and projected, 1950–2100) (sources: Historical world uranium production from 1945 to 2000 is from NEA (2006). World uranium production from 2001 to 2011 is from WNA (2013b). World nuclear electricity consumption from 1965 to 2012 is from BP (2013). For projections from 1950 to 2100, see text).

of the century, world nuclear electricity is projected to more than double from the current level, reaching about 5,500 terawatt-hours (about 470 million tonnes of oil equivalent).

Nuclear fuel recycling

Under the current technology, nuclear electricity generation is limited by the available uranium resources.

In theory, the spent nuclear fuel still contains about 95 percent of the original energy content. Reprocessed and recycled fuel could be used for nuclear electricity generation (WEC 2010: 211). But, in practice, the recycling of nuclear spent fuel is very expensive and associated with high risks of terrorism and nuclear weapon proliferation.

Currently, the most important form of nuclear fuel recycling is through the so-called "MOX" fuel. MOX fuel is a mixture of plutonium and uranium oxides, with the plutonium extracted from the spent nuclear fuel. The worldwide capacity of annual plutonium recycling was reported to be about 2,500 tonnes of natural uranium equivalent (Dittmar 2009a: 3).

But the recovery of plutonium is very expensive and consumes substantial amounts of energy, materials, and equipment. The extracted plutonium could be easily converted for military purposes. The spent MOX fuel cannot be reprocessed again. Thus, even for nuclear reactors that operate with 100 percent MOX fuel, it saves the uranium resources required to generate a given amount of energy only by about 10 percent (Leeuwen 2012: 59–60).

Nuclear breeder reactors

Theoretically, the fissile material from uranium may be increased by 60–100 times if the technology of breeder reactors can be mastered and operated on commercial scales.

There are two approaches of breeder technology. The first approach uses U_{238} (an uranium isotope) to "breed" plutonium, which serves as the fissile material. The reaction is sustained by fast prompt neutrons and therefore is known as "fast reaction." The second approach uses thorium to "breed" U_{233}, with U_{233} being the fissile material.

The world has built only eight fast breeder reactors and six have already been shut down. Currently, only two small fast reactors with a total generating capacity of 0.7 gigawatts are operating. Two fast breeder reactors with a combined capacity of 1.2 gigawatts are now under construction.

The expectation has been that the fast breeder reactors can "breed" more fissile materials than they consume. But a few fast breeder reactors that were designed to have positive breeding gains have been shut down. The currently operating Russian fast reactor actually has negative breeding gains. This means that the fast reactors will continue to rely upon new fissile materials (made from uranium or plutonium) to provide their initial fuel loads.

The fast breeder reactors are very expensive to build. Germany invested €3.5 billion on a small fast breeder reactor, which was only one-fifth the size of a conventional nuclear power plant. The reactor never started operation.

A fast breeder reactor needs to be started with a fuel that contains twice as much natural uranium equivalent as a conventional nuclear reactor. The fissile material needs to be enriched five times more than the conventional fissile material. The highly enriched fissile material can be easily converted to military uses.

The fast breeder reactors have serious safety concerns, making Chernobyl-style nuclear incidents more likely to happen (Dittmar 2009b: 11–13).

According to Dr. Michael Dittmar, a researcher with the Institute of Particle Physics of ETH Zurich, the fast breeder reactors currently face "a large number of unresolved technological problems" and "huge efforts, including many basic research questions with an uncertain outcome, are needed before a large commercial breeder prototype can be designed" (Dittmar 2009b: 1).

From 1977 to 1982, the US Atomic Energy Commission operated a research reactor as a thorium breeder reactor. The reactor was started with highly enriched U_{233}. After five years of operation, the reactor was measured to have achieved a breeding gain of 1.3 percent. The initial concentration of fissile material was very large and, if it was used in a conventional nuclear reactor, it could generate five times more electricity than it had during the thorium breeder experiment. No further thorium breeder experiment has been performed since then.

Many more tests are needed before a large-scale prototype thorium breeder reactor can be constructed. Some possible problems with the thorium breeder reactors include the high cost of fuel fabrication, the contamination of thorium and U_{233} by other radioactive materials, and the risk of nuclear weapon proliferation (Dittmar 2009b: 10–11, 15–17).

Nuclear fusion

Nuclear fusion reaction is based on energy liberated by the fusion of atoms. It is the energy source of the sun and other stars. A hydrogen bomb is designed to explode with uncontrolled nuclear fusion reactions. Peaceful and commercial applications require the nuclear fusion reactions to be controlled.

Currently, nuclear fusion scientists are able to achieve a fusion operation that lasts only a few seconds and the energy output has been less than the energy input. Scientists from several of the world's largest countries are cooperating on a project, which is expected to cost 10 billion dollars. The scientists hope to demonstrate that nuclear fusion can produce electricity at a rate of 0.15 megawatt for 400 seconds by 2025. By comparison, a conventional nuclear power plant can operate on a gigawatt scale in a near steady state for 80 percent of the year.

The material that surrounds a full-scale nuclear fusion reactor needs to survive an extremely high neutron flux over years. No known material today comes close to meeting the requirements.

Large-scale nuclear fusion experiments and operations require large quantities of tritium, which create serious radiation protection problems as well as weapon proliferation risks.

A small nuclear fusion reactor that has an electricity generating capacity of 0.3 gigawatt needs to consume 56 kilograms of tritium a year. Currently, tritium is extracted from some heavy water reactors in Canada at a cost of 30 million dollars per kilogram. By 2027, the old heavy water reactors will retire and the world will have accumulated 27 kilograms of tritium. Tritium has a very high decay rate of 5 percent a year. Thus, by 2050, only seven kilograms of the accumulated tritium will be left, not enough even for a prototype nuclear fusion reactor to operate for two months (Dittmar 2009b: 17–24).

Given these and some other considerations, Dittmar concluded that "commercial fusion power will never become a reality" (Dittmar 2009b: 1).

Nuclear accidents and radioactivity pollution

Nuclear energy production generates radioactivity at all stages: uranium mining and processing, nuclear electricity generation, nuclear waste disposal, and nuclear power plant decommissioning. A nuclear reactor with a generating capacity of one gigawatt produces each year an amount of radioactivity that is equivalent to 1,000 nuclear bombs (Leeuwen 2012: 68).

Radioactivity cannot be destroyed and only decreases by natural decay. The radiation emitted by radioactive substances is hazardous to human beings. A severe accident, such as what happened in Chernobyl or Fukushima, could kill millions of people if it happened in densely populated areas such as Western Europe or China.

The nuclear waste remains radioactive and needs to be securely isolated from the biosphere for many thousands of years. However, currently, none of the nuclear waste that has been generated is stored in a permanent safe place. Any significant expansion of nuclear electricity could lead to potentially intractable nuclear waste problems (Leeuwen 2012: 69–71).

Renewable energies

All renewable energies, with the exception of geothermal energy, originally derive from solar energy. The theoretical amount of solar energy is enormous. The total solar radiation absorbed by the earth's land surface amounts to 790,000 EJ (EJ = exajoule, 1 EJ = 10^{18} joules, or 23.88 million tonnes of oil equivalent) (Smil 2010a: 109).

By comparison, the world's total primary energy consumption is currently about 12 billion tonnes of oil equivalent, or 500 EJ. Thus, the solar energy potentially available on the world's land surface is roughly 1,600 times the world's current energy consumption. If 1 percent of the land surface can be utilized and 10 percent of the solar energy in the utilized area can be captured, it would translate into 790 EJ, more than sufficient to replace the world's total energy supply.

The theoretical wind resources are large. The global wind flux at 80 meters above ground is estimated to be 2,200–2,500 EJ. But given land and technical constraints, only a small fraction of the potential wind resources can be captured and utilized.

The global economic potential of hydroelectric power is estimated to be about 30 EJ. The global ocean waves dissipated along the coasts have a kinetic energy of 90 EJ, of which only a small fraction can be harvested. Only about 2 EJ of the tidal energy is dissipated along the coasts (Smil 2010a: 109–110).

The global terrestrial photosynthesis proceeds have an annual rate of 1,900 EJ (Smil 2010a: 110). The total annual "net primary production" of terrestrial biomass is estimated to be 1,260 EJ (IPCC 2011: 222). Net primary production is the portion of the gross photosynthesis proceeds that is available for biomass growth. About 40 percent of it is already committed to various human uses for the production of food, feed, and fiber. The rest provides essential environmental services to diverse ecological systems. Any further significant increase in the human appropriation of the global net primary productivity could fatally undermine many ecological systems and lead to global ecological collapse (Smil 2010a: 115–116).

The global geothermal flux is about 1,300 EJ. But about 80 percent of that is through the ocean floor and cannot be accessed. The technical potential of geothermal electricity may be no more than 4 EJ by the mid-twenty-first century (Smil 2010a: 110).

Thus, among the world's renewable energy resources, only solar energy has the technical potential that may be substantially greater than the world's current energy supply.

Electricity generating costs

Table 5.1 compares the current electricity generating costs of different technologies.

A coal-fired power plant of one gigawatt generating capacity, with a capacity utilization rate of 50 percent, can generate 4,380 gigawatt-hours of electricity in a year.

The capital invested in the coal plant is estimated to be 2.9 billion dollars (capital cost estimates are from EIA 2013e). Annual fixed cost is assumed to include depreciation of fixed capital, maintenance, and interests. These are assumed to be 10 percent of the capital invested. It follows that the annual fixed cost is 290 million dollars.

The coal plant is assumed to generate electricity with an efficiency of 40 percent. To generate 4,380 gigawatt-hours of electricity, it requires 10,950 gigawatt-hours of thermal energy or 0.94 million tonnes of oil

Table 5.1 Cost estimates of electricity generating technologies (1 gigawatt of generating capacity, 2012 dollars)

	Coal	Natural gas	Nuclear	Wind	Solar photovoltaic
Capacity utilization rate (%)	50	50	80	25	15
Ann. generation (GWH)	4,380	4,380	7,008	2,190	1,314
Capital cost (million $)	2,900	1,000	5,500	2,200	3,900
Ann. fixed cost (million $)	290	100	550	220	390
Ann. fuel cost (million $)	192	188	27	0	0
Ann. total cost (million $)	482	288	577	220	390
Ave. unit cost ($ per KWH)	0.110	0.066	0.082	0.100	0.297

Notes
Capacity utilization rate: Based on the observed world average capacity utilization rates.
Capital cost: Capital cost estimates are from EIA (2013e: 6).
Annual fixed cost: Annual fixed cost is assumed to be 10 percent of the capital cost (assuming 5 percent for depreciation and maintenance and 5 percent interest rate).
Annual fuel cost: Coal and natural gas power plants are assumed to have 40 percent generating efficiency; coal price is assumed to be 100 dollars per tonne; natural gas price is assumed to be five dollars per thousand cubic feet; nuclear power plants are assumed to consume 180 tonnes of uranium a year and the uranium price is assumed to be 150 dollars per kilogram.
Annual total cost: Annual total cost is the sum of annual fixed cost and annual fuel cost.
Average unit cost: Average unit cost is the annual total cost divided by the annual electricity generation.

equivalent. Given the current world average quality of coal, 0.94 million tonnes of oil equivalent equals the energy content of 1.92 million tonnes of coal. Assuming that the coal price is 100 dollars per tonne, the annual fuel cost is calculated to be 192 million dollars.

The average unit cost is calculated by dividing the annual total cost by the annual electricity generated. For coal-fired electricity, it is calculated to be 11 cents per kilowatt-hour.

Given the current costs, natural gas-fired electricity is the cheapest, with an average unit cost of 6.6 cents per kilowatt-hour. Nuclear electricity appears to be relatively cheap. But the nuclear cost calculation does not include the costs of nuclear waste disposal and nuclear power plant decommissioning.

Wind electricity is about 50 percent more expensive than natural gas-fired electricity, and solar electricity (based on the solar photovoltaic technology) costs 4.5 times as much as natural gas-fired electricity.

The world currently has a total installed electricity generating capacity of about 5,000 gigawatts. Using the capital cost of the coal-fired power plant as a reference, the total capital invested in the world's electric power sector is about 15 trillion dollars. This is about 21 percent of the world's current GDP (about 70 trillion dollars).

Assuming that the power plants have an average depreciation rate of 2.5 percent and the electric power sector's growth rate is 2.5 percent, the world's annual investment on new power plants amounts to 750 billion dollars (15 trillion dollars × 5% = 0.75 trillion dollars), or 1.1 percent of the world GDP.

The world electric power sector now has an average capacity utilization rate of about 50 percent. Wind electricity has an average capacity utilization rate of about 25 percent. If the world's current electricity consumption were to be provided entirely by wind electricity, it would require 10,000 gigawatts of wind power plants. The total capital required would need to be 22 trillion dollars, which equals 31 percent of the world's current GDP. The annual investment cost on new wind power plants would need to be 1.1 trillion dollars, or 1.6 percent of the world GDP.

Solar electricity has an average capacity utilization rate of about 15 percent. If the world's current electricity consumption were to be provided entirely by solar electricity, it would require 16,500 gigawatts of solar power plants. The total capital required would be 64 trillion dollars, which equals 91 percent of the world's current GDP. The annual investment cost on new solar power plants would need to be 3.2 trillion dollars, or 4.6 percent of the world GDP.

Solar electricity: future generating costs

There are two different types of solar electricity generation: solar thermal electricity and solar photovoltaic electricity. Currently, one gigawatt of solar thermal electricity costs 5.1 billion dollars and one gigawatt of solar photovoltaic electricity costs 3.9 billion dollars.

Solar thermal electricity uses solar thermal collectors to heat a water boiler and make steam, which is in turn used to run a conventional generator with a steam turbine. According to the EIA (2013e: Table 23–1), "mechanical equipment supply and installation" accounts for 53 percent of the solar thermal power plant cost. Other costs account for 47 percent. Other costs include construction of buildings and foundations, electrical instrumentation and control, project indirect costs, and the owner's costs (research and development costs, legal costs, and insurance costs, etc.). These are conventional cost items that are unlikely to be affected significantly by future technological progress.

Within the "mechanical equipment supply and installation," the generator accounts for about half of the cost and the solar thermal collectors account for the other half. The prices of high-temperature solar thermal collectors (the collectors used for solar thermal electricity generation) have fluctuated wildly since the 1980s, with no clear trend (EIA 2012a).

The solar photovoltaic electricity uses semiconductor panels to convert the solar energy directly from light into electricity. The costs of solar panels (under the category of "mechanical equipment supply and installation") account for 47 percent of the solar photovoltaic power plant cost; other costs account for 53 percent (EIA 2013e: Table 24–2).

From 1989 to 2010, the average solar module price declined from 5.14 dollars per watt to 1.96 dollars per watt (EIA 2012b). In the near future, the solar panel costs are likely to keep falling as the solar technology progresses and the solar panel manufacturing relocates to cheap labor sites, such as China. But other cost items (such as civil structural material and installation, electrical instrument and control, contingency costs, and the owner's costs) are based on conventional technologies and may not be significantly reduced.

Suppose that the solar panel price can be reduced by 90 percent from the current level but other costs remain the same, the overall capital cost of solar photovoltaic electricity would only fall by 42 percent.

Assuming that, in the near future, the solar electricity capital cost can be reduced by half, the annual investment cost on new solar power plants would still amount to 2.3 percent of the world GDP if the world's electricity generation were to be provided entirely by solar electricity.

According to the World Bank (2013), the world's total gross fixed capital formation accounts for about 20 percent of the world GDP. After subtracting residential investment and government investment, business investment accounts for about 10 percent of the world GDP. That is, about one-quarter of the world's business investment would have to be spent on the new solar power plants (given the above assumptions).

In the long run, the supply of solar and other renewable electricity will be constrained by the availability of land, the availability of physical resources, and certain technical factors. As the available land and resources become scarcer, the costs of solar and other renewable electricity will tend to rise.

The cost of rooftop solar photovoltaic electricity

Currently, most of the solar photovoltaic electricity is generated from rooftop installations. Rooftop photovoltaic equipment can be directly installed on residential and commercial buildings. It does not require the building of new infrastructure and transmission lines.

The Wall Street Journal published an interesting report on "The Economics of Installing Solar" in a special section on energy on September 17, 2012 (Chernova 2012). The report was based on calculations made by Clean Power Research, a research firm based in Seattle.

A solar power system helps the homeowner to save money by reducing electricity purchases from the utility. The homeowner's cumulative saving is the difference between the cumulative reduction of electricity cost and his or her initial investment.

According to the report, a solar power system installed on a house in Brooklyn, New York with an initial investment of about 9,700 dollars will bring about a cumulative saving of 33,500 dollars after 25 years. In Denver, an initial investment of 19,300 dollars will bring about a cumulative saving of 13,100 dollars. In Los Angeles, the initial investment is 14,100 dollars and the cumulative saving is 21,500 dollars. In Minneapolis, the initial investment is 11,400 dollars and the cumulative saving is 11,100 dollars. In Portland, Oregon, where a smaller system is assumed, the initial investment is 8,900 dollars and the cumulative saving is 4,200 dollars.

For Brooklyn, Denver, Los Angeles, and Minneapolis, a solar power system of five kilowatts is assumed and the system cost before tax credits and rebates is said to be 27,500 dollars. The unit capital cost is 5.5 dollars per watt. On a gigawatt scale, this would correspond to 5.5 billion dollars per gigawatt, significantly more expensive than the capital cost of a solar photovoltaic power plant estimated by the Energy Information Administration.

For the system installed in Brooklyn, the federal, state, and local government credits add up to 12,000 dollars and the state government provides an additional tax rebate of 7,500 dollars. After correcting for the federal tax adjustment on the state tax rebate, government tax credits and rebate reduce the original system cost by 17,800 dollars, or by 65 percent. For Los Angeles, Minneapolis, Denver, and Portland, the subsidy to original system cost ratio is 49 percent, 59 percent, 30 percent, and 28 percent, respectively.

The Brooklyn solar system has the highest cumulative rate of return. The cumulative saving-to-investment ratio is 3.5. The implied average annual compound rate of return is 6.2 percent. That is, if an investor were to invest the same 9,700 dollars on a stock or a bond with an annual rate of return of 6.2 percent and were to reinvest the investment income every year, after 25 years the investor should have received the same cumulative return as he or she would receive from an investment in the Brooklyn solar system.

For Los Angeles, Minneapolis, Denver, and Portland, the cumulative saving to investment ratio is 1.5, 1, 0.7, and 0.5, respectively. The corresponding average annual compound rate of return is 3.8 percent, 2.8 percent, 2.1 percent, and 1.6 percent, respectively. In 2012, the US average new-home mortgage interest rate was 3.7 percent, the lowest in history (ERP 2013). At this rate, only the Brooklyn solar system would make clear economic sense and the Los Angeles solar system is barely economic. In Minneapolis, Denver, and Portland, the homeowner would do better to use the money to pay back some of his or her mortgage than to invest in the solar system.

In Minneapolis and Portland, if there were no government subsidy, the cumulative saving that could be achieved by installing the solar power system would actually be negative as the cumulative electricity cost reduction turns out to be smaller than the original system cost. In Brooklyn, Los Angeles, and Denver, the average annual compound rate of return on the solar power system would be 1.8 percent, 1.1 percent, and 0.7 percent, respectively, if there were no government subsidy. It would not make economic sense to invest in the solar power system if there were no government subsidy.

For the study, Clean Power Research assumed that the homeowner in each example filed taxes as a single person and had an annual income of 140,000 dollars, almost three times the American median household income. It appears that the current US government programs for rooftop solar photovoltaic electricity essentially use tax revenues to subsidize wealthy capitalist or upper middle class families so that they can make money while living "green" lifestyles.

Land availability

In June 2011, the Working Group III of the Intergovernmental Panel on Climate Change published a special report that provided highly optimistic estimates of the future technical potentials of various renewable energies (IPCC 2011). The Working Group III estimated that the maximum technical potential of electricity generation from geothermal, hydro, ocean, and wind energies would be 2,072 EJ. The maximum technical potential of primary energy from biomass and solar energy was estimated to be 500 EJ and 48,837 EJ, respectively. Assuming that 35 percent of the biomass primary energy can be converted to liquid fuels, 500 EJ of primary biomass energy implies 175 EJ of biofuels. Assuming that 7.5 percent of the solar primary energy can be converted to electricity (the land area used is assumed to be twice the area of the solar collectors and the conversion efficiency is assumed to be 15 percent), 48,837 EJ of primary solar energy implies 3,663 EJ of solar electricity. Thus, according to the Working Group III, the total maximum technical potential of electricity and liquid fuels from renewable sources amounts to about 6,000 EJ, or 12 times the world's present energy consumption.

The Working Group III also provided minimum estimates. The total minimum technical potential of electricity and liquid fuels from renewable sources was estimated to be about 400 EJ, or about 80 percent of the world's present energy consumption (IPCC 2011: 12).

The Working Group III also cited predictions of the likely renewable energy contribution by the mid-twenty-first century. These predictions are much more modest. About half of the studies cited by the Working Group III predicted that the renewable energy contribution by the mid-twenty-first century would be no more than 173 EJ. The maximum prediction for the renewable energy contribution by the mid-twenty-first century was 400 EJ (IPCC 2011: 20). The Working Group III's measurement of renewable energy included 30 EJ of traditional biomass and the Working Group III appeared to have used thermal equivalent rather than electrical energy content to measure the contribution of renewable electricity. Using this book's measurement of renewable energies, the Working Group III in effect predicted that, by the mid-twenty-first century, the renewable electricity and liquid fuels would contribute no more than 60 EJ based on the median estimate, or no more than 150 EJ based on the maximum estimate.

In an earlier study, Lightfoot and Green (2002) assumed that 1 percent of the world's unused land, or 390,000 square kilometers, would be used for solar electricity generation, 4 percent of the land with wind speed higher than 5.1 meters per second at 10 meters above the surface, or 1.2

million square kilometers, would be used for wind electricity generation, and 8.95 million square kilometers would be used for biomass production. Under these assumptions, Lightfoot and Green estimated that the total potential of renewable electricity and liquid fuels by 2100 would be 365 EJ.

In a later study, Green *et al.* (2007) pointed out that, when resource constraints and technical problems such as storage and electric grid integration were taken into account, the realistic potential of renewable energies by 2100 would be no more than 150–175 EJ.

Steel requirements

The building of renewable electric power plants and biofuel processing plants requires the consumption of nonrenewable mineral resources. Iron is the least expensive and most widely used metal. Steel is an alloy based primarily on iron and is an essential material for modern economic life (USGS 2012a; World Coal Association 2012). In this sub-section, I use the steel requirement as the limiting factor to evaluate how the future potential of renewable energies may be limited by the available nonrenewable mineral resources.

According to studies by the US National Renewable Energy Laboratory, the steel requirement for a coal-fired power plant was estimated to be 50,700 tonnes per gigawatt of generating capacity (Spath, Mann, and Kerr 1999: 24) and the steel requirement for a natural gas combined cycle power plant was estimated to be 31,000 tonnes per gigawatt of generating capacity (Spath and Mann 2000: 8).

By comparison, renewable electric power plants require larger amounts of material inputs per unit of generating capacity. According to a report published by the US Geological Survey, under the current technology, a wind power plant requires 115,000 tonnes of stainless steel per gigawatt of generating capacity. The steel requirement may be reduced to 103,000 tonnes per gigawatt of generating capacity with the next generation technology (Wilburn 2011: 12).

According to a report made by the SunPower Corporation, the steel requirements of solar photovoltaic power plants range from 83,000 tonnes to 145,000 tonnes per gigawatt of generating capacity (Campbell 2008: 14).

According to a presentation made by Professor Hans Müller-Steinhagen at the 2008 Annual Stockholders Meeting of Heat Transfer Research, Inc., a solar thermal power plant with a generating capacity of 100 megawatts typically required 25,000 tonnes of steel. This translates into a steel requirement of 250,000 tonnes per gigawatt of generating capacity

(Müller-Steinhagen 2008: 15). Professor Müller-Steinhagen is the director of the Institute for Technical Thermal Dynamics of the German Aerospace Centre.

According to the *Historical Statistics for Mineral and Material Commodities*, compiled by the US Geological Survey, the cumulative world steel production from 1943 to 2011 was 43 billion tonnes (USGS 2012b). Assuming that 70 percent of the historical steel production was "primary steel" made from iron and the rest consisted of recycled steel, the cumulative world production of primary steel was about 30 billion tonnes.

Currently, the world has about 5,000 gigawatts of installed electric power generating capacity. Assuming that the average steel content of the world's power plants is 50,000 tonnes per gigawatt (taking the coal-fired power plant's steel requirement as a reference), the total steel content embodied in the world's current electric power plants is 250 million tonnes, or 0.8 percent of the world's cumulative primary steel production.

The world's cumulative iron ore production from 1905 to 2011 was 65 billion tonnes and the cumulative pig iron production from 1910 to 2010 was 32 billion tonnes (USGS 2012b). The world's current iron ore reserves are 170 billion tonnes, with the iron content estimated to be 80 billion tonnes (USGS 2012a). Thus, the observed recoverable iron resources are about 110 billion tonnes. Making the assumption that all future iron resources will be used for primary steel production, the world's ultimate cumulative production of primary steel will be about 110 billion tonnes.

Assuming optimistically that 5 percent of the world's ultimate cumulative production of primary steel will be used for electric power plant construction and further assuming that the worn-out power plants can be replaced indefinitely by new power plants built from recycled steel, the total steel content embodied in the world's electric power sector may eventually rise to 5.5 billion tonnes. This would be 3.7 times the world steel production in 2011.

Assuming that the average steel requirement for renewable electric power plants will be 100,000 tonnes per gigawatt, 5.5 billion tonnes of steel content implies 55,000 gigawatts of generating capacity. Future renewable energies are likely to be dominated by wind and solar electricity, which have low capacity utilization rates. Assuming that the future average capacity utilization rate is 20 percent, 55,000 gigawatts of generating capacity can generate 96,360 terawatt-hours of electricity in a year, which equals about 8.3 billion tonnes of oil equivalent or 350 EJ.

Thus, only the minimum estimate of the world renewable energy potential made by the Working Group III of IPCC is consistent with the world's remaining iron resources.

Liquid fuels

Most renewable energies are best used to generate electricity. If liquid fuels are to be made from electricity through hydrogen, there will be major technical difficulties. Hydrogen has very low energy density by volume. This makes the transportation of hydrogen extremely difficult. It was estimated that it would take 15 times as many tankers to transport hydrogen as it would need to deliver the same amount of energy in the form of petroleum product. Significant energy losses happen as electricity is converted to hydrogen, hydrogen is compressed and pumped over long distance, and hydrogen is reconverted into end-use electricity via fuel cell. The cumulative energy loss from electricity to end use is estimated to be about 80 percent (Trainer 2007: 93–100).

Biomass is the only renewable energy that can be converted to liquid fuels or chemical inputs without major technical obstacles. Currently, biofuels are mainly made from corn, sugarcane, and palm oil, which competes with food supply. In 2011, the US produced 28.5 million tonnes of biofuels (573,000 barrels per day), accounting for only 0.7 percent of the world's total oil consumption (BP 2013). In the same year, the US used about 130 million tonnes of corn for fuel ethanol production, accounting for 5.5 percent of the world's total grain production (EPI 2012b, 2012c). At this rate, just to provide 5 percent of the world's oil consumption, it would consume about 40 percent of the world's total grain production. This is clearly impossible.

In the long run, if biofuels were to make a significant contribution to the world energy supply, it will have to be based on either cellulosic material or algae. Suppose that 1.5 billion hectares of land were committed to the production of cellulosic biomass (about the same size as the world's current arable land area). The average yield for very large-scale biomass production is assumed to be seven tonnes per hectare (by comparison, the current world average grain yield is about three tonnes per hectare). The cellulosic biomass has an average heat content of 20 gigajoules per tonne or 20 EJ per gigatonne. Given these assumptions, the world biomass potential may be 10.5 billion tonnes with 210 EJ of primary energy. If 40 percent of the primary biomass energy can be converted to biofuels, the world potential of biofuel production would be about 85 EJ, or two billion tonnes of oil equivalent (Trainer 2007: 75).

Under ideal conditions, algae can achieve much higher growth rates than terrestrial plant crops. Algae can be grown on ponds, lakes, water channels, and in the ocean, and does not need to compete with arable land. Algae production does not require fresh water. Both waste water and sea water can be used (Mórrígan 2010: 82–86).

Nevertheless, very large areas would still be needed if algae were to make a significant contribution to world liquid fuels consumption. Assuming that algae yield is 10 grams per square meter per day, or 36.5 tonnes per hectare per year and the oil content of algae is 30 percent, the biofuel yield from algae would be about 11 tonnes per hectare (Mórrígan 2010: 83). To provide 2.2 billion tonnes of biofuels (equaling about 55 percent of the world's current oil consumption), it would take 200 million hectares.

Assuming that the capital cost of algae production is 100,000 dollars per hectare (Mórrígan 2010: 85), the total capital cost would need to be 20 trillion dollars, significantly greater than the world's current total capital invested in the electric power sector. Assuming that the annual costs of depreciation, interests, operation and management, and the inputs of nutrients equal 15 percent of the capital cost, the cost of the biofuel made from algae would be 190 dollars per barrel.

Algae production requires massive inputs of nutrients. The availability of nutrients could prove to be the limiting factor to large-scale algae production. At a minimum, phosphorous needs to account for 1 percent of the algal biomass by weight (Mórrígan 2010: 84). To produce 7.3 billion tonnes of algae (200 million hectares × 36.5 tonnes per hectare), it would require at least 73 million tonnes of phosphorous. The phosphorous content of phosphate rock is 8.5–13 percent (Global Phosphorous Network 2012). Assuming that the phosphorous content is 10 percent, the annual requirement of phosphate rock would have to be 730 million tonnes. The world annual phosphate rock production is about 170 million tonnes and the world phosphate rock production may peak in the 2030s (Mórrígan 2010: 116–120). Thus, to replace just about one-half of the world's current oil consumption with biofuels made from algae, it would require 4.3 times the world's current phosphate rock production.

I assume that the world's future potential of biofuel production will be two billion tonnes of oil equivalent. Given the land, water, and nutrition constraints, this assumption may prove to be too optimistic.

Liquid fuels-constrained renewable energy potential

Beyond the twenty-first century, with the depletion of nonrenewable energy resources, eventually both electricity and the liquid fuels will have to be provided entirely from renewable energy resources.

Currently, liquid fuels account for about 50 percent of the world's final consumption of commercially produced energy and electricity accounts for about 20 percent. So the liquid fuels–electricity ratio is 2.5 : 1.

In 2010, industry, transport, and the "other sectors" (including agriculture, services, and the residential sector) each accounted for about 30 percent of the world's total final energy consumption (excluding consumption of traditional biomass). In addition, non-energy uses (coal, oil, and natural gas used as chemical inputs) accounted for 10 percent (IEA 2012a).

In the future, electricity may be able to replace natural gas and coal for most of their final uses in the industrial, commercial, and residential sector. But electricity clearly cannot serve as a chemical input. Hydrocarbons may be synthesized from carbon dioxide and hydrogen using electricity (Biello 2011). But the processes would involve substantial energy losses (see the discussion on making hydrogen from electricity in the previous section).

In the transportation sector, electricity may be able to replace gasoline and provide the main fuel for passenger road transportation in the future. However, given the constraints of material resources and economic cost considerations, it is by no means certain that the world's entire passenger car fleet can be replaced with electric cars.

According to Gaines and Nelson (2009: 7), the lithium requirement for full electric cars with a range of 100 miles ranges from three kilograms per battery to 13 kilograms per battery. If the electric car were to have a range comparable to today's typical gasoline-fueled cars (about 300 miles), the lithium requirement needs to be between nine kilograms per battery and 39 kilograms per battery. Assuming that the lithium requirement is 10 kilograms per battery, to replace the world's current fleet of about one billion cars, it would require 10 million tonnes of lithium.

The world's current lithium reserves are 13 million tonnes and the annual production in 2011 was only 34,000 tonnes. At the current lithium production rate, it would take about 300 years to replace the world's current car fleet with electric cars. Just to replace the world's existing car fleet, about three-quarters of the world's current lithium reserves would be depleted. This raises the question of how to provide fuel for the expansion of the world passenger car fleet as the global economy grows.

Given the limitation of lithium resources and some fundamental technical difficulties, it would be even less likely that freight road transportation, sea transportation, and air transportation could be electrified (Heinberg 2011: 159–160).

In 2010, motor gasoline accounted for 25 percent of the world's total petroleum consumption, or 42 percent of the total transportation fuel (using motor gasoline as a proxy for the fuel used for passenger road transportation) (EIA 2013a).

Assuming that in the future about 50 percent of the transportation fuel can be electrified, at the maximum, electricity can provide 75 percent of the future world energy consumption (including energy consumption by industry, services, the residential sector, and half of the transportation). The other 25 percent will have to be provided by liquid fuels (including energy consumption by the chemical industries and half of the transportation). Thus, at the maximum, the future electricity–liquid fuels ratio may rise to $3:1$.

Since the future biofuel potential is two billion tonnes of oil equivalent and other renewable energies are best used to generate electricity, the maximum future renewable energy potential implied by the liquid fuels constraint is eight billion tonnes of oil equivalent.

Intermittency

Solar electricity and wind electricity are intermittent. Solar and wind electricity fluctuate in accordance with changes in natural conditions. They do not generate constant flows of electricity. Nor can they increase or decrease in response to demand changes. Thus, solar and wind electricity cannot serve as base-load electricity. Moreover, their output peaks do not necessarily match the demand peaks; although, in the summer, daily output peaks of solar electricity often coincide with peak demands for electricity around noon time. Unless large-scale storage technologies can be developed in the future, solar and wind cannot become the main sources of electricity generation without large-scale back up by fossil fuels.

Suppose that an electric grid system needs to meet a maximum demand of two gigawatts and an average demand of one gigawatt. The annual electricity generation needs to be one gigawatt × 8,760 hours = 8,760 gigawatt-hours. But the short-term electricity demand could vary between zero and two gigawatts. The ratio between the maximum and the average electricity demand used in this example is similar to the current ratio for the world electric power sector.

The maximum wind and solar generating capacity the system can have is two gigawatts. If the system includes more than two gigawatts of solar and wind electricity, there will be times when both the solar and the wind electricity are operating at full capacity and generating more than two gigawatts of electricity. The extra electricity will have to be dumped.

Suppose that the system includes one gigawatt of wind electricity and one gigawatt of solar electricity. The wind power plant has an average capacity utilization rate of 25 percent and the solar power plant has an average capacity utilization rate of 15 percent. The total annual electricity generation from wind and solar would be 3,504 gigawatt-hours, or 40 percent of the annual electricity demand. The other 60 percent of the electricity demand has to be provided by fossil fuels (see the discussion of "integration limits" in Trainer 2011).

This calculation has not taken into account the fact that there will be times when the combined electricity generation from wind and solar is greater than the demand even when the wind and solar electricity are operating at less than full capacity. In those cases, additional wind or solar electricity needs to be dumped.

Within the fossil fuels, natural gas-fired electricity is best suited to provide back-up for fluctuating renewable electricity as the gas turbines can be turned on or off quickly. If coal-fired electricity is used to provide back-up, the coal-fired steam turbines need to stay warm and consume coal even when no electricity is being generated (Trainer 2007: 32–33).

Based on this chapter's projection, the world natural gas production is projected to peak in 2034 and decline to about 700 million tonnes of oil equivalent by 2100 (compared to the current world natural gas production of about three billion tonnes of oil equivalent). Assuming that the world's entire natural gas production in 2100 will be used for electricity generation and the generating efficiency is 40 percent, the world's natural gas-fired electricity generation would be about 3,300 terawatt-hours (or about 280 million tonnes of oil equivalent) by 2100.

Further assuming that the natural gas-fired electricity generation accounts for 50 percent of the total electricity generation by 2100 and the rest of the electricity generation comes from renewable sources, the world potential of renewable electricity generation by 2100 would be no more than 280 million tonnes of oil equivalent.

Solar thermal electricity

Compared to wind and solar photovoltaic electricity, intermittency may be less of a problem for solar thermal electricity. Heat received by the solar thermal collectors during the sunny daytime may be stored in oil, molten salt, or crushed rock, to be used for electricity generation during the night-time or cloudy days (Trainer 2007: 46).

Currently, a solar thermal electric power plant typically has a capacity utilization rate of 25 percent (Trainer 2007: 45). Suppose that, in the future, the solar thermal electricity will serve as the main source of electricity generation. The average capacity utilization rate of the solar thermal power plants needs to be raised to about 50 percent, comparable to the current average capacity utilization rate of conventional thermal power plants.

For the output to double, the total solar heat collected needs to double accordingly. According to the information provided by EIA (2013e: Table 23–1), it can be estimated that the solar thermal collectors and construction account for about 40 percent of the total capital cost of solar thermal electricity. To double the amount of solar heat collected, the capital cost associated with solar heat collection is likely to double and the overall capital cost of a solar thermal power plant is likely to increase by about 40 percent. Similarly, Trainer (2012) summarized several estimates and concluded that a doubling of the solar heat collection field would lead to an increase in the solar thermal plant capital cost of 40–46 percent. The current capital cost of a solar thermal power plant is about five billion dollars per gigawatt. To double the capacity utilization rate, the capital cost would have to rise to about seven billion dollars.

For the solar thermal electricity output to match the demand, excess solar heat during sunny daytime needs to be stored to meet the demand during nighttime or cloudy days. According to Trainer (2012), even in the best solar region in Australia, there are likely to be four continuous cloudy days during the winter. Thus, to provide continuous electricity supply to meet demand during cloudy days may require a storage facility that can provide up to four days of electricity.

Suppose a storage facility that is capable of providing four days of electricity is to be built. For a solar thermal power plant with a generating capacity of one gigawatt, heat energy capable of generating 48 gigawatt-hours of electricity needs to be stored (assuming that the average daily electricity output is 12 gigawatt-hours). Assuming a generating efficiency of 40 percent, 120 gigawatt-hours of heat energy needs to be stored. According to Trainer (2012), the current storage cost is about 90 dollars per kilowatt-hour of heat energy, though in the future it may be reduced by three-quarters. Assuming that the future storage cost is 25 dollars per kilowatt-hour of heat energy. The capital cost of the storage facility would be 3 billion dollars.

The combined capital cost of a solar thermal electric power plant with one-gigawatt generating capacity, 50 percent capacity utilization rate, and a 48-hour storage facility would be about 10 billion dollars. If the world's current electric power sector (about 5,000 gigawatts) were to be replaced by such solar thermal electric power plants, the total capital cost would be 50 trillion dollars, or 70 percent of the world GDP.

Even with expensive storage facilities, solar thermal electricity would still have to deal with the problem of large seasonal variations. Even at the best sites, the winter output of solar thermal electricity is only about a half of the summer output (Trainer 2011). If a solar thermal electric power plant is built to operate with an average capacity utilization rate of 50 percent during the summer, then it can only achieve an average capacity utilization rate of 25 percent during the winter. If an electric power system typically needs to have an average capacity utilization rate of about 50 percent, then solar thermal electricity can only meet half of the winter's electricity demand and the other half would have to be met from other sources (such as natural gas).

If the solar thermal electric power plant is built to have an average capacity utilization rate of 50 percent during the winter, it needs to collect twice as much solar heat as a plant with an average capacity utilization rate of 25 percent during the winter. Its capital cost needs to be increased by another 40 percent.

How about regulating the electric power demand so that the winter demand for electricity is limited to about a half of the summer demand? In that case, the rest of the economy would find its capital stock significantly underutilized in the winter.

Suppose that the future electric power system is based on solar thermal electricity and natural gas-fired electricity. Solar thermal electricity provides the entire electricity supply in the summer and the winter electricity output is divided equally between solar thermal electricity and natural gas-fired electricity. Thus, about one-quarter of the world's future electricity generation would be provided by natural gas.

As explained in the previous sub-section, the world's natural gas-fired electricity generation by 2100 would be no more than 3,300 terawatt-hours. It follows that the solar thermal electricity generation by 2100 would be no more than 9,900 terawatt-hours (about 850 million tonnes of oil equivalent).

Renewable energy potential: summary

According to the IPCC Working Group III, the maximum technical potential of renewable electricity and liquid fuels amounts to 6,000 EJ (about 144 billion tonnes of oil equivalent) and the minimum technical potential amounts to 400 EJ (about 9.6 billion tonnes of oil equivalent) (IPCC 2011: 12)

Assuming that the world's ultimate cumulative production of primary steel will be 110 billion tonnes and 5 percent of it will be used for the building of renewable electric power plants, the maximum potential of renewable electricity is estimated to be 55,000 gigawatts of generating capacity, or 96,000 terawatt-hours of annual electricity generation (which equals 8.3 billion tonnes of oil equivalent).

If one assumes that the future renewable electricity will be dominated by solar thermal electricity and the steel requirement for a solar thermal electric power plant is assumed to be 250,000 tonnes per gigawatt (Müller-Steinhagen 2008: 15), then the maximum potential of solar thermal electricity would be 22,000 gigawatts of generating capacity. Further assuming that the solar thermal electric power plants have an average capacity utilization rate of 50 percent, the maximum potential solar thermal electricity generation would be 96,000 terawatt-hours, the same as the above estimate.

Assuming that the world's biofuels potential will be two billion tonnes of oil equivalent and the future electricity–liquid fuels ratio is 3 : 1, the liquid-fuels constrained world renewable energy potential is estimated to be eight billion tonnes of oil equivalent.

When the problem of intermittency and the availability of natural gas are taken into account, the intermittency-constrained renewable electricity potential may be only 0.3–0.9 billion tonnes of oil equivalent.

If one excludes the IPCC's maximum estimate as utterly unrealistic and makes the optimistic assumption that the intermittency problem can be overcome through development of storage technology, then the other estimates of the world renewable energy potential range from eight to 10 billion tonnes of oil equivalent (including renewable electricity and liquid fuels). I assume that the world's long-term potential of total renewable energy production will be 10 billion tonnes of oil equivalent. Figure 5.8 compares the historical and projected world renewable energy production from 2000 to 2100.

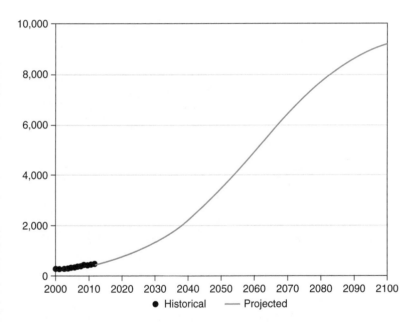

Figure 5.8 World renewable energy production (historical and projected, million TOE, 2000–2100) (sources: Renewable energy production is defined as the sum of hydroelectricity, other renewable electricity, and biofuel production. For hydroelectricity and other renewable electricity, production is assumed to be the same as consumption and their energy is measured by electrical energy content. Data for hydroelectricity consumption, other renewable electricity consumption, and biofuel production from 2000 to 2012 are from BP (2013). For projections from 2000 to 2100, see text. "TOE" stands for "tonnes of oil equivalent").

Peak energy

Figure 5.9 shows the historical and projected world primary energy consumption from 1950 to 2100. World primary energy consumption is the sum of oil consumption, natural gas consumption, coal consumption, nuclear energy consumption, and the consumption of renewable energies. The renewable energies include renewable electricity and biofuels. Nuclear and renewable electricity is measured by electrical energy content. For projections from 2013 to 2100, energy consumption is assumed to equal energy production.

World energy consumption is projected to peak around 2060 at 16.5 billion tonnes of oil equivalent, about 44 percent higher than the world

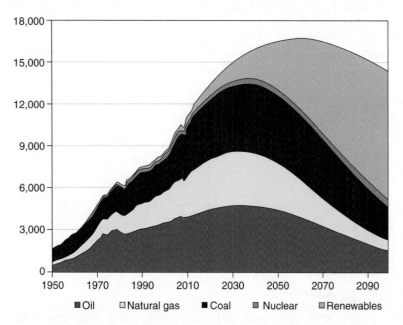

Figure 5.9 World primary energy consumption (million tonnes of oil equivalent, 1950–2100) (sources: World consumption of oil, natural gas, and coal from 1950 to 1964 are estimated from EPI (2012d). World consumption of oil, natural gas, coal, nuclear energy, and renewable energies from 1965 to 2012 are from BP (2013), with nuclear and renewable electricity measured by electrical energy content. From 2013 to 2100, world consumption of oil, natural gas, coal, nuclear energy, and renewable energies are assumed to be the same as their respective production. For the future coal production, 1 tonne of coal is assumed to equal 0.49 tonne of oil equivalent. For world energy production projections, see the text of Chapter 5).

energy consumption in 2012. By 2100, world energy consumption is projected to decline to 14.2 billion tonnes of oil equivalent, about 14 percent below the peak level.

Table 5.2 summarizes the average annual growth rates of different types of energy by decade from 1951 to 2100.

Table 5.3 summarizes the shares of different types of energy in world energy consumption from 1950 to 2100. Coal is projected to regain the title of the world's largest source of energy by the 2030s and will keep the title until the late 2050s. The fossil fuels will account for more than half of the world's total energy consumption until the 2070s. The renewable energies will account for about one-fifth of the world energy consumption by 2050 and about two-thirds by 2100.

Energy efficiency

Energy efficiency is the ratio of economic output (usually measured by gross domestic product or GDP) over energy consumption. The inverse of energy efficiency is known as the "energy intensity."

Lightfoot and Green (2001) studied the long-term potential of world energy efficiency improvement and concluded that, by 2100, the world

Table 5.2 World energy consumption by type, average annual growth rates (historical and projected, 1951–2100) (%)

	Oil	Natural gas	Coal	Nuclear	Renewables
Historical:					
1951–1960	7.2	9.3	2.8	n.a.	n.a.
1961–1970	7.9	8.5	0.9	n.a.	n.a.
1971–1980	2.8	3.7	1.8	24.8	3.8
1981–1990	0.6	3.2	2.1	10.9	3.2
1991–2000	1.3	2.1	0.6	2.6	2.4
2001–2010	1.1	2.8	4.0	0.7	5.0
Projected:					
2011–2020	1.2	2.0	2.1	0.3	5.9
2021–2030	0.6	0.9	1.0	1.6	5.8
2031–2040	0.0	−0.1	0.5	1.4	5.3
2041–2050	−0.6	−1.1	−0.1	1.2	4.6
2051–2060	−1.2	−2.0	−0.6	1.0	3.7
2061–2070	−1.7	−2.7	−1.1	0.7	2.7
2071–2080	−2.1	−3.2	−1.5	0.5	1.8
2081–2090	−2.4	−3.6	−1.	0.2	1.1
2091–2100	−2.7	−3.9	−2.2	−0.1	0.7

Sources: See Figure 5.9.

Table 5.3 World energy consumption by type, share of total (historical and projected, 1950–2100) (%)

	Oil	Natural gas	Coal	Nuclear	Renewables
Historical:					
1950	30	9	60	n.a.	n.a.
1960	37	14	49	n.a.	n.a.
1970	47	19	31	0	2
1980	47	21	29	1	2
1990	42	24	29	2	3
2000	42	25	27	3	3
2010	36	26	32	2	4
Projected:					
2020	34	26	32	2	6
2030	32	26	32	2	9
2040	30	24	31	2	14
2050	27	20	30	2	21
2060	24	16	28	2	30
2070	20	13	25	3	39
2080	17	9	22	3	48
2090	14	7	19	3	57
2100	11	5	17	3	64

Sources: See Figure 5.9.

average energy intensity could be reduced to 40 percent of the 1990 level, implying that the long-term potential energy efficiency could be increased to 250 percent of the 1990 level. Baski and Green (2007) developed the study by taking into account economic structural changes and found that, by 2100, the world average energy efficiency could be increased to 300–450 percent of the 1990 level.

The world average energy efficiency depends on three factors: how much of the world's primary energy supply is transformed into usable energy available for final consumption; how the final energy consumption is distributed between different economic sectors; and the energy efficiency in each economic sector.

Table 5.4 shows the approximate values of the world's energy transformation efficiency in 2000. In 2000, about 70 percent of the world's primary energy supply is transformed into usable energy available for final consumption. The theoretical maximum improvement in this area is about 40 percent, which would bring the average transformation efficiency to near 100 percent.

Table 5.5 shows the approximate sectoral distribution of world energy consumption in 2000 and the possible improvement of world average

Table 5.4 The world average efficiency of energy transformation, 2000 (approximate values) (%)

	Share of world primary energy consumption	Transformation efficiency
Electricity	40	40
Liquid, gaseous, and solid fuels	60	90
Total	100	70

Table 5.5 Sectoral distribution of world energy consumption, 2000 (approximate values) (%)

	Energy share	Output share	Future energy share	Future output[a]
Transportation	30	5	30	5
Industry	40	30	25	19
Residential	15	5	15	5
Services	15	60	30	120
Total	100	100	100	149

Note
a One unit of "future output" represents 1 percent of world economic output in 2000.

energy efficiency through a "dematerialization" of the world economy (a shift of the world economic output from industry toward the services).

Table 5.5 assumes that 15 percent of world energy consumption can be transferred from the industrial sector to the services. Since the services sector has an energy efficiency that is 5.3 times the industrial sector energy efficiency, such a transfer would bring about an increase in the world average energy efficiency of about 50 percent, holding everything else constant. However, this is purely an accounting exercise. In reality, it would be very difficult to accomplish a doubling of the energy available for the services sector while reducing the energy use by the industrial sector by nearly 40 percent. The implicit assumption that the energy consumption in the transportation and the residential sector could stay constant as the services output doubles may also be unrealistic.

Table 5.6 shows the maximum potential levels of energy efficiency in the world's main economic sectors based on the studies of Lightfoot and Green (2001) and Baksi and Green (2007). The maximum potential of the world's average efficiency in final energy use is estimated to be 315 percent of the world's average efficiency in 2000.

Table 5.6 Energy efficiency potentials in the world's main economic sectors (approximate values)

	Energy share in 2000 (%)	Maximum efficiency as % of efficiency in 2000
Transportation	30	300
Industry	40	300
Residential	15	400
Services	15	300
Total	100	315

Sources: Lightfoot and Green (2001: 11) and Baski and Green (2007: 6462).

If one sums up the cumulative effects of the above three exercises, it leads to the following calculation: $1.4 \times 1.5 \times 3.15 = 6.615$. That is, theoretically, the world's maximum energy efficiency in the future can be 660 percent of the world energy efficiency in 2000. In 2000, the world economy's average energy efficiency was about 5,600 dollars per tonne of oil equivalent (in constant 2005 international dollars). It follows that the theoretical maximum energy efficiency is about 37,000 dollars per tonne of oil equivalent.

In reality, it is impossible to achieve the theoretical maximum, if simply because some energy losses in the transformation processes are inevitable. The assumed 50 percent improvement in energy efficiency that may result from the economy's "dematerialization" could also prove to be too optimistic.

I assume that the long-term potential world average energy efficiency will be 30,000 dollars per tonne of oil equivalent. Given this assumption, Figure 5.10 shows the historical and projected world average energy efficiency from 1980 to 2100. World energy efficiency is projected to rise to about 15,000 dollars per tonne of oil equivalent by 2100. That is, given the existing trend of energy efficiency improvement, only about half of the long-term efficiency potential can be achieved by the end of the century.

The limits to global economic growth

Figure 5.11 shows the historical and projected world economic growth rates from 1901 to 2100.

Table 5.7 summarizes the average annual growth rates of world energy consumption, world carbon dioxide emissions (from fossil fuels burning), world GDP, energy efficiency, and emissions efficiency.

The normal operations of the capitalist world system depend on stable and sustained economic growth. From 1913 to 1950, the capitalist world system almost collapsed as it struggled to survive the Great Depression

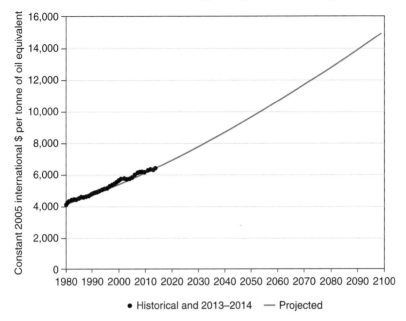

Figure 5.10 World energy efficiency (historical and projected, dollars per TOE,
1980–2100) (sources: World energy efficiency is calculated as world
GDP divided by world energy consumption. World GDP from 1980
to 2011 is from the World Bank (2013). World GDP in 2012, 2013,
and 2014 are based on the International Monetary Fund's projections
(IMF 2013). For world energy consumption from 1980 to 2012 and
the projected world energy consumption in 2013 and 2014, see Figure
5.9. For energy efficiency projections from 2000 to 2100, see text).

and two world wars. But according to the data compiled by Angus Maddison (2010), during the period, the world economy actually achieved an
average annual growth rate of 1.8 percent. Since the Second World War,
the world economic growth rate has fallen below 2 percent only during
major economic crises.

Future world GDP can be calculated by multiplying the projected world
energy consumption by the projected world energy efficiency. World
annual economic growth rates are projected to fall below 2 percent by the
2030s. Historical experience suggests that the capitalist world system may
suffer from major instabilities and crises after 2030.

Toward the end of the century, the world economic growth rate will
approach zero. Chapter 1 of this book argues that the capitalist world
system is inherently driven to pursue the "endless accumulation of capital"
or infinite economic growth.

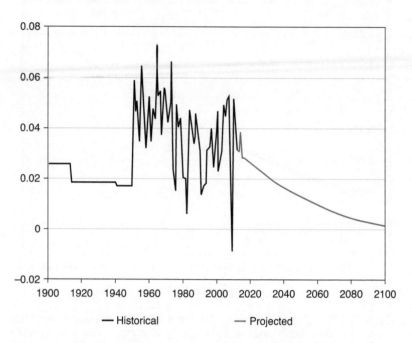

Figure 5.11 World economic growth (historical and projected, annual rate of
change, 1901–2100) (sources: Historical world economic growth rates
from 1901 to 1980 are from Maddison (2010). World economic
growth rates from 1981 to 2011 are from the World Bank (2013).
World economic growth rate in 2012 and projected world economic
growth rates in 2013 and 2014 are from IMF (2013). From 2014 to
2100, world economic growth rates are calculated from projected
GDP which is the product of projected world energy consumption and
projected world energy efficiency (see Figures 5.9 and 5.10)).

Can the capitalist world system survive as the global economy
approaches a zero-growth steady state?

Can capitalism survive the end of growth?

The capitalist economy is based on the private ownership of the means
of production and the market economic relations. The market, or the
interaction of supply and demand between private capitalist producers
and consumers, is the basic mechanism through which large-scale and
complex social division of labor is carried out in a capitalist economic
system.

Table 5.7 World energy consumption, carbon dioxide emissions, and GDP: average annual growth rates (historical and projected, 1951–2100) (%)

	Energy consumption	CO₂ emissions	World GDP	Energy efficiency	Emissions efficiency
Historical:					
1951–1960	5.0	4.6	4.7	−0.3	0.1
1961–1970	5.4	5.1	5.0	−0.3	−0.1
1971–1980	2.8	2.6	3.8	1.0	1.2
1981–1990	1.8	1.6	3.2	1.4	1.6
1991–2000	1.3	1.2	2.9	1.6	1.8
2001–2010	2.5	2.6	3.5	1.0	0.9
Projected:					
2011–2020	1.9	1.8	3.0	1.1	1.2
2021–2030	1.2	0.8	2.3	1.2	1.5
2031–2040	0.7	0.2	1.8	1.1	1.7
2041–2050	0.4	−0.5	1.4	1.1	1.9
2051–2060	0.1	−1.0	1.1	1.0	2.2
2061–2070	−0.1	−1.5	0.8	1.0	2.4
2071–2080	−0.3	−1.9	0.6	0.9	2.6
2081–2090	−0.5	−2.3	0.4	0.8	2.7
2091–2100	−0.6	−2.5	0.2	0.8	2.8

Sources: For world energy consumption, energy efficiency, and world GDP, see Figures 5.9, 5.10, and 5.11. World carbon dioxide emissions from fossil fuels burning from 1950 to 1964 are from EPI (2012d). Emissions from 1965 to 2012 are from BP (2013). Projections of carbon dioxide emissions from 2012 to 2100 are based on the projected consumption of oil, natural gas, and coal. "Emissions efficiency" is defined as the ratio of world GDP over the world carbon dioxide emissions.

Under the market relations, the capitalists are inevitably compelled to compete against one another. To survive and prevail in competition, each capitalist is motivated to use a large portion of the profit to make investment in order to increase the scale of production or improve technology. Thus, under capitalism, there is a powerful tendency for the stock of invested capital to keep growing.

The capitalist profit is a part of the overall economic output. If the overall economic output ceases to grow, sooner or later the profit will have to stop growing. In the short run, the profit growth may be sustained despite zero economic growth by raising the share of profit in the output. But this cannot last very long, as the rising profit share will be resisted by the working class and other social groups and the profit, of course, can never rise above 100 percent of the output.

If the profit does not grow but the capital stock keeps growing, then the profit rate or the rate of return on capital (which is the ratio of profit over the capital stock) will have to keep falling. Mathematically, if the capital stock approaches infinity, the profit rate will approach zero. As capitalism is an economic system based on the pursuit of profit, it obviously cannot function with a profit rate approaching zero. This is the fundamental reason why capitalism cannot possibly survive a steady state global economy with zero economic growth.

In addition to this fundamental reason, there are several secondary reasons that also rule out the possibility that a capitalist economic system can be viable with zero economic growth.

First, because of capitalist competition, the capitalists are constantly pressured to reduce the costs of production, especially labor costs. This has led to a long-term tendency for labor productivity to rise. With rising labor productivity, the economic output needs to keep growing in order to provide adequate employment to the population. For example, in a capitalist economy with a population growth rate of 1 percent and a labor productivity growth rate of 2 percent, the economic growth rate needs to be at least 3 percent in order to keep the unemployment rate from rising. If the economic growth rate falls to zero but the labor productivity keeps rising, the unemployment rate would keep rising and it would be impossible for the capitalist system to maintain social stability.

Second, under capitalism, there is a tendency for wealth and income to be concentrated in a small group of wealthy capitalists, leaving the rest of the society with a smaller share. If there is economic growth, the working class and other social groups may be able to achieve rising living standards despite having a smaller share of the total income. However, if economic growth comes to an end, rising inequality would translate directly into absolute declines of living standards for the great majority of society. The situation would be socially and politically unsustainable.

Third, modern capitalism cannot function without sophisticated financial institutions. A necessary condition for the normal operation of the modern financial institutions is for them to deliver positive interest rates. For an individual or a business with a net debt position (that is, the value of the debt is greater than the value of the assets), a positive interest rate normally leads to growth of debt. If the debtor's current income exactly equals current spending and the debtor borrows money just to pay for the interest expense, the debt would grow at the same rate as the interest rate.

In the current capitalist economy, growth of debt would not be a serious problem so long as the debt grows in the same proportion as the income so that the debtor's debt–income ratio stays constant. However, in a zero economic growth environment, any growth of debt would result in rising debt–income ratio and therefore would be unsustainable. In such an environment, the scope of financial markets would be greatly limited and, without sophisticated financial institutions, capitalism as we know it will cease to exist.

To summarize, a global steady state with zero economic growth will be fundamentally incompatible with capitalism, which is an economic system based on the endless accumulation of capital or infinite economic growth. This raises the question of how the post-capitalist economic system can be made compatible with the end of economic growth and how the transition from capitalism to post-capitalism might take place.

6 Peak energy and the limits to China's economic growth

In recent years, China has become the driving engine for global economic growth. China's ability to sustain economic growth in the coming decades depends on its ability to increase domestic energy production, the possibility to import a larger share of world energy production, and the pace of energy efficiency improvement. This chapter argues that China will have to confront insurmountable limits in all three areas.

From 1950 to 1980, the Chinese economy grew at an average annual rate of 7.1 percent and China's modern energy consumption grew at an average annual rate of 10.3 percent. During the 1980s and the 1990s, China achieved rapid improvements in energy efficiency. From 1980 to 2000, the Chinese economy grew at an average annual rate of 9.9 percent and energy consumption grew at an average annual rate of 4.3 percent. Since 2000, China's economic growth has again become energy intensive. From 2000 to 2012, the Chinese economy grew at an average annual rate of 10.2 percent and the energy consumption grew at an average annual rate of 8.7 percent.

Figure 6.1 shows China's historical energy consumption and gross domestic product from 1950 to 2012.

Coal

In 2012, coal accounted for 73 percent of China's primary energy consumption. In the next few decades, coal will continue to dominate China's energy supply.

From 2000 to 2012, China's coal production grew at an average annual rate of 8.4 percent. In 2012, China produced 3.65 billion tonnes of coal (1.83 billion tonnes of oil equivalent), accounting for 46 percent of the world's coal production by volume (BP 2013).

Based on the historical coal production data provided by Rutledge (2011) and BP (2013), from 1896 to 2012, China's cumulative coal production was 62 billion tonnes.

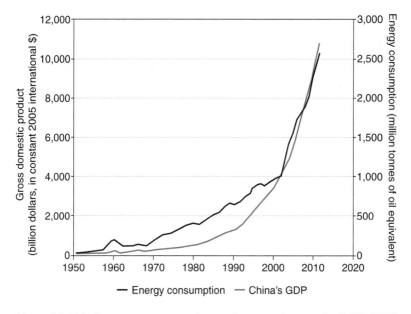

Figure 6.1 China's energy consumption and economic growth (1950–2012) (sources: China's GDP in constant 2005 international dollars is from the World Bank (2013). China's GDP before 1980 is calculated from China's economic growth rates. The economic growth rates in 1951 and 1952 are from National Bureau of Statistics of China (1985). The economic growth rates from 1953 to 1980 are from China Data Online (2013a). China's energy consumption data from 1965 to 2012 are from BP (2013). Before 1965, China's energy consumption is assumed to equal energy production. China's coal production, oil production, natural gas production, and hydroelectricity generation from 1950 to 1964 are from China Data Online (2013b)).

The BP *Statistical Review of World Energy* reported that China's coal reserves were 114.5 billion tonnes in 2012 (BP 2013). The coal reserves cited by BP were based on the Chinese government's report to the World Energy Council in 1992 but the information had not been updated since then (Heinberg 2009: 60–61).

In 2002, the Chinese Ministry of Land and Natural Resources reported that China's coal reserves were 189 billion tonnes (Heinberg 2009: 61).

The coal reserves are defined as the economically recoverable coal that can be produced after the subtraction of mining losses. The coal reserve base is the economically recoverable coal before subtracting mining losses. Since 2001, the *Statistical Yearbook of China* has published annually China's coal "reserve base" (National Bureau of Statistics of China 2012 and various years). In 2002, China's reserve base was reported to be 332 billion tonnes. A comparison of the reserves reported by the Chinese Ministry of Land and Natural Resources and the reserve base implies a recovery factor of 57 percent.

In this section, I estimate China's coal reserves from 2001 to 2011 by assuming that the coal reserves were 60 percent of the reserve base.

Before 2001, the *Statistical Yearbook of China* published annually China's "identified coal resources." In 2001, the identified coal resources were 1.02 trillion tonnes, or three times the reserve base (which was 334 billion tonnes in 2001). For the period 1981–2000, I assume that China's coal reserves were 20 percent of China's identified coal resources.

The observed recoverable coal resources are defined as the sum of the cumulative production and the estimated reserves. Figure 6.2 shows the evolution of China's observed recoverable coal resources from 1981 to 2011. The observed recoverable coal resources tended to rise from the 1980s to the early 2000s. From 2004 to 2009, the observed recoverable coal resources stayed just below 250 billion tonnes.

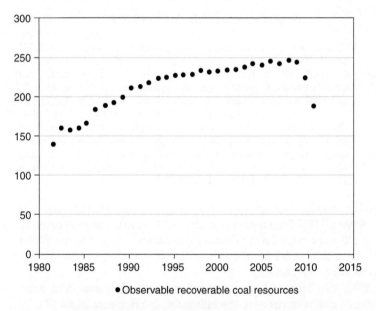

● Observable recoverable coal resources

Figure 6.2 China's observed recoverable coal resources (billion tonnes, 1981–2011) (sources: The observed recoverable coal resources are the sum of cumulative coal production and the coal reserves. Data for China's historical coal production are from Rutledge (2011) and BP (2013). China's coal reserves are estimated from China's coal reserve base and identified coal resources. See text).

In 2010 and 2011, the *Statistical Yearbook of China* reported large downward adjustments of China's coal reserve base. As a result, China's observed recoverable coal resources declined from 243 billion tonnes in 2009 to 188 billion tonnes in 2011.

I assume that China's ultimately recoverable coal resources will be 250 billion tonnes. Given this assumption, China's coal production is projected to peak in 2026 with a production level of 4.9 billion tonnes. Figure 6.3 shows China's historical and projected coal production from 1950 to 2100.

Oil

In 2012, oil accounted for 19 percent of China's energy consumption. Domestic oil production accounted for 43 percent of China's oil consumption.

From 2000 to 2012, China's oil production grew at an average annual rate of 2.1 percent. In 2012, China produced 208 million tonnes of crude oil and natural gas liquids, accounting for 5 percent of the world's oil production (BP 2013).

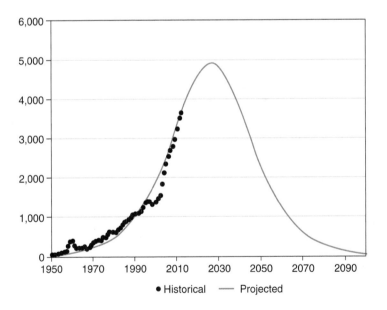

Figure 6.3 China's coal production (historical and projected, million tonnes, 1950–2100) (sources: Data for China's historical coal production are from Rutledge (2011) and BP (2013). For projections from 1950 to 2100, see text).

Based on the historical oil production data provided by China Data Online (2013b) and BP (2013), China's cumulative oil production up to 2012 was 5.9 billion tonnes. China's proved oil reserves were 2.4 billion tonnes in 2012 (BP 2013). Thus, China's observed recoverable oil resources were 8.3 billion tonnes in 2013.

In the section on "China" in Chapter 4, the Hubbert linearization exercise indicates China's ultimately recoverable oil resources to be 16.5 billion tonnes. Assuming that China's ultimately recoverable oil resources will be 16.5 billion tonnes, China's oil production is projected to peak in 2023 with a production level of 225 million tonnes. Figure 6.4 shows China's historical and projected oil production from 1950 to 2100.

Natural gas

In 2012, natural gas accounted for 5 percent of China's energy consumption. Domestic natural gas production accounted for 75 percent of China's natural gas consumption.

From 2000 to 2012, China's natural gas production grew at an average annual rate of 12.1 percent. In 2012, China produced 107 billion cubic

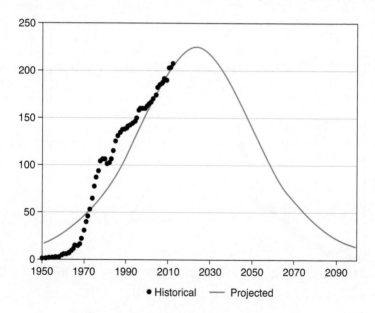

Figure 6.4 China's oil production (historical and projected, million tonnes, 1950–2100) (sources: Data for China's historical oil production are from China Data Online (2013b) and BP (2013). For projections from 1950 to 2100, see the section on "China" in Chapter 4).

meters of natural gas or 97 million tonnes of oil equivalent, accounting for 3 percent of the world natural gas production (BP 2013).

Based on the historical natural gas production data from China Data Online (2013b) and BP (2013), China's cumulative natural gas production up to 2012 was 1.1 billion tonnes of oil equivalent. China's natural gas proved reserves in 2012 were 2.8 billion tonnes of oil equivalent. As of 2012, China's observed recoverable natural gas resources were 3.9 billion tonnes of oil equivalent.

According to the *China Energy Development Report*, China's technically recoverable conventional natural gas resources are 22 trillion cubic meters (Zhao and Gan 2010: 89). According to the International Energy Agency, China's technically recoverable unconventional natural gas resources amount to 50 trillion cubic meters (including 36 trillion cubic meters of shale gas, nine trillion cubic meters of coalbed methane, and three trillion cubic meters of tight gas). China's total conventional and unconventional natural gas resources are about 72 trillion cubic meters or 65 billion tonnes of oil equivalent.

In the section on "Natural Gas" in Chapter 5, the world's remaining economically recoverable natural gas resources are estimated to be about 250 billion tonnes of oil equivalent (340 billion tonnes of ultimately recoverable resources less 90 billion tonnes of cumulative production). Compared to the technically recoverable resources of 675 billion tonnes of oil equivalent, the implied recovery factor is about 37 percent. Applying the same recovery factor to China's technically recoverable natural gas resources, China's remaining economically recoverable natural gas resources are estimated to be about 24 billion tonnes of oil equivalent.

I assume that China's ultimately recoverable natural gas resources will be 25 billion tonnes of oil equivalent. Given this assumption, China's natural gas production is projected to peak in 2045 with a production level of 597 million tonnes of oil equivalent. Figure 6.5 shows China's historical and projected natural gas production from 1950 to 2100.

Nuclear electricity

In 2012, nuclear electricity accounted for 0.3 percent of China's energy consumption (nuclear electricity is measured by electrical energy content) (BP 2013). In 2011, nuclear electricity accounted for 1.9 percent of China's electricity generation (EIA 2013a).

From 2000 to 2012, China's nuclear electricity consumption grew at an average annual rate of 15.8 percent (BP 2013). In 2012, China generated 93 terawatt-hours of nuclear electricity. As of January 2013, China had 13 gigawatts of nuclear electricity generating capacity (WNA 2013a).

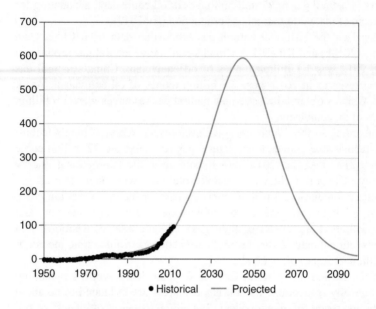

Figure 6.5 China's natural gas production (historical and projected, million TOE,
1950–2100) (sources: Data for China's historical natural gas production are from China Data Online (2013b) and BP (2013). For projections from 1950 to 2100, see text. "TOE" stands for "tonnes of oil
equivalent").

According to the World Nuclear Association, China currently has 30
gigawatts of nuclear generating capacity under construction, 60 gigawatts
being planned, and 123 gigawatts being proposed. In total, 213 gigawatts of
nuclear generating capacity are being constructed, planned, or proposed in
China, accounting for about one-third of the world's total nuclear generating
capacity currently being constructed, planned, or proposed (WNA 2013a).

If all of China's constructed, planned, and proposed nuclear power
plants become operational by 2030 and none of the currently operating
nuclear power plants retires, China's total nuclear generating capacity will
reach 226 gigawatts by 2030. The total uranium requirement will be about
41,000 tonnes (assuming that 1 gigawatt of nuclear generating capacity
consumes 180 tonnes of uranium in a year), or about 75 percent of the
world's uranium production in 2011 (WNA 2013b).

As of 2011, China's total identified uranium resources were 166,100
tonnes. In addition, China had 7,700 tonnes of undiscovered uranium
resources. The total identified and undiscovered uranium resources were
about 174,000 tonnes (NEA 2012: 18, 29).

In 2011, China produced 1,500 tonnes of uranium, which could provide the fuel for eight gigawatts of nuclear generating capacity (WNA 2013b). If China were to have 226 gigawatts of nuclear generating capacity and the uranium consumption were to be provided entirely from domestic sources, China's domestic uranium resources would be completely depleted within five years.

Uranium is a nonrenewable resource and large-scale development of nuclear industry involves serious safety, security, and pollution concerns. I assume that, in the long run, China's nuclear electricity generation will approach zero.

Renewable energies

The renewable energies include hydroelectricity, other renewable electricity (wind, solar, biomass, and geothermal), and biofuels. In 2012, renewable energies accounted for 3.4 percent of China's energy consumption (with renewable electricity measured by electrical energy content).

From 2000 to 2012, China's renewable energy consumption grew at an average annual rate of 13.4 percent. In 2012, China's total renewable energy consumption was 88 million tonnes of oil equivalent (calculated using data from BP 2013).

In 2010, China's hydroelectricity generating capacity reached about 220 gigawatts (EIA 2013a). In 2012, China's hydroelectricity consumption was about 860 terawatt-hours and accounted for 84 percent of China's total renewable energy consumption. According to the *China Energy Development Report*, China's economic potential of hydroelectric power was estimated to be about 400 gigawatts (Wang *et al.* 2010: 242). Assuming a capacity utilization rate of 40 percent, China's long-term potential of hydroelectricity generation will be about 1,400 terawatt-hours, or 120 million tonnes of oil equivalent.

China's wind electricity potential was estimated to be 950 gigawatts (including 800 gigawatts of onshore potential and 150 gigawatts of offshore potential) (Wang *et al.* 2010: 232). Assuming a capacity utilization rate of 25 percent, China's long-term potential of wind electricity generation will be about 2,100 terawatt-hours, or 180 million tonnes of oil equivalent.

The total solar energy absorbed by the world's land surface is about 790,000 EJ (Smil 2010a: 109). But only a small fraction of the theoretical solar resources can be economically utilized. Lightfoot and Green (2002) assumed that 1 percent of the world's unused land would be utilized and found that the world's long-term potential of solar electricity generation would be about 180 EJ.

The total solar energy absorbed by China's land surface is about 1,700 billion tonnes of coal equivalent, or 47,500 EJ (Wang *et al.* 2010: 235), or about 6 percent of the world's terrestrial solar resources. I assume that China's potential of solar electricity generation is also 6 percent of the world potential: $180 \, EJ \times 6\% = 10.8 \, EJ$; 10.8 EJ corresponds to 260 million tonnes of oil equivalent, 3,000 terawatt-hours, or the electricity generation by 2,300 gigawatts of solar power plants (assuming a capacity utilization rate of 15 percent).

China's biomass resources (including forest waste and agricultural crop residues) were estimated to be about 500 million tonnes of coal equivalent, or about 330 million tonnes of oil equivalent (Wang, Lu, and Xu 2010: 237). If all of these resources were utilized and one assumes a conversion efficiency of 40 percent, 130 million tonnes of biomass electricity or bio-fuels may be produced.

As explained in Chapter 5, other forms of renewable energy (such as geothermal, ocean waves, and tides) are likely to be insignificant.

China's total long-term potential of nuclear and renewable energies adds up to about 700 million tonnes of oil equivalent. This estimate has not taken into account the resources, liquid fuels, and intermittency constraints and could turn out to be too optimistic.

Figure 6.6 shows China's historical and projected production of nuclear and renewable energies from 2000 to 2100.

Net energy imports

In this chapter, "net energy imports" is defined as the difference between a country's total energy consumption and its total energy production. Inventory changes are ignored.

From the 1970s to the 1990s, China was a net energy exporter. In 2000, China's net energy imports accounted for only 0.5 percent of the world's total energy consumption. By 2012, the share had increased to 3.1 percent. In the long run, China's ability to import energy will be limited by the economic resources at China's disposal, China's geopolitical capabilities, and resources depletion in the rest of the world.

Figure 6.7 compares the US net energy imports and China's net energy imports as a share of the world energy consumption from 1970 to 2012. The US net energy imports share averaged 5.1 percent from 1970 to 2012 and peaked at 7.4 percent in 2000.

The US is the world's hegemonic power. Its ability to import energy resources from the rest of the world indicates the maximum extent to which a country can rely upon imported energy to meet its own energy demand.

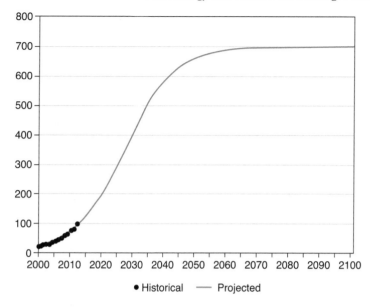

Figure 6.6 China's nuclear and renewable energies production (million TOE, 2000–2010) (sources: For 2000–2012, China's production of nuclear and renewable energies is assumed to equal consumption. Data for China's nuclear and renewable energy consumption are from BP (2013). For projections from 2000 to 2100, see text. "TOE" stands for "tonnes of oil equivalent").

In 2012, the US net energy imports as a share of world energy consumption fell to 3.1 percent. At the current trend, China should overtake the US to become the world's largest net energy importer in 2013.

I assume that China's net energy imports will rise to 3.5 percent of the world's energy consumption by 2015. From 2016 to 2100, I assume that China's net energy imports share will stay at 3.5 percent. The future world energy consumption is based on the projections made in Chapter 5.

Energy efficiency

China's energy efficiency grew at an average annual rate of 4.4 percent from 1980 to 1990, at a rate of 6.3 percent from 1990 to 2000, and at a rate of 1.3 percent from 2000 to 2012. In 2012, China's energy efficiency (the ratio of GDP over primary energy consumption) was about 4,200 dollars per tonne of oil equivalent (in constant 2005 international dollars), or 66 percent of the world average level.

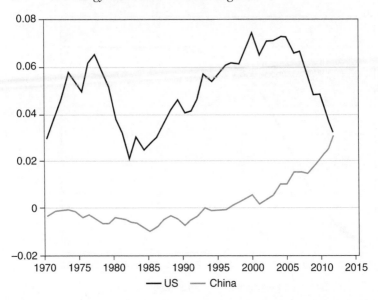

Figure 6.7 Net energy imports as share of world energy consumption (US and China, 1970–2012) (sources: Net energy imports equal energy consumption less energy production. Energy consumption data for the world, US, and China from 1970 to 2012 are from BP (2013). For the US and China, oil and natural gas production from 1970 to 2012 and coal production from 1981 to 2012 are from BP (2013). Coal production data from 1970 to 1980 are from Rutledge (2011)).

In Chapter 5, it is assumed that the long-term potential world energy efficiency will be 30,000 dollars per tonne of oil equivalent. The same assumption is applied to the projection of China's future energy efficiency. Figure 6.8 shows China's historical and projected energy efficiency from 1980 to 2100.

China's energy efficiency is projected to rise to about 25,000 dollars per tonne of oil equivalent by 2100, about 70 percent higher than the projected world average energy efficiency by 2100.

China's projected energy efficiency by the end of the century is much higher than the projected world energy efficiency. This is because the projections are based on the energy efficiency trends from 1980 to 2012. Over the period, China's energy efficiency grew more rapidly than the world average energy efficiency. But as China's energy efficiency approaches the world average, China's efficiency improvement is likely to slow down. Thus, the current projection of China's energy efficiency may prove to be too optimistic.

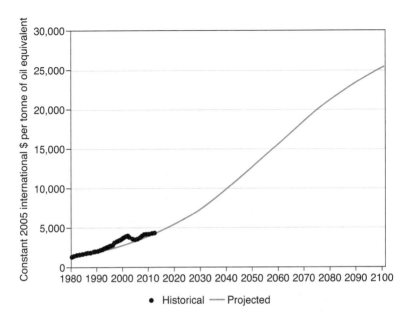

Figure 6.8 China's energy efficiency (historical and projected, dollars per TOE, 1980–2100) (sources: Energy efficiency is the ratio of GDP over primary energy consumption. China's historical GDP data from 1980 to 2011 are from the World Bank (2013), updated to 2012 using information from IMF (2013). Historical energy data are from BP (2013). For projections from 1980 to 2100, see text).

The limits to China's economic growth

Figure 6.9 shows China's historical and projected primary energy consumption from 1950 to 2100. China's primary energy consumption is projected to peak in the early 2030s at about 3.9 billion tonnes of oil equivalent (about 50 percent larger than the current level). China's energy consumption is projected to decline rapidly from the 2040s to the 2070s. After about 2080, the decline of energy consumption slows as the renewable energies and energy imports help to stabilize the total energy supply. By 2100, China's primary energy consumption is projected to fall to less than 1.3 billion tonnes of oil equivalent, about one-third of the peak level.

Table 6.1 summarizes the average annual growth rates by decade of China's different forms of energy production and net energy imports from 1951 to 2100. Table 6.2 shows the shares of different forms of energy

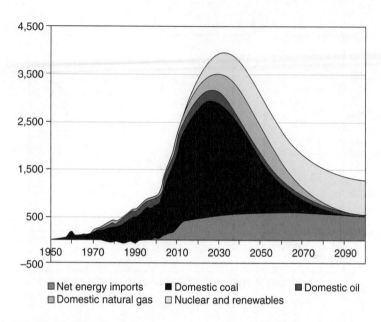

4,500

3,500

2,500

1,500

500

1950   1970   1990   2010   2030   2050   2070   2090

−500

■ Net energy imports   ■ Domestic coal   ■ Domestic oil
□ Domestic natural gas   □ Nuclear and renewables

Figure 6.9 China's primary energy consumption (million tonnes of oil equivalent,
1950–2100) (sources: For the period 1950–1964, China's energy consumption is assumed to equal China's energy production. The coal production data from 1950 to 1980, the oil production data from 1950 to
1964, and the natural gas production data from 1950 to 1969 are from
China Data Online (2013b). China's energy consumption data from
1965 to 2012, coal production data from 1981 to 2012, oil production
data from 1965 to 2012, and natural gas production data from 1970 to
2012 are from BP (2013). For projections from 2013 to 2100, see text).

production and net energy imports in China's total energy consumption
from 1950 to 2100.

Domestic coal production will account for more than half of China's
total energy consumption until 2040. The contribution of nuclear and
renewable energies is projected to rise to about one-fifth by 2050 and to
more than 50 percent by the 2090s. Toward the end of the century, about
two-fifths of China's energy consumption is projected to come from net
energy imports.

Figure 6.10 shows China's historical and projected economic growth
rates from 1951 to 2100. China's future GDP is the product of the projected energy consumption and the projected energy efficiency. Table 6.3
reports the historical and projected average annual growth rates by decade

Table 6.1 China's energy production and net energy imports, average annual growth rates (historical and projected, 1951–2100) (%)

	Domestic coal	Domestic oil	Domestic natural gas	Nuclear and renewables	Net energy imports
Historical:					
1951–1960	24.9	38.5	64.9	24.9	n.a.
1961–1970	−1.1	19.4	10.7	12.5	n.a.
1971–1980	5.8	13.2	17.4	9.2	n.a.
1981–1990	5.7	2.7	0.7	8.1	n.a.
1991–2000	2.5	1.6	5.9	6.7	n.a.
2001–2010	8.9	2.2	13.3	13.7	17.7
Projected:					
2011–2020	3.6	1.0	8.3	10.9	7.0
2021–2030	0.5	−0.3	7.2	7.1	1.2
2031–2040	−2.5	−1.7	4.1	3.4	0.7
2041–2050	−4.7	−2.9	−0.2	1.2	0.4
2051–2060	−6.1	−3.7	−4.2	0.4	0.1
2061–2070	−6.8	−4.3	−6.9	0.1	−0.1
2071–2080	−7.2	−4.7	−8.2	0.0	−0.3
2081–2090	−7.4	−5.0	−8.7	0.0	−0.5
2091–2100	−7.5	−5.1	−9.0	0.0	−0.6

Sources: See Figure 6.9.

Table 6.2 China's energy production and net energy imports, share of total energy consumption (historical and projected, 1950–2100) (%)

	Domestic coal	Domestic oil	Domestic natural gas	Nuclear and renewables	Net energy imports
Historical:					
1950	99	1	0	0	0
1960	97	3	0	0	0
1970	89	15	1	1	-7
1980	76	26	3	1	-6
1990	83	21	2	2	-9
2000	73	17	3	2	5
2010	73	9	4	3	11
Projected:					
2020	68	7	6	6	14
2030	61	6	10	11	13
2040	50	5	15	16	15
2050	37	4	18	21	19
2060	26	4	15	29	25
2070	17	3	10	38	32
2080	9	2	5	46	37
2090	2	2	2	52	39
2100	2	1	1	56	40

Sources: See Figure 6.9.

Table 6.3 China's energy consumption, carbon dioxide emissions, and GDP: average annual growth rates (historical and projected, 1951–2100) (%)

	Energy consumption	CO_2 emissions	GDP	Energy efficiency	Emissions efficiency
Historical:					
1951–1960	25.2	25.1	11.3	−11.1	−11.0
1961–1970	−0.3	−0.2	3.9	4.2	4.0
1971–1980	7.5	7.2	6.2	−1.2	−0.9
1981–1990	4.7	4.8	9.3	4.4	4.3
1991–2000	3.9	3.7	10.4	6.3	6.5
2001–2010	8.9	8.8	10.5	1.5	1.6
Projected:					
2011–2020	4.3	3.9	7.2	2.9	3.2
2021–2030	1.5	0.9	4.8	3.2	3.9
2031–2040	−0.4	−1.4	2.5	2.9	3.9
2041–2050	−1.9	−3.0	0.5	2.5	3.7
2051–2060	−2.7	−4.0	−0.6	2.1	3.5
2061–2070	−2.5	−4.0	−0.8	1.7	3.3
2071–2080	−1.8	−3.2	−0.5	1.3	2.8
2081–2090	−1.1	−2.3	−0.1	1.0	2.2
2091–2100	−0.7	−1.6	0.0	0.7	1.6

Sources: For energy consumption, energy efficiency, and GDP, see Figures 6.8, 6.9, and 6.10. For the period 1950–1964, one tonne of oil is assumed to emit 2.95 tonnes of carbon dioxide; one tonne of oil equivalent of natural gas is assumed to emit 2.17 tonnes of carbon dioxide; one tonne of oil equivalent of coal is assumed to emit 3.75 tonnes of carbon dioxide. Emissions from 1965 to 2012 are from BP (2013). For the period 2013–2100, one tonne of oil is assumed to emit 3.07 tonnes of carbon dioxide; one tonne of oil equivalent of natural gas is assumed to emit 2.35 tonnes of carbon dioxide; one tonne of oil equivalent of coal is assumed to emit 3.96 tonnes of carbon dioxide; net energy imports are assumed to have the same emissions intensity as oil. "Emissions efficiency" is defined as the ratio of GDP over the carbon dioxide emissions from fossil fuels burning.

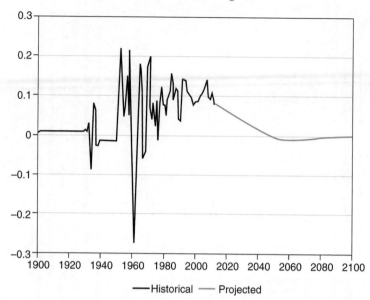

Figure 6.10 China: economic growth rates (historical and projected, 1901–2100)
(sources: China's historical economic growth rates from 1901 to 1950
are from Maddison (2010). Economic growth rates in 1951 and 1952
are from National Bureau of Statistics of China (1985). Economic
growth rates from 1953 to 1980 are from China Data Online (2013a).
Economic Growth rates from 1981 to 2012 are from the World
Bank (2013) and IMF (2013). Projected economic growth rates in
2013 and 2014 are from IMF (2013). For projections from 2015 to
2100, see text).

of China's energy consumption, carbon dioxide emissions from fossil fuels
burning, and economic output from 1951 to 2100.

China's economic growth rates are projected to fall steadily from 2015
to 2050. After 2030, China's economic growth rate will fall below 3.5
percent. Since 1976, China's official economic growth rate has not fallen
below 4 percent, except in 1990, when the Chinese economy struggled in
the aftermath of the political crisis in 1989. After 2050, the Chinese
economy will enter into a quasi-steady state as the economic growth rates
fluctuate around zero.

Since the 1980s, China has been transformed into a capitalist society
based on the production for profit and capital accumulation. Chinese capitalism has relied upon rapid economic growth to maintain economic and
political stability. As the economic growth rate falls below politically sens-
itive levels, will Chinese capitalism remain a viable social system?

7   The crisis of Chinese capitalism

China was the greatest beneficiary of the global capital relocation that took place in the 1990s and the early 2000s. Since the last global economic crisis, China has emerged as the driving engine of the global capitalist economy, accounting for about 40 percent of the global economic growth and three-quarters of the global energy consumption growth (see Chapter 1). The future of the capitalist world system to a large degree depends on what will happen to China in the next few decades.

China's rapid economic growth has been driven by rapid capital accumulation, which has in turn been motivated by high profit rates. China's capitalist accumulation has been based on the exploitation of a large, cheap labor force and the rapid depletion of fossil fuel resources (especially coal). However, as explained in the previous chapter, the depletion of fossil fuels will impose insurmountable limits to China's economic growth. Moreover, the Chinese working class is emerging as a new social force that will demand a growing range of economic and political rights. The combination of these factors will lead to an inexorable decline of the profit rate and a structural crisis for Chinese capitalism, a crisis that cannot be overcome within the system's own framework.

The tendency for the rate of profit to fall

Capitalism is an economic system based on the production for profit. The capitalists make investments in order to make profits. The profits also provide the financial means to finance capital accumulation. Thus, the rate of return on capital or the profit rate is a crucial indicator for the capitalist economy. Historically, periods of major capitalist crises and instabilities were invariably associated with substantial declines of the profit rate.

In the literature of Marxist political economy, there has been a long-time controversy over the hypothesis known as "the tendency for the rate of profit to fall." In *Capital*, volume 3, Marx hypothesized that, as capitalism developed, there was a tendency for the rate of profit to fall. If the tendency were not checked, eventually it would bring capitalist accumulation to an end and lead to the demise of capitalism.

In the context of labor theory of value, Marx argued that, as the capitalists adopted new technologies by substituting machines for labor, the social labor time embodied in the "means of production" (capital goods such as machines and buildings) would grow more rapidly than the present labor time employed in the current production. This would result in rising "organic composition of capital." If the "rate of surplus value" (which measured the degree of capitalist exploitation of the workers) stayed constant, rising organic composition of capital would translate into a falling profit rate (Marx 1967[1894]: 211–266).

In terms of modern economic languages, Marx essentially hypothesized that, in the long run, there would be a tendency for the economy's capital stock to grow more rapidly than economic output. Unless this tendency was offset by rising profit share of the output, the rising capital–output ratio would eventually translate into declines of the profit rate.

The growth rate of the capital stock is the ratio of the net investment in capital stock over the existing capital stock. Net investment equals gross investment less depreciation of fixed capital, or the total addition of new capital less the wearing out of the old capital.

The capitalist net investment needs to be financed by the capitalist profit:

Net Investment = Profit × The Ratio of Accumulation

"The ratio of accumulation" is defined as the share of the capitalist profit that is used for net investment rather than capitalist consumption. Therefore, the growth rate of the capital stock depends on the level of the profit rate:

The Profit Rate = Profit / Capital Stock

The Capital Stock Growth Rate = Net Investment/Capital Stock = Profit × The Ratio of Accumulation/Capital Stock = Profit Rate × The Ratio of Accumulation

Figure 7.1 illustrates the relationship between the profit rate and capitalist investment and how the equilibrium profit rate is determined. In the hypothetical economic model, depreciation rate is assumed to be 5 percent. For the economy to function normally, the capitalists need to make at least as much investment as depreciation to replace the old capital stock that wears out. Any investment above depreciation would result in growth of capital stock.

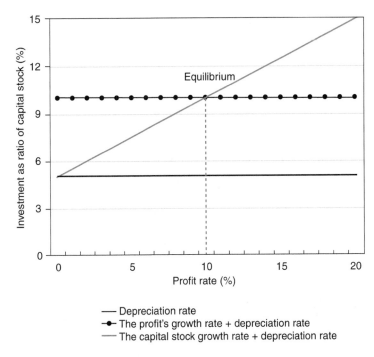

Figure 7.1 The profit rate and investment.

Note
A hypothetical economic model.

The ratio of accumulation is assumed to be 50 percent. Thus, the growth rate of the capital stock equals 50 percent of the profit rate. The profit's growth rate is assumed to be 5 percent. If the capital stock growth rate is greater than the profit's growth rate, the capital stock would grow more rapidly than the profit and the profit rate would tend to fall. Marx's hypothesis would be validated. In Figure 7.1, this happens when the profit rate is greater than 10 percent. However, if the capital stock growth rate is smaller than the profit's growth rate, the profit rate would tend to rise and Marx's hypothesis would not apply. In Figure 7.1, this happens when the profit rate is smaller than 10 percent.

Either way, there would be a tendency for the profit rate to converge toward 10 percent. At 10 percent, the profit rate is at equilibrium and the profit's growth rate equals the capital stock growth rate:

The Capital Stock Growth Rate = The Profit's Growth Rate

Or,

The Profit Rate × The Ratio of Accumulation = The Profit's Growth
Rate

It follows that:

The Equilibrium Profit Rate = The Profit's Growth Rate / The Ratio of
Accumulation

The growth rate of the capitalist profit depends on both the economic
growth rate and how the share of the capitalist profit in the overall economic output changes over time. Theoretically, the capitalist profit share
can neither go above 100 percent nor fall below 0 percent. In reality, the
profit share tends to fluctuate within a range that is determined by the pre-
vailing social institutions and the class struggle. It can neither rise indefinitely nor fall indefinitely. Thus, in the long run, the profit's growth rate
will be determined primarily by the economic growth rate.

So long as the profit's growth rate is positive, there would be a limit to
how much the profit rate can fall. However, as the previous chapters have
argued, in the long run, there will be a tendency for both the global economic growth rate and China's economic growth rate to fall toward zero
as the fossil fuels decline. If the profit's growth rate falls to zero and the
ratio of accumulation remains positive, the equilibrium profit rate would
inevitably fall toward zero.

Obviously, a capitalist economy cannot function with zero profit rate.
Marx's original hypothesis made in the nineteenth century may eventually
prove to be correct in the twenty-first century.

Profit, accumulation, and crisis

In reality, major capitalist crises happened even as the average profit rate
stayed in the positive territory. Because of capitalist competition, the total
capitalist profits are distributed unevenly among the capitalists. Even if the
economy-wide average profit rate remains positive, large sections of capitalists may suffer from negative rates of return on their individual capitals
if the average profit rate falls below certain critical levels. If a sufficiently
large number of capitalists stop making investment or become bankrupt,
they could drag the rest of the economy into a major crisis.

Investment in fixed capital involves the commitment of large sums of
capital sunk in buildings and durable capital equipment that will last many
years or decades. Because of the fundamental uncertainty about the future,

capitalists cannot rationally calculate the future rates of return on capital. Thus, the level of investment is inevitably influenced by the capitalists' subjective "expectations." If the average profit rate falls below certain levels, the capitalist confidence could be fatally undermined, leading to a general collapse of investment (Keynes 1964[1953]: 147–164).

Figure 7.2 shows the US economy's average profit rates and the economic growth rates (shown in five-year moving averages) from 1929 to 2012. The total economy's average profit rate is measured as the ratio of "net operating surplus" over the net stock of total fixed assets. Net operating surplus includes all property incomes (corporate profits, net interest payments, rent, and proprietors' incomes). Historically, the US average profit rate fell persistently below 8 percent only during three periods: the 1930s, the 1970s, and from 2007 to 2009. In each case, the US capitalist economy suffered from a major crisis.

Figure 7.3 shows China's historical and projected profit rate from 1993 to 2100. From 1993 to 2011, China's total economy profit rate averaged 11.1 percent. During the same period, the US profit rate averaged 8.5

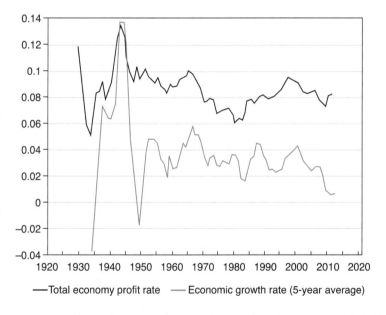

Figure 7.2 The profit rate and economic growth (US economy, 1929–2012) (sources: Total economy profit rate is defined as the ratio of "net operating surplus" over the net stock of total fixed assets. Data for national income distribution and economic growth rates are from BEA (2013a). Data for fixed assets are from BEA (2013b)).

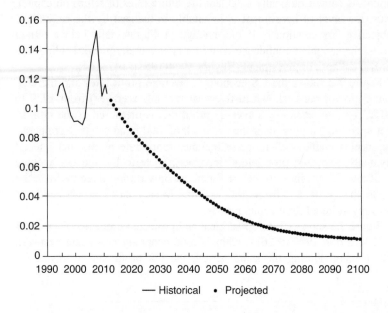

Figure 7.3 China's total economy profit rate (historical and projected, 1993–2100)
(sources: Total economy profit rate is defined as the ratio of "net operating surplus" over the net stock of total fixed assets. Net operating
surplus from 1993 to 2011 is from China's "Gross Domestic Product
by Income Approach" (National Bureau of Statistics of China 2012 and
various years). China's net stock of fixed assets from 1993 to 2011 is
estimated from fixed capital formation and depreciation of fixed capital.
Data for fixed capital formation are from National Bureau of Statistics
of China (2012). Depreciation from 1993 to 2011 is from China's
"Gross Domestic Product by Income Approach" (National Bureau of
Statistics of China 2012 and various years). For projections from 2012
to 2100, see text).

percent. China's average profit rate was 31 percent higher than the US
average profit rate.

In the projection, the profit (net operating surplus) is assumed to grow
at the same rate as the economy. The economic growth rates are based on
the projection of Chapter 6 (see Figure 6.10). The projection assumes that
China's ratio of accumulation will be 100 percent—that is, 100 percent of
the capitalist profit would be used for net investment. This is similar to
China's observed ratios of accumulation (China's observed ratios of accumulation averaged 103 percent from 1993 to 2011). Given this assumption, China's profit rate is projected to fall below 8 percent by the early
2020s. Based on the US experience, if the total economy profit rate falls

below 8 percent and fails to recover, the capitalist economy is likely to enter into a major crisis.

Postponing the crisis?

China's current ratio of accumulation is very high. In 2011, China's net investment rose to about 120 percent of the total profit. If China's ratio of accumulation can be substantially lowered, the equilibrium profit rate corresponding to any given economic growth rate will be raised and the capitalist crisis can be postponed for some years. This section evaluates this possibility.

A country's total national expenditures include consumption, investment, government spending, and net exports (that is, exports less imports). The total national incomes include wages, profits, and taxes. Total national expenditures should equal total national incomes. Therefore:

Consumption + Investment + Government Spending + Net Exports = Wages + Profits + Taxes

Rearrange the terms:

Profits = Investment + (Consumption − Wages) + (Government Spending − Taxes) + Net Exports

That is, the capitalist profit is the sum of investment, government deficit, trade surplus, and the total household consumption less wages. The capitalists would always consume a portion of their profits. On the other hand, the working class households may save a portion of their wages. If the capitalist consumption is exactly offset by the working class savings, consumption would equal wages. Moreover, if both the government sector and the trade sector are in balance, the total capitalist profit would exactly equal the investment.

For investment to be less than the capitalist profit, the sum of consumption, government spending, and trade surplus must be greater than the sum of wages and taxes. On the other hand, if the sum of consumption, government spending, and trade surplus are less than the sum of wages and taxes, investment will be greater than the capitalist profit.

Figure 7.4 shows China's macroeconomic structure from 1990 to 2011. From 1990 to 2011, China's household consumption as a share of GDP declined from 49 percent to 35 percent, government consumption stayed around 14 percent, gross fixed capital formation (that is, gross fixed investment) increased from 25 percent to 46 percent, change in inventories

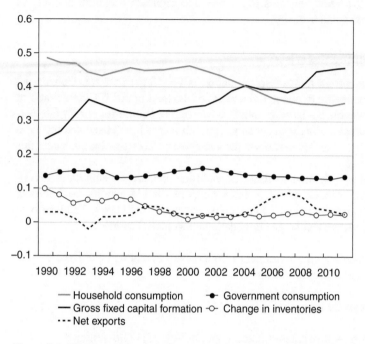

Figure 7.4 China's macroeconomic structure (share of GDP, 1990–2011) (sources: Data for China's GDP from the expenditures approach and its component are from National Bureau of Statistics of China (2012)).

(treated as a form of investment in the national income and product accounting) declined from 10 percent to 3 percent. Net exports increased from 2.6 percent of GDP in 1990 to 8.8 percent in 2007. By 2011, China's trade surplus fell to 2.6 percent of GDP.

Figure 7.5 shows China's national income distribution from 1993 to 2011. From 1993 to 2011, China's compensation of laborers as a share of GDP declined from 51 percent to 40 percent. By 2011, the compensation of laborers recovered to 45 percent of the GDP. Net producer taxes (government taxes on production and imports less subsidies) increased from 14 percent in 1993 to 16 percent in 2011. Depreciation of fixed capital increased from 12 percent in 1993 to 16 percent in 2003 and fell to 13 percent in 2011. Net operating surplus (the sum of all property incomes) fell from 24 percent in 1993 to 19 percent in 2001. In the early 2000s, the net operating surplus rose sharply. By 2007, net operating surplus reached 31 percent of China's GDP. In 2011, net operating surplus was 27 percent of China's GDP.

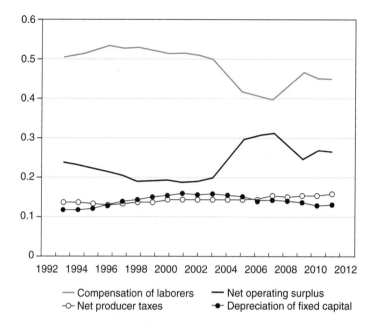

Figure 7.5 China's national income distribution (share of GDP, 1993–2011)
(sources: Data for China's national income distribution are from
China's "Gross Domestic Product by Income Approach" (National
Bureau of Statistics of China 2012 and various years)).

In 2011, the net producer taxes were greater than the government consumption by 2 percent of GDP. Thus, the net contribution from the government sector to the capitalist profit was –2 percent of GDP. Net exports
and change in inventories together contributed 5 percent of GDP. But this
was more than offset by the working class household savings. Total wages
were higher than household consumption by 10 percent of GDP.

As explained above, the investment will be greater than the capitalist
profit if the sum of consumption, government spending, and trade balance
are less than the sum of wages and taxes. Indeed, after subtracting depreciation of fixed capital (13 percent of GDP), the net fixed capital formation
in 2011 was 33 percent of GDP, greater than the net operating surplus (27
percent of GDP).

For China's ratio of accumulation to fall from the current level, net investment has to fall relative to the capitalist profit. To offset this, household consumption, government consumption, and net exports need to rise relative to
GDP. By how much could the ratio of accumulation fall in the future?

Net exports

Currently, the Chinese economy grows more rapidly than the rest of the world. As the Chinese economy grows rapidly, China's demands for imported energy, raw materials, and capital equipment are likely to grow in proportion with the Chinese economy. On the other hand, as western capitalist economies struggle with stagnation and recession, the Chinese exports will have to struggle with stagnating and declining foreign markets.

In the future, as China's exports slow down and imports continue to grow rapidly, it is unlikely for China to maintain large trade surpluses. I assume that, in the long run, China's trade will move toward balance between exports and imports. Other things being equal, the change from a trade surplus of about 3 percent of GDP to trade balance will result in a reduction of the capitalist profit by 3 percent of GDP.

Government consumption

In 2011, China's government consumption was smaller than the government taxes on production and imports (also known as the indirect taxes) by about 2 percent of GDP. If the government consumption were to be increased relative to GDP, how could it be financed? If it is to be financed by higher income taxes, the increase in government consumption would be offset by decline in household consumption as the household disposable income falls.

If the increase in government consumption is to be financed by borrowings, it would lead to rising government debt. The long-term government debt–GDP ratio is determined by the following formula:

Long-Term Debt–GDP Ratio = Primary Deficit–GDP Ratio / (Economic Growth Rate + Inflation Rate – Nominal Interest Rate)

The "primary deficit" is the government deficit before the interest payments. By 2050, China's economic growth rate is projected to decline to toward zero. The nominal interest rate normally should be higher than the inflation rate. Making the generous assumption that the real interest rate will be 0 percent (that is, the nominal interest rate equals the inflation rate), the denominator in the above formula will be zero. In this case, any positive primary deficit will imply explosive growth of government debt–GDP ratio toward infinity.

I assume that, in the long run, China's government consumption will equal net producer taxes. Other things being equal, the change in the government sector balance from 2 percent of GDP to zero will increase the capitalist profit by 2 percent of GDP.

Household consumption

In 2011, China's household consumption was 35 percent of the GDP. According to China's household surveys, in 2011, China's average household saving rate was 29 percent (National Bureau of Statistics of China 2012). The implied household sector saving was 14 percent of GDP.

Making the assumption that in the future the household sector saving rate will be reduced by half, the household consumption may be increased by 7 percent of GDP.

Lowering the ratio of accumulation?

In the future, household consumption and government consumption together may be increased by 9 percent of GDP. But net exports may fall by 3 percent of GDP. These changes would allow the capitalist net investment to fall by 6 percent of GDP without reducing the share of the capitalist profit in the GDP.

In 2011, China's net investment accounted for 33 percent of China's GDP. If the net investment is to be reduced by 6 percent of GDP, China's net investment would be 27 percent of GDP. Assuming that China's net operating surplus stays at 27 percent of GDP, the ratio of accumulation would fall from about 120 percent in 2011 to 100 percent in the future.

The above analysis suggests that, in the future, Chinese capitalism will have great difficulty in lowering the ratio of accumulation to much below 100 percent. If this turns out to be the case, it is unlikely that the major crisis of Chinese capitalism can be postponed beyond the 2020s.

The current projection assumes that the Chinese capitalist class will be able to maintain its current share in the national income. The capitalist profit is assumed to stay constant at 27 percent of China's GDP. However, as the Chinese working class emerges as a new political and social force, the capitalist profit may be further reduced as the working class demands higher wages and a growing range of economic and social benefits.

The rise of the Chinese working class

China's capitalist accumulation has been based on the ruthless exploitation of hundreds of millions of Chinese workers. Labor income is about 45 percent of China's GDP, compared to about 55 percent in the United States. In 2005, the Chinese workers' wage rate was 5 percent of the US level, 6 percent of the South Korean level, and 40 percent of the Mexican level (Li 2009a: 108).

Since the early 1980s, about 160 million migrant workers have moved from the rural areas to the urban areas in search of employment (National Bureau of Statistics of China 2013). China's export manufacturing is largely based on the exploitation of migrant workers. A study of the workers' conditions in the Pearl River Delta (an area that includes Guangzhou, Shenzhen, and Hong Kong) found that about two-thirds of workers worked more than eight hours a day and never took weekends off. Some workers had to work continuously up to 16 hours. The capitalist managers routinely used corporal punishment to discipline the workers. About 200 million Chinese workers work in hazardous conditions. There are about 700,000 serious work-related injuries in China every year, claiming more than 100,000 lives (Hart-Landsberg 2011).

In *The Communist Manifesto*, Marx and Engels argued that the working class struggle against the capitalists followed several stages of development. At first, the struggle was carried on by individual workers against the capitalists who directly exploited them. With the development of capitalist industry, the working class increased in number and became concentrated in greater masses. The workers' strength grew and they began to form unions to fight the capitalists as a collective force (Marx and Engels 1972). The same law of motion is operating in China today. As more and more migrant workers settle in the cities and increasingly regard themselves as wage workers rather than peasants, a new generation of working class with growing class consciousness is emerging. Both the official government documents and the mainstream media now recognize the rise of the "second generation migrant workers."

According to the Chinese mainstream media, currently there are about 100 million second generation migrant workers, defined as migrant workers born after 1980. They moved to the cities soon after completing their high school or middle school education. Most of these people had no experience in agricultural production. They identified more with the cities than the countryside. Compared to the "first generation," the second generation migrant workers tend to have better education and higher expectations in employment; they demand better material and cultural living standards, and are less likely to tolerate harsh working conditions (Baidu Online Encyclopedia 2011).

In recent years, waves of strikes and labor unrests have hit China's manufacturing industries, forcing the capitalists to accept wage increases. Mainstream Chinese scholars are worried about the possibility that China is entering a new period of intense strikes that will bring China's cheap labor regime to an end and threaten China's social stability (Chan 2010).

China's capitalist development is preparing the objective conditions that favor the growth of working class organizations. After many years of rapid accumulation, the massive reserve army of cheap labor in China's rural areas begins to be depleted.

From 2000 to 2010, China's prime labor force aged between 20 to 29 years, from which the bulk of the cheap unskilled workers in the manufacturing industries were recruited, declined by 15 percent (Wang 2011). From 2010 to 2020, China's working-age population aged between 18 to 22 years is expected to fall by 40 million and the working-age population aged between 20 to 40 years is expected to fall by 100 million (Luo 2010).

According to a report by the Boston Consulting Group and the Swiss Reinsurance Company, China's working-age population is expected to start declining in 2015. From 2010 to 2050, China's working-age population will decline at an average annual rate of 0.7 percent. On the other hand, China's population that is 60 years old or older is expected to grow from 165 million in 2010 to 440 million in 2050. The demographic change could impose a substantial burden on the Chinese economy, leading to surging pension costs and government deficits, or alternatively leaving millions uncovered by pensions, healthcare, and long-term care (BCG and Swiss Re 2012).

From 1980 to 2011, non-agricultural employment as a share of China's total employment increased from 31 percent to 65 percent (National Bureau of Statistics of China 2012). According to a report by the Chinese Academy of Social Sciences, in 2000, about 80 percent of the non-agricultural labor force consisted of wage workers (CASS 2002). Thus, the growth of non-agricultural employment may be used as a proxy for the growth of the working class.

Figure 7.6 compares the share of non-agricultural employment in total employment in China, Brazil, South Korea, and Poland. In the 1980s, the share of non-agricultural employment rose above 70 percent in Brazil, South Korea, and Poland. In each of the three countries, a militant working-class movement emerged and forced the ruling elites to make major political changes.

A similar development is now taking place in China. China's non-agricultural employment share is now about 65 percent. If China follows its own trend from 1980 to 2011, China's non-agricultural employment as a share of total employment should surpass the critical threshold of 70 percent before 2020.

If the historical experience of Brazil, South Korea, and Poland could be taken as a guide, the Chinese capitalist class will have to make political and economic concessions as the Chinese working class emerges as a powerful social and political force. However, unlike in the 1980s when

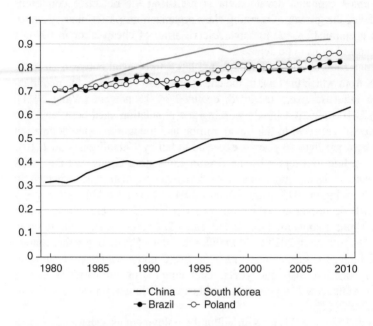

Figure 7.6 Non-agricultural employment as share of total employment (selected countries, 1980–2010) (sources: National Bureau of Statistics (2012); World Bank (2013)).

neoliberal capitalism was on the rise, in the future both Chinese capitalism and global capitalism will have to confront insurmountable structural crises.

By the 2020s, Chinese capitalism may enter into a permanent structural crisis due to the depletion of energy resources and the irreversible decline of the profit rate. Any concession from the capitalist class would further reduce the profit and intensify the crisis. On the other hand, if the capitalist class fails to make the necessary concessions, the growing working-class militancy could eventually lead to the downfall of the existing social system.

China's environmental crisis

The pursuit of endless accumulation of capital is in fundamental conflict with the requirements of environmental sustainability. Decades of rapid capital accumulation have led to massive environmental degradation in China.

China has 16 out of the 20 most polluted cities in the world. The aquifers in 90 percent of Chinese cities are polluted. Seventy-five percent of the river water flowing through China's urban areas is unsuitable for drinking or fishing. About 30 percent of the river water is unfit for agricultural or industrial use. Desertification has engulfed about one quarter of China's land area. About 40 percent of China's arable land has been degraded and 10 percent of China's arable land has been contaminated (Wen and Li 2006; Economy 2007).

The pervasive air, water, and land pollution has already become an urgent public health problem. Every year, between 400,000 and 800,000 Chinese people die prematurely due to respiratory diseases related to air pollution. Near 200 million Chinese people are sick from drinking contaminated water (Economy 2007).

According to the *China Ecological Footprint Report 2010*, in 2007, China's per capita ecological footprint (the productive land and water area required to produce the resources consumed and to absorb the waste generated) was 2.2 hectares, or about 81 percent of the world average. However, China's ecological footprint is now more than twice as much as China's own bio-capacity (the productive land and water area available). Thus, China is now running a huge ecological deficit against its own available resources and the size of China's ecological deficit has steadily grown since the 1970s (WWF 2010).

China's consumption of resources and generation of material waste have already overwhelmed China's own ecological systems. Unless this pattern is reversed in the near future, the current model of development will inevitably lead to a general ecological collapse inside China.

According to Li, Y. (2009), China's agricultural water demand is likely to increase to 463 billion cubic meters in 2030. On the other hand, the available water supply is expected to be 420 billion cubic meters in 2030. Thus, there is likely to be a water deficit of 43 billion cubic meters in the agricultural sector, or about 10 percent of the expected agricultural water demand in 2030.

According to a report prepared by the 2030 Water Resources Group (a consortium sponsored by the International Finance Corporation and several international companies), China's total water demand is projected to increase to 818 billion cubic meters under the "business as usual" scenario. But China's total water supply is expected to be 619 billion cubic meters by 2030, implying a 25 percent aggregate water deficit (WRG 2009: 15).

Like modern agriculture in the rest of the world, contemporary Chinese agriculture is heavily dependent on fossil fuels, mechanization, and irrigation. The intensive applications of chemical fertilizers, perennial irrigation, and mechanized tilling have led to widespread soil erosion. According to

Ye *et al.* (2010), under "business as usual," China's grain yields may decline by 11 percent from 2005 to 2030 and by 15 percent from 2005 to 2050 due to soil erosion. As a result, China may face a food deficit of 14 percent of the expected food demand by 2030 and a food deficit of 18 percent by 2050.

China: the weakest link of the global capitalist chain?

Historically, the wealth of the capitalist world system has been concentrated in the core countries comprising a small minority of the global population. As a result of several rounds of global capital relocation that have taken place since the early twentieth century, the geographical zone of semi-periphery has been greatly expanded. With the massive expansion of the population that demands comparatively high levels of resources consumption, the pressure of rising resources and labor costs now threaten to overwhelm not only the global capitalist system but also the global ecological system.

China has been the main beneficiary of the latest round of global capital relocation. China's economic growth has been based on high investment, intense exploitation of a large cheap labor force, massive resources consumption, and environmental degradation. None of these conditions can be sustained beyond the near future.

Years of rapid economic growth have led to fundamental transformations of the Chinese society. As the Chinese working class emerges as a powerful political and social force, it will inevitably demand more economic, political, and social rights and challenge China's current capitalist system.

Given the energy constraints, both China's economic growth rates and the profit rates are set to decline in the coming decades. A permanent economic crisis could begin in the 2020s. On the other hand, China's resources consumption and pollution generation have been proceeding at such a rate that China's own ecological systems may soon be overwhelmed.

With the world's largest manufacturing economy (which will soon become the world's largest economy), the world's largest and possibly the most exploited industrial working class, as well as the world's largest energy consumption and greenhouse gas emissions, China is where the global economic, social, and ecological contradictions are concentrated.

By the 2020s, China's economic, social, and environmental contradictions are likely to converge, leading to a structural crisis that can no longer be resolved within the capitalist system. China could very well prove to be the weakest link of the global capitalist chain.

How China's coming economic, social, and environmental crisis will be resolved may determine not only China's but also the world's future.

8 China and climate change

All human societies depend on the earth's ecological systems for survival and development. Human societies use renewable and nonrenewable resources for material production and consumption. The human production processes, in addition to producing useful goods and services, generate material waste or pollution. To sustain the normal functioning of the ecological systems, the human consumption of nonrenewable resources should be minimized, the human consumption of renewable resources should stay within the ecological systems' natural regenerative capacities, and the material waste generated by human activities needs to stay within the ecological systems' natural absorptive capacities (Huesemann 2003).

Thus, to maintain ecological sustainability, the human environmental impact (resources consumption and pollution) must stabilize at a level that is within the ecological systems' natural limits. However, the capitalist economic system is based on the production for profit and endless accumulation of capital. The normal operation of capitalism leads to unlimited expansion of material production and consumption. The basic laws of motion of capitalism are in fundamental conflict with the requirement of ecological sustainability.

This may be illustrated by the following formula:

$$\text{Environmental Impact} = \text{GDP} \times \text{Impact Intensity}$$

"Impact intensity" is defined as the environmental impact per unit of GDP. Under capitalism, economic output normally tends to grow. Unless the environmental effect of economic growth is more than offset by declining impact intensity, capital accumulation (economic growth) will result in growing environmental impact and eventually lead to ecological collapse.

After centuries of relentless capital accumulation, many aspects of the global ecological system are now on the verge of collapse. In particular, climate change, caused by greenhouse gases emitted by human consumption of fossil fuels, is now threatening the survival of human civilization. The global average temperature is now about 0.8°C (0.8 degree Celsius) higher than in the late nineteenth century and has risen by 0.5°C since the 1970s. Many scientists argue that, if global warming rises above 2°C (relative to the pre-industrial time), dangerous climate feedbacks may be triggered, leading to the release of more greenhouse gases from the oceans and terrestrial ecological systems. In the event of runaway global warming, much of the world would cease to be inhabitable and catastrophic declines of global population could happen (Spratt and Sutton 2008).

Limits to technological progress

Is it possible for the global ecological crisis to be resolved within the historical framework of capitalism? According to the defenders of the existing system, capitalism is an exceptionally innovative system. With proper incentives, capitalists would be motivated to develop environmentally friendly technologies that help to reduce environmental impact per unit of economic output, allowing capitalism to achieve both endless accumulation of capital and ecological sustainability.

However, in reality, economic growth rate is almost always higher than the reduction rate of impact intensity, so that the global consumption of most natural resources and the generation of most pollutants keep growing exponentially. Why has capitalist technological progress failed to deliver ecological sustainability?

All human activities inevitably consume some material resources and generate some material waste. Thus, the environmental impact per unit of economic output can never fall to zero. In the long run, if economic output grows toward infinity, it is inevitable that the overall environmental impact will grow beyond the ecological limit.

In addition to this fundamental reason, the pace of technological progress is also limited by the pace of capital replacement. New technologies that reduce the environmental impact per unit of economic output need to be embodied in new capital equipment and buildings. However, only a fraction of the existing capital can be replaced each year.

Table 8.1 illustrates the relationship between the new capital's impact intensity reduction and the whole economy's impact intensity reduction. The rate of reduction of environmental impact is then calculated as the economic growth rate less the rate of impact intensity reduction.

For example, if the economic growth rate is 3 percent, then the growth rate of capital stock needs to be 3 percent. In addition, 5 percent of the old capital stock is assumed to wear out every year. Thus, the total new capital

Table 8.1 Capital replacement and environmental impact reduction (%)

Economic growth rate	New capital as % of capital stock[a]	Impact intensity reduction of new capital		
		12.5	25	50
Total economy impact intensity reduction:				
0	5	−0.6	−1.3	−2.5
1	6	−0.8	−1.5	−3.0
2	7	−0.9	−1.8	−3.5
3	8	−1.0	−2.0	−4.0
4	9	−1.1	−2.3	−4.5
5	10	−1.3	−2.5	−5.0
Total economy environmental impact change:				
0	5	−0.6	−1.3	−2.5
1	6	0.2	−0.5	−2.0
2	7	1.1	0.2	−1.5
3	8	2.0	1.0	−1.0
4	9	2.9	1.7	−0.5
5	10	3.7	2.5	0.0

Note
a Assuming that depreciation rate is 5 percent.

would be 8 percent of the old capital stock. If the new capital's impact intensity is 12.5 percent lower than the old capital, the total economy's impact intensity would fall by 1 percent ($8\% \times 12.5\% = 1\%$). But since the economy grows at 3 percent a year, the environmental impact would grow at an annual rate of 2 percent ($3\% - 1\% = 2\%$).

If the new capital's impact intensity is 12.5 percent lower than the old capital, then the economic growth rate would have to stay below 1 percent to prevent environmental impact from rising. If the new capital's impact intensity is 25 percent lower than the old capital, the economic growth rate would have to stay below 2 percent to prevent environmental impact from rising. But a modern capitalist economy often needs an economic growth rate of 3 percent or more to prevent the unemployment rate from rising and a global economic growth rate lower than 2 percent is usually considered to be a global recession. In both cases, ecological sustainability is incompatible with the economic growth rate required for capitalist stability.

Only with the very optimistic assumption that the new capital reduces impact intensity by 50 percent compared to the old capital could the economy grow by up to 5 percent a year without increasing environmental impact.

"Ecological footprint" measures human demands on the earth's ecological systems by calculating the areas required for resources consumption and pollution absorption. According to *The Living Planet Report 2012*, in 1961, the world's total ecological footprint was 7.1 billion hectares and, in 2008, the world's total ecological footprint was 18.2 billion hectares (WWF *et al.* 2012: 38, 40). From 1961 to 2008, the world's total ecological footprint grew at an average annual rate of 2 percent. During the same period, the world economy grew at an average annual rate of 3.8 percent. The implied average annual rate of impact intensity reduction was 1.8 percent. The implied new capital's impact intensity reduction rate was 20 percent (assuming a depreciation rate of 5 percent; 1.8%/(5%+3.8%)=20.5%).

In 2008, the earth's total bio-capacity (which measures the nature's capacity to produce renewable resources and absorb pollution) was only 12 billion hectares. In other words, the global material consumption has overshot the earth's bio-capacity and now it would take about 1.5 years for the earth's ecological systems to regenerate the resources which the world uses up in just one year (WWF *et al.* 2012: 38).

To prevent global ecological collapse, the global ecological footprint needs to be brought back to within the earth's bio-capacity within a reasonable period of time. The longer the period during which the ecological footprint exceeds the bio-capacity, the greater the risk of collapse. Suppose the goal is to eliminate global ecological overshoot by 2050. The global ecological footprint needs to be reduced by 34 percent from 2008 to 2050, with an average annual rate of reduction of 1 percent. Table 8.1 indicates that this can only be accomplished with near zero economic growth if the new capital's impact intensity reduction is 25 percent.

On the other hand, if the global economy and the Chinese economy keep growing through the rest of the twenty-first century, rising levels of resources consumption and environmental degradation will overwhelm many dimensions of the global ecological system. In particular, without a fundamental decarbonization of the Chinese and the global economy, global climate catastrophes could threaten the survival of human civilization.

The twenty-first century—toward climate catastrophes?

It is now widely understood that human economic activities have led to the emission of greenhouse gases (mainly carbon dioxide emissions from fossil fuels consumption) that have contributed to long-term global warming. Rising global temperatures and the related impacts on the earth's ecological systems threaten to bring about global ecological catastrophes.

In the decade 2003–2012, the global land and ocean surface temperatures averaged 14.6°C. This was 0.8°C higher than the global average temperature during 1881–1890 and 0.5°C higher than during 1971–1980 (NASA 2013).

If global warming rises above 2°C (relative to the pre-industrial time), dangerous climate feedbacks may be triggered, leading to the release of more greenhouse gases from the soil and the oceans. For this reason, 2°C warming is generally considered by scientists as the "safe limit" beyond which global warming may be out of human control.

A 3°C warming would destroy the Amazon rainforest, leading to a further warming of 1.5°C. Southern Africa, Australia, Mediterranean Europe, and the western US would turn into deserts. Sea levels would eventually rise by 25 meters and billions of people could become environmental refugees (Spratt and Sutton 2008: 26–32; Hansen 2010: 140–171).

According to James Lovelock, one of the world's leading earth system scientists, if the atmospheric concentration of carbon dioxide rises above 500 parts per million (ppm), the world is likely to be set for runaway global warming. Algae, the ocean's largest carbon sink, would die out. The algal failures could lead to a sudden upward jump in global temperature. The global average temperature could reach 24°C, or more than 10°C warmer than the pre-industrial time. In that event, only Northern Europe, Siberia, Canada, and Antarctica may remain inhabitable. Catastrophic declines of global population would take place (Lovelock 2007: 26–35, 48–65; Spratt and Sutton 2008: 31). It would not be exaggerating to say that the very survival of human civilization for centuries to come is at stake.

Table 8.2 summarizes the potential consequences of various degrees of global warming.

The global emissions budget

The gases in the atmosphere that contribute to global warming are known as the "greenhouse gases." Long-lived greenhouse gases in the atmosphere include carbon dioxide, methane, nitrous oxide, and some minor gases. The greenhouse gases in the atmosphere are measured by their atmospheric concentration. Because carbon dioxide is the most important greenhouse gas, other greenhouse gases are often converted into carbon dioxide equivalent (CO_2-equivalent) to reflect their contributions to global warming.

In the pre-industrial time, the atmospheric concentration of all long-lived greenhouse gases was about 280 parts per million (ppm) of CO_2-equivalent. According to the Intergovernmental Panel on Climate Change (IPCC), the "climate sensitivity" or the extent of global warming that would result from a doubling of the greenhouse gases in the atmosphere is estimated to be 3°C. Thus, according to the IPCC climate sensitivity, if the

Table 8.2 Global warming scenarios

Global warming scenarios	1–2°C	3–4°C	5–6°C
Drought and desertification	Frequent heat waves	Widespread drought and desertification	Much of the world ceases to be inhabitable
Sea ice and ice sheets	Disappearing of Arctic sea ice	Melting of Greenland ice sheets	Melting of Antarctic ice sheets
Sea level rise	Several meters	25 meters	75 meters
Eco-systems	One third of species become extinct	Amazon rainforest burns down	Massive species extinction
Human impact	Half a billion people at risk of starvation	Billions become environmental refugees	Catastrophic decline of global population
Climate feedbacks	Possible initiation of soil and ocean carbon feedbacks	Arctic permafrost and ocean algae endangered	Runaway global warming

Sources: Spratt and Sutton (2008: 26–32); Hansen (2010: 140–171).

atmospheric concentration of CO_2-equivalent rises to 550 ppm, it should lead to an increase in global average temperature of 3°C from the pre-industrial time (IPCC 2007: 227–229).

However, new developments in climate science suggest that the IPCC is likely to have underestimated the potential of global warming. Based on the study of paleoclimate data, James Hansen, one of the world's leading climate scientists, concluded that when "slow" climate feedbacks (such as ice sheet disintegration and vegetation migration) were taken into account, the observed long-term climate sensitivity was about 6°C rather than 3°C (Hansen 2010: 140–171). Given the Hansen climate sensitivity, an atmospheric concentration of CO_2-equivalent of 550 ppm would lead to a long-term global warming of about 6°C.

In 2012, the atmospheric concentration of carbon dioxide reached 394 ppm (carbon dioxide only, other greenhouse gases not included). From 1750 to 2012, the atmospheric concentration of carbon dioxide increased by 116 ppm. Since 1980, the atmospheric concentration of carbon dioxide has been rising at an average rate of 1.7 ppm a year (EPI 2012e; NOAA 2013).

Figure 8.1 shows the historical evolution of atmospheric concentration of carbon dioxide from 1000 to 2012, in comparison with the global average temperatures from 1880 to 2012.

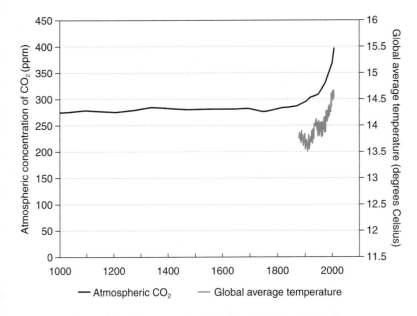

Figure 8.1 Atmospheric concentration of carbon dioxide and global average temperature (1000–2012) (sources: Data for atmospheric concentration of carbon dioxide from 1000 to 2011 are from EPI (2012e), updated to 2012 using data from NOAA (2013); global average temperatures from 1880 to 2012 are from NASA (2013)).

According to the European Environment Agency (2012), the total greenhouse gases regulated by the Kyoto Protocol reached 439 ppm CO_2-equivalent in 2009, which was 161 ppm higher than in 1750. Without any further increase in greenhouse gases, the current level of greenhouse gases already implies a long-term warming of 2–4°C.

Table 8.3 summarizes the various scenarios of climate stabilization. Under Scenario I, atmospheric concentration of carbon dioxide eventually stabilizes at 350 ppm and the total greenhouse gases stabilize at 450 ppm of CO_2-equivalent. This will lead to a long-term global warming of 2°C under the IPCC climate sensitivity but a 4°C warming under the Hansen climate sensitivity.

As more than 2°C global warming would significantly increase the risk of dangerous climate feedbacks and anything beyond 3°C warming would be devastating for human civilization, a responsible global climate policy should really aim at an atmospheric concentration of CO_2-equivalent of no more than 450 ppm. To achieve this objective, the cumulative carbon

Table 8.3 Climate stabilization scenarios and emissions budgets (Gt: billion tonnes)

Climate stabilization scenarios	Scenario I	Scenario II	Scenario III
Atmospheric CO_2	350 ppm	450 ppm	550 ppm
Atmospheric CO_2-equivalent	450 ppm	550 ppm	700 ppm
Global warming[a]			
IPCC climate sensitivity	2°C	3°C	4°C
Hansen climate sensitivity	4°C	6°C	8°C
Approximate twenty-first century emissions budgets:			
Global budgets			
Cumulative CO_2 emissions budget	1,000 Gt	2,000 Gt	3,000 Gt
Less: early twenty-first century emissions	400 Gt	400 Gt	400 Gt
Remaining CO_2 emissions budget	600 Gt	1,600 Gt	2,600 Gt
China's budgets			
Cumulative CO_2 emissions budget	210 Gt	420 Gt	630 Gt
Less: early twenty-first century emissions	80 Gt	80 Gt	80 Gt
Remaining CO_2 emissions budget	130 Gt	340 Gt	550 Gt

Sources: IPCC (2007: 198–199, 227–229); Hansen (2010: 140–171).

Note

a Long-term equilibrium temperature increase relative to the pre-industrial time.

dioxide emissions from fossil fuels burning over the entire twenty-first century needs to be no more than 1 trillion tonnes.

However, over the period 2001–2012, about 360 billion tonnes of carbon dioxide has already been emitted from fossil fuels burning. To limit the global carbon dioxide emissions in the rest of the twenty-first century to no more than 640 billion tonnes, the global emissions will have to fall at an annual rate of 5 percent from 2013 to 2100 (if emissions reduction starts in 2013). If the global capitalist economy were to keep growing at 3 percent a year, the global emissions intensity of GDP (the ratio of carbon dioxide emissions to GDP) would have to fall at an annual rate of 8 percent. This will clearly be impossible. Even with zero economic growth, an annual reduction of emissions by 5 percent cannot be accomplished even if one makes the most heroic assumption of the pace of technological progress (see Table 8.1). Thus, for all practical purposes, it is no longer possible to keep long-term global warming to less than 2°C (also see Anderson and Bows 2011).

According to IPCC (2007: 198–199), to keep atmospheric concentration of CO_2-equivalent at no more than 550 ppm (which implies long-term global warming of 3–6°C), the cumulative carbon dioxide emissions from fossil fuels burning over the entire twenty-first century need to be less than two trillion tonnes.

Figure 8.2 compares the historical world carbon dioxide emissions from 2000 to 2012, the future carbon dioxide emissions from 2013 to 2100 based on the fossil fuels consumption projected in Chapter 5, and the emissions trajectory that would be consistent with an atmospheric concentration of CO_2-equivalent of no more than 550 ppm.

From 2000 to 2012, world carbon dioxide emissions from fossil fuels burning grew from 25 billion tonnes to 34 billion tonnes. World carbon dioxide emissions are projected to peak in the late 2030s, with emissions reaching 43 billion tonnes. The cumulative carbon dioxide emissions over the twenty-first century are projected to be 3.4 trillion tonnes.

The carbon dioxide "airborne" ratio is the proportion of carbon dioxide emissions that end up in the atmosphere. Over the past half a century, the average observed airborne ratio was 56 percent (Hansen 2010: 119–120). Assuming that the future average airborne ratio will be 50 percent, with 3.4 trillion tonnes of cumulative emissions, 1.7 trillion tonnes of the emitted carbon dioxide will eventually stay in the atmosphere. One "ppm" of atmospheric carbon dioxide equals roughly 7.8 billion tonnes. Thus, over the course of the twenty-first century, about 220 ppm of carbon dioxide will

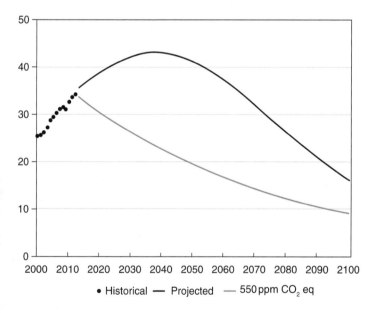

Figure 8.2 World carbon dioxide emissions (historical and projected, billion tonnes, 2000–2100) (sources: World carbon dioxide emissions from fossil fuels burning from 2000 to 2012 are from BP (2013). For projections from 2013 to 2100, see text).

be added to the atmosphere. In 2000, the atmospheric concentration of CO_2 was 370 ppm. The projected emissions trajectory therefore implies a long-term atmospheric concentration of carbon dioxide of 590 ppm. In the long run, the non-CO_2 greenhouse gases are likely to rise to 100–150 ppm of CO_2-equivalent (see Table 8.3). When all greenhouse gases are included, the atmospheric concentration of CO_2-equivalent will rise to about 700–750 ppm, leading to a long-term global warming of 4–8°C.

According to the scientists' assessment, a long-term global warming of 4–8°C will lead to a global sea level rise of 75 meters, massive species extinction, and catastrophic declines in global population (see Table 8.2). This would lead to the end of human civilization as we know it.

To keep the long-term global warming at no more than 3–6°C (this would still carry a significant risk of runaway global warming), the world needs to immediately start reducing the levels of carbon dioxide emissions. If the world carbon dioxide emissions start to fall in 2013, the emissions need to fall at an annual rate of 1.5 percent from 2013 to 2100 to keep the cumulative emissions over the twenty-first century to no more than two trillion tonnes (see Figure 8.2). If the global economy operates with zero growth, then the required rate of reduction of emissions intensity of GDP would need to be 1.5 percent.

In the 1980s and the 1990s, the world economy had achieved an average annual emissions intensity reduction rate of 1.6–1.8 percent (see the average annual growth rates of "emissions efficiency" in Table 5.7; emissions efficiency is the inverse of emissions intensity of GDP). Thus, if the global economic system can be fundamentally transformed to operate with zero economic growth, the long-term global warming may be limited to no more than 3–6°C with reasonable efforts of technological progress.

Climate stabilization: the political conditions

Climate stabilization at a reasonable level (consistent with the preservation of human civilization) is a global common good that cannot be accomplished without serious and committed international cooperation.

However, in the capitalist world system, states are under constant and intense pressures to compete against one another in economic and military terms. The states that prevail in the competition would consolidate and possibly improve their relative positions in the world system. The states that fail in the competition would not only suffer from declining relative positions but also face the risk of collapse, revolution, or disintegration. To succeed in the interstate competition, all states are pressured to mobilize all available resources to maximize the rates of economic growth within a politically meaningful period of time (which often means 5–10 years).

Policies designed to reduce the consumption of fossil fuels are likely to reduce the short-run economic growth rates and undermine the immediate interests of the capitalist class. In the medium- and the long-run, serious climate stabilization policies may require zero or negative economic growth rates. On the other hand, the benefits of climate stabilization are to be shared by the entire global population and will not be strongly felt until several generations later.

In this context, it is not surprising that most national states have little enthusiasm for the global project of climate stabilization. In fact, the political conditions required for serious international cooperation on climate stabilization may not be established until the current capitalist world system is replaced by a new world system that is based on the pursuit of basic needs and ecological sustainability rather than endless accumulation of capital.

China's emissions budget

Whether the global political conditions required for climate stabilization can be made ready will depend on the development of the global class struggle in the coming decades. The previous chapter argues that, in one or two decades, economic, political, and environmental crises may converge in China, and China may prove to be the weakest link in the global capitalist chain. Given China's important position in the capitalist world system, if China's future crisis is resolved in a way that is favorable for the Chinese working class, the global balance of power may be turned to the favor of the international working classes. Such a development may pave the way for a new world system organized for social and ecological sustainability.

Assuming that the political conditions for climate stabilization are present, the global emissions budget would still need to be distributed among countries based on the principle of equity and some practical considerations

From 1751 to 2008, the world's cumulative carbon dioxide emissions were about 1.3 trillion tonnes (EPI 2012a). Of the world's cumulative emissions, the US accounted for 27 percent, the European countries accounted for 31 percent, Russia accounted for 7 percent, Japan accounted for 4 percent, Canada and Australia accounted for 3 percent, China accounted for 9 percent, and the rest of the world accounted for 14 percent (Hansen 2010: 189).

If the global emissions budget were to be distributed based on the consideration of equity alone, every person in the world should be entitled to an equal portion in the global total emissions, including both the historical and the future emissions. In 2000, the Chinese population was 21 percent of the world population. If year 2000 is taken as the reference year, China would be entitled to 21 percent of the world's historical and future emissions budget. The world historical cumulative emissions were 1.3 trillion tonnes and the world's remaining emissions budget from 2009 to 2100 is 1.7 trillion tonnes (to limit global warming to no more than 3–6°C). Thus, the world's total historical and future emissions budget would be three trillion tonnes and China would be entitled to total historical and future emissions of 620 billion tonnes. Subtracting China's historical emissions (9 percent of 1.3 trillion tonnes) from the 620 billion tonnes, China's remaining emissions budget from 2009 to 2100 would be 500 billion tonnes.

However, under this approach, the US would be entitled to only 5 percent of the world's historical and future emissions budget, which would equal 150 billion tonnes. Before 2009, the US had already emitted 350 billion tonnes of carbon dioxide (27 percent of 1.3 trillion tonnes). Thus, the US would have to not only immediately reduce emissions to zero but also make compensation for the historical emissions debt of 200 billion tonnes. This is obviously not practical. If this approach is applied to Europe, Japan, Canada, Australia, or Russia, the implications would be similar.

An alternative approach is to decide that every person at the beginning of the twenty-first century (year 2000) was entitled to an equal portion of the global emissions budget over the twenty-first century. From the peripheral countries' perspective, this approach may be seen as unfair because it allows the core countries to write off their historical emissions debt. But it avoids the obvious impracticality of forcing the core countries to immediately achieve zero emissions. By assigning every person an equal portion of the global future emissions budget, it by and large retains the equity principle.

The global emissions budget over the twenty-first century would be 2 trillion tonnes if global warming is to be limited to no more than 3–6°C. Given China's population share in 2000, China is entitled to 21 percent of the global emissions budget, or 420 billion tonnes of carbon dioxide emissions over the twenty-first century. From 2001 to 2012, China had already emitted about 75 billion tonnes of carbon dioxide. Thus, China's remaining emissions budget is 345 billion tonnes for carbon dioxide emissions from 2013 to 2100.

Figure 8.3 shows China's historical carbon dioxide emissions from fossil fuels consumption from 2000 to 2012, the projected emissions based on China's projected fossil fuels consumption from 2013 to 2100 (see Chapter 6), and the emissions trajectory consistent with China's emissions budget over the twenty-first century (which would allow China to meet its global obligation of limiting global warming to no more than 3–6°C).

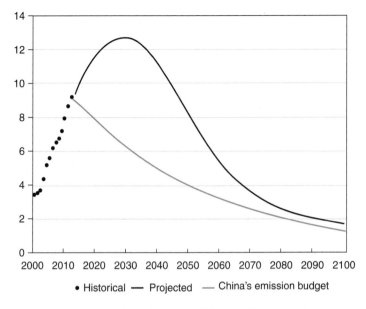

Figure 8.3 China's carbon dioxide emissions (historical and projected, billion tonnes, 2000–2100) (sources: China's carbon dioxide emissions from fossil fuels burning from 2000 to 2012 are from BP (2013). For projections from 2013 to 2100, see text).

From 2000 to 2012, China's carbon dioxide emissions from fossil fuels consumption increased from 3.4 billion tonnes to 9.2 billion tonnes. China's emissions are projected to peak in the late 2020s, with carbon dioxide emissions reaching 12.7 billion tonnes. Under the current projection, China's cumulative emissions over the twenty-first century will be 680 billion tonnes.

To limit China's cumulative carbon dioxide emissions over the twenty-first century to 420 billion tonnes, China's carbon dioxide emissions need to fall at an annual rate of 2.2 percent from 2013 to 2100 (assuming that emissions reduction starts in 2013).

Climate stabilization and the limits to China's economic growth

Suppose that China starts reducing carbon dioxide emissions in 2013 and China's emissions fall by 2.2 percent annually from 2013 to 2100.

From 2013 to 2080, all required emission reductions are assumed to take place through the reduction of domestically produced coal. Coal has the highest emissions intensity per unit of energy among all types of energy. Thus, emissions reduction through reduction of coal consumption is more efficient than other forms of emissions reduction.

By 2080, even with domestic coal production reduced to zero, the emissions remain higher than what are allowed by China's emissions budget. After 2080, additional emission reductions are assumed to take place through the reduction of net energy imports (which are assumed to have the same emissions intensity as oil).

Figure 8.4 shows China's historical and future energy consumption. The future energy consumption projections are the same as in Figure 6.9 except that domestic coal production and net energy imports are reduced so that China's cumulative carbon dioxide emissions over the twenty-first century would stay within the budget of 420 billion tonnes.

China's total energy consumption is projected to peak in 2013 at 2.6 billion tonnes of oil equivalent. Despite the rapid expansion of nuclear and renewable energies, it is insufficient to offset the required decline of fossil

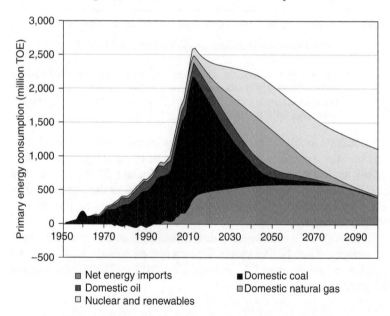

Figure 8.4 China's primary energy consumption (historical and climate stabilization projects, 1950–2100) (sources: For China's historical energy consumption from 1950 to 2012 and China's projected oil production, natural gas production, nuclear energy production, and renewable energies production from 2013 to 2100, see Figure 6.9. For climate stabilization projections for domestic coal production and net energy imports, see text).

fuels. By 2100, the total energy consumption is projected to fall to 43 percent of the peak level.

Figure 8.5 shows China's historical economic growth rates from 2000 to 2012, the projected economic growth rates from 2013 to 2100 under business as usual (see Figure 6.10), and the projected economic growth rates with major decarbonization effort staring from 2013. The projected energy consumption with decarbonization from 2013 to 2100 is based on Figure 8.4. The projected energy efficiency is the same as in Figure 6.8.

To meet China's climate stabilization obligations, China's economic growth rate is required to fall sharply from 7.8 percent in 2012 to 1.5 percent in 2014. With optimistic assumptions of renewable energies and energy efficiency growth, China's economic growth rate is projected to rise gradually to 2.9 percent by 2030. From the 2040s to the 2070s, the projected economic growth rates with decarbonization would actually be higher than that under business as usual. Toward the end of the century, both sets of projected economic growth rates would approach zero.

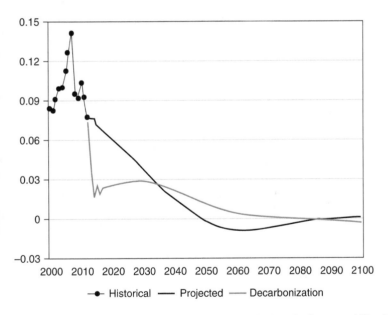

Figure 8.5 China's economic growth rates (historical and climate stabilization projections, 2000–2010) (sources: For China's historical economic growth rates from 2000 to 2012 and projected economic growth rates without decarbonization policy from 2013 to 2100, see Figure 6.10. For projected economic growth rates with emissions reduction from 2013 to 2100, see text).

9 Transition to the end of growth

In the nineteenth century, the rise of the capitalist world system to global supremacy coincided with the decline of the historical Chinese empire. By the mid-twentieth century, China was reduced to a peripheral member of the capitalist world system and one of the world's most impoverished countries. Since then, China has achieved a great economic revival. By the early twenty-first century, China becomes the driving engine of global economic growth and is set to regain the title of the world's largest economy in a few years.

As China regains the big power status within the capitalist world system, the system itself is in a structural crisis that can no longer be resolved. Capitalism is a unique historical system driven by the pursuit of endless economic growth. The pursuit of infinite economic growth has been made possible by the massive exploitation of fossil fuels. With the depletion of fossil fuels and the threat of global climate catastrophes, the world is confronted with the urgent task of a fundamental energy transformation. But neither the renewable energies nor the improvement of energy efficiency can deliver infinite economic growth. Moreover, with realistic rates of technological progress, reasonable climate stabilization can be achieved only with zero economic growth.

China is at the center of the global energy contradictions. Moreover, China's relentless capitalist accumulation has generated overwhelming social and environmental contradictions within China. Without fundamental changes, the combination of these contradictions will lead to the collapse of China's existing social system in one or two decades.

Crisis and collapse?

Without fundamental changes, the most likely scenario is for China to continue on the current path of capitalist accumulation. The Chinese government will undertake further "economic reforms." The remaining state-owned enterprises will be privatized. Without serious adjustment of economic and social policies, inequality in income and wealth distribution will keep rising. Environmental conditions will continue to deteriorate. With mass consumption depressed, the economy will depend on excessively high levels of investment to sustain growth.

In Chapter 7, it is argued that these tendencies are likely to result in a general economic, social, and environmental crisis in the 2020s, leading to the collapse of the Chinese economy. Given China's central position in the global division of labor, a collapse of the Chinese economy may lead to the collapse of the global economy.

A general collapse of the Chinese and the global economy might help to reduce greenhouse gas emissions and postpone global climate catastrophes. But people in China and the rest of the world will suffer from massive declines of living standards. The economic collapse is likely to be followed by social and political collapses. Class and ethnic conflicts, wars, and revolutions will turn into a web of vicious spirals with the end outcome inherently difficult to predict.

Reform within capitalism?

Chapter 7 argues that, by the 2020s, the Chinese working class will emerge as a powerful political and social force. Under the pressure of the growing working class power, the Chinese government may be forced to undertake serious economic, political, and social reforms. The Chinese workers will be provided with a growing range of political and social rights. Wealth and income will be redistributed from the capitalist class to the working class. Environmental regulations will be imposed on the capitalist enterprises to prevent further environmental degradations.

These social democratic policies would help to accommodate the demands of the Chinese working class and address some local and national environmental problems. However, the underlying economic system would remain capitalist. Eventually, the depletion of fossil fuels will impose limits on China's economic growth and reduce the capitalist profit rate. The various social democratic policies will lead to higher wages and taxes, further reducing the capitalist profits. As the profit rate falls below a certain critical level, the capitalist investment will collapse, leading to a structural crisis that cannot be overcome within the capitalist system.

Transition to the end of growth

By the 2020s, as China's oil production peaks, large sections of the Chinese population will understand that the existing model based on the ruthless exploitation of nonrenewable resources is unsustainable. As global warming advances and extreme climate events happen more frequently, popular awareness of climate change may reach a critical turning point leading to a general desire for fundamental change.

As the Chinese and the global capitalist crisis deepen, there will be growing understanding that the existing social system is fundamentally flawed and the environmental crisis cannot be resolved within the system. In this context, a general social consensus may be formed, demanding the transition from the existing failed capitalist system to a new social system based on ecological sustainability.

Commitment to zero growth

Infinite economic growth is fundamentally incompatible with ecological sustainability. Commitment to zero economic growth should be the basic premise of any post-capitalist social system. In the early phase of the post-capitalist transition, society may take the initial step of committing to very slow economic growth. With an annual economic growth rate of 1–2 percent and very aggressive efforts to promote renewable energies and energy efficiency, it may be possible to achieve an annual reduction of carbon dioxide emissions by 2–3 percent for several years. This would keep the economy on track to achieve long-term reasonable climate stabilization.

Macroeconomic balancing

Assuming that the economic growth rate is 2 percent, the depreciation rate is 5 percent, and the total economy capital–GDP ratio is $3:1$ (implying an economy-wide profit rate of 9 percent if the profit share is 27 percent), the required investment–GDP ratio would be 21 percent $(3 \times (2\% + 5\%) = 21\%)$. Currently, China's investment–GDP ratio is about 45 percent. Thus, investment as a share of China's GDP needs to be lowered by 24 percentage points. To offset the decline of investment, consumption as a share of China's GDP needs to rise by 24 percentage points.

Currently, household consumption accounts for only 35 percent of China's GDP and labor income accounts for about 45 percent. For consumption to rise as a share of GDP, labor income needs to rise and the household saving rate needs to be lowered.

Currently, the Chinese households save about one-third of their disposable incomes. The high saving rate reflects the general insecurity caused by expensive urban housing, healthcare, education, and insufficient pensions. Greater social spending in these areas will increase the general social security and encourage the households to spend a greater proportion of their incomes.

According to the World Bank (2013), in 2009, the Chinese government spending on healthcare accounted for 2.3 percent of the GDP, compared to the world average of 6.1 percent. In 2008, the world average public sector spending on education as a share of GDP was 4.4 percent. By comparison, in 2011, the Chinese government spending on education accounted for 3.5 percent of the GDP (National Bureau of Statistics of China 2012).

China needs to increase its government spending on healthcare and education by about 5 percent of GDP to match the world average levels of spending.

One hundred million jobs for the Chinese workers

China currently has a total labor force of about 760 million, including 360 million in the urban sector and 400 million in the rural sector. The large rural surplus labor force reduces the Chinese workers' bargaining power, allowing the capitalists to maintain the current super exploitative regime.

Suppose the Chinese government would spend 5 percent of GDP on a massive public employment program. Given China's current GDP (about 50 trillion Yuan, or 8 trillion dollars), 5 percent of GDP equals 2.5 trillion Yuan (or 400 billion dollars). Given the Chinese private sector's current average annual wage rate (about 25,000 Yuan, or 4,000 dollars), the public employment program could create up to 100 million jobs.

The public employment program would help to directly redistribute about 5 percent of GDP from capitalist profits to wages. Moreover, by absorbing a large portion of the unemployed and underemployed population, it would help to increase the bargaining power for the entire working class, contributing to further income redistribution from capital to labor.

The massive public employment program can be used to construct numerous social and environmental projects, such as building social housing, pollution cleaning, experimenting organic agriculture, building renewable power plants, and electrification of transportation.

Preparing for peak oil

According to this book's projections (see Chapters 4 and 5), world oil production is likely to peak in the 2030s (and possibly earlier). Under the current trend, China will be ill prepared for peak oil. China is set to surpass the US to become the world's largest oil importer in a few years. By the 2040s, the minimum prices acceptable to the main oil exporters will exceed the maximum prices affordable by the Chinese economy. Failure to prepare for peak oil is likely to have devastating economic and social consequences.

In 2010, China consumed 69 million tonnes of gasoline, 17 million tonnes of kerosene (including jet fuels), 146 million tonnes of diesel oil, and 38 million tonnes of fuel oil (National Bureau of Statistics of China 2012).

Diesel fuels are mainly used to power trucks, trains, ships, and various heavy machines in industry and agriculture. Under the current and likely future technology, it would be difficult or impossible to replace diesel fuels with electricity for most of these uses (though railways can be electrified). Diesel fuels can be replaced by liquid fuels made from coal or natural gas. But China's coal production may peak in the 2020s and natural gas production may peak in the 2040s. Large-scale making of liquid fuels from coal or natural gas would also involve massive energy losses and greenhouse gas emissions.

Gasoline is mainly used for personal cars, light trucks, and buses, and can be replaced by electricity with less technical difficulty. China's gasoline consumption grew at an average annual rate of 6.1 percent from 2000 to 2010 (EIA 2013a). At this trend, China's gasoline consumption is likely to rise to 120 million tonnes by 2020. In terms of energy content, 120 million tonnes of oil equals about 1,400 terawatt-hours. But electric devices are more efficient than internal combustion engines. Currently, the best gasoline engines have an efficiency of 40 percent (Smil 2010a: 9); the lithium-ion batteries have a net efficiency of about 75 percent (after subtracting self-discharge losses) (Smil 2010b: 26). Thus, one unit of electrical energy can replace approximately two units of gasoline energy. It would take about 700 terawatt-hours of electricity to replace 120 million tonnes of gasoline.

Suppose the electricity used to replace gasoline consumption is to be generated by solar. One gigawatt of solar power plant can generate about 1.3 terawatt-hours of electricity in a year (assuming a capacity utilization rate of 15 percent). It would take about 540 gigawatts of solar power plants to generate 460 terawatt-hours of electricity.

At the current construction cost, it takes 3.9 billion dollars to build 1 gigawatt of solar generating capacity (see Table 5.1). Thus, the total capital cost would amount to 2.1 trillion dollars, or about one-quarter of China's GDP. If the construction is going to be completed within a five-year plan, the annual investment cost would be about 5 percent of China's GDP.

Financing the transition

The above public spending and investment programs amount to about 15 percent of China's GDP. The Chinese capitalist income (measured by the "net operating surplus") is more than 25 percent of GDP. This would provide the financial resource base from which the proposed public spending and investment programs can be financed.

In 2011, the state-owned enterprises accounted for 26 percent of China's industrial output value and 27 percent of the profits, but paid for 47 percent of the total taxes on the industrial sector enterprises (National Bureau of Statistics of China 2012). In other words, the foreign and domestic private enterprises accounted for about three-quarters of the output value but paid only about one half of the total taxes. Raising the effective tax rates on the private enterprises to the same levels as the state-owned enterprises would double China's tax revenue from the business sector.

In 2011, China's various business taxes accounted for 13 percent of the GDP. Thus, simply by demanding the private capitalist enterprises pay the same tax rates as the state-owned enterprises, an additional tax revenue of 13 percent of GDP can be raised.

In 2011, the individual income taxes collected by the Chinese government equaled only 1.3 percent of the GDP. It would not be unreasonable for the Chinese government to raise the individual income tax revenue to about 3 percent of GDP by improving tax collection on wealthy capitalist individuals.

Under the current global division of labor, China specializes in labor-intensive and energy-intensive manufacturing. In effect, China subsidizes the transnational corporations and the core countries' consumers by exploiting cheap labor and cheap energy. A smaller exports sector would help China to reduce resources consumption and environmental degradation. China should remove the export subsidies and impose higher taxes on trade.

Socialization of investment

Back to the 1930s, economic instability rather than ecological unsustainability was considered to be the fatal flaw of the capitalist system.

John Maynard Keynes wrote the *General Theory of Employment, Interest, and Money* to analyze the capitalist instability. Toward the end of *The General Theory*, Keynes proposed that "a somewhat comprehensive socialisation of investment will prove the only means of securing an approximation of full employment" (Keynes 1964[1953]: 378). However, Keynes insisted that the proposed socialization of investment would not require social ownership of the means of production.

After the Second World War, instead of practicing "socialization of investment," the core capitalist economies have adopted "Keynesian" macroeconomic policies. In recessions, the government would increase fiscal deficits to stabilize capitalist profits and the central bank would print money to stabilize financial markets.

The big government interventions have largely succeeded in preventing the 1930s-style depressions. However, by socializing the investment risks within an economic system of privatized profits, the big government capitalism encourages the capitalists to undertake increasingly riskier investment and financing activities (Minsky 2008[1986]; Pollin and Dymski 1994; Li 2009b).

Periodic financial crises forced governments to intervene. Each round of intervention led to a higher level of government debt. The Great Recession of 2009 forced the western governments to spend trillions of dollars or euros to bail out the financial sector. Nearly every core capitalist government is now confronted with unsustainable debt–GDP ratios.

Within the capitalist system, it is hard to see how the dilemma can be resolved. On the one hand, socialization of investment risks has become indispensable for the stabilization of modern capitalism. On the other hand, the lack of social control over investment has led to growing financial instability and increasingly unsustainable government debts. The underlying contradiction has led to progressively more destructive economic and financial crises. Contrary to what Keynes argued, the eventual resolution of the dilemma may require nothing short of a comprehensive socialization of the basic means of production.

Socialization of investment is required not only for achieving economic stability but also for ecological sustainability. As economic growth approaches zero and the capitalist profit rate falls toward zero, there will be less incentives for the capitalists to undertake productive investment.

In a capitalist economy, as investment falls, economic output would fall below the full employment level and a large portion of the labor force would be unemployed. In the post-capitalist transition, the government should follow Keynes's advice, using "socialization of investment" to approach full employment. Public investment will increase, offsetting the decline of private investment. As public investment gradually replaces private investment, most of the means of production will be socialized.

The increase in public investment will not be used to generate economic growth. As socially owned enterprises (which may include state-owned enterprises, community-owned enterprises, or cooperatives) take over the bulk of the economy, the profits of the socially owned enterprises will be collected as taxes or contributions to communities and used for public consumption or to finance the energy transition.

Final reflection: is there an alternative to socialism?

After centuries of relentless capital accumulation, the global ecological system is now on the verge of collapse. Whether the global economy, society, and political system can be transformed and ecological sustainability achieved will be the ultimate challenge humanity will have to confront during the twenty-first century.

To achieve global ecological sustainability, consumption of nonrenewable resources must be minimized, consumption of renewable resources needs to be limited to within the natural regenerative capacities, and the generation of pollution needs to be limited to within the natural absorptive capacities. Thus, the overall environmental impact has to be stabilized at a level that is ecologically sustainable. Since the environmental impact per unit of economic output cannot fall to zero, ultimately, a stable environmental impact can only be achieved with a stable economic output—that is, with zero economic growth.

For the economy to operate with zero growth, the surplus product (a society's total product less the replacement of the means of production used up and the population's basic consumption; see Chapter 1) must be committed to socially useful consumption rather than capital accumulation.

Under capitalism, the social division of labor takes place through the market. The surplus product takes the form of "surplus value" or profit. Under the pressure of market competition, all capitalists are compelled to use a large portion of their profits for capital accumulation. The drive for endless accumulation of capital is fundamentally incompatible with ecological sustainability. Throughout this book, it has been argued that capitalism needs to have a certain level of positive economic growth to maintain economic and social stability and no capitalism can function with persistent zero economic growth.

The argument regarding the incompatibility between capitalism and ecological sustainability can also be applied to any market-based economic system. So long as the social division of labor takes place through the market, market competition would force the individuals to use the surplus product under their control to promote capital accumulation, in order to prevail in competition.

In the pre-capitalist societies, the surplus product was concentrated in a small group of elites who used the surplus product for luxury consumption, wars, religious activities, or public works. Capitalism has brought about fundamental transformations to human societies. Literacy and basic education have been extended to the entire population. Large sections of the population in every country are politically active. Democratic forms of government and a certain set of "human rights" have become the basic political standard. It is unlikely that, in the post-capitalist world, people will accept a return to the pre-capitalist form of social system.

Only with social control over the surplus product can society collectively decide how to use the surplus product. Society could then decide to use the surplus product not for economic growth but for democratically decided social needs, such as education, culture, science, and environmental improvement. Society could also decide to reduce the size of the surplus product. This would allow people to work fewer hours and spend more time on creative activities.

Social control over the surplus product presupposes social ownership of the means of production. Thus, ecological sustainability can only be achieved through some form of socialism.

In the twentieth century, socialist experiments were limited to the periphery and semi-periphery of the capitalist world system. The socialist states remained a part of the capitalist world system and were forced to compete with the capitalist states in economic growth and industrialization.

The conventional wisdom is that the socialist states had failed largely because the socialist economies were hopelessly inefficient. The mainstream economic literature has greatly exaggerated the inefficiency of the socialist economies. As Chapter 2 discussed, the socialist economies' growth performance was largely comparable to the capitalist peripheral and semi-peripheral economies. The economic crisis of the socialist economies in the 1980s was part of the more general crisis of the historical semi-periphery (see Figure 2.3).

In any case, in the twenty-first century, the fundamental question for humanity is no longer about how to compete successfully within the capitalist world system, but about how to replace capitalism with a fundamentally different, new social system and rebuild global ecological sustainability.

In this context, capitalism has ceased to be a viable historical option. The real question for humanity in the twenty-first century is not whether there is any alternative to capitalism, but whether there is any alternative to socialism if human civilization were to survive beyond the twenty-first century.

Bibliography

Aleklett, Kjell (with Michael Lardelli). 2012. *Peeking at Peak Oil*. New York: Springer.

Anderson, Kevin and Alice Bows. 2011. "Beyond Dangerous Climate Change: Emission Scenarios for a New World," *Philosophical Transactions of the Royal Society* 369(1934): 20–44. http://rsta.royalsocietypublishing.org/content/369/1934/20.full.

APIC. Arab Petroleum Investment Corporation. 2012. "Economic Commentary," *APICORP Research* 7(8–9), August–September. www.apic.com/Research/Commentaries/Commentary_V7_N8-9_2012.pdf.

Arrighi, Giovanni, Po-keung Hui, Ho-fung Hung, and Mark Selden. 2003. "Historical Capitalism, East and West," in Giovanni Arrighi, Takeshi Hamashita, and Mark Selden (eds.), *The Resurgence of East Asia: 500, 150 and 50 Year Perspectives*, pp. 259–333. London and New York: Routledge.

Baidu Online Encyclopedia. 2011. "Xinshengdai Nongmingong (The New Generation Migrant Workers)." http://baike.baidu.com/view/2967908.htm.

Baker, Dean, Gerald Epstein, and Robert Pollin. 1998. "Introduction," in Dean Baker, Gerald Epstein, and Robert Pollin (eds.), *Globalization and Progressive Economic Policy*, pp. 1–35. Cambridge: Cambridge University Press.

Ban, Zoltan. 2012. "The Controversy over Peak Oil, Oil Prices, and Technological Advances," *Sustainable Economics*, May 21. http://zoltansustainableecon.blogspot.com/2012/05/controversy-over-peak-oil-oil-prices.html.

Barnosky, Anthony D., Elizabeth A. Hadly, Jordi Bascompte, Eric L. Berlow, James H. Brown, Mikael Fortelius, Wayne M. Getz, John Harte, Alan Hastings, Pablo A. Marquet, Neo D. Martinez, Arne Mooers, Peter Roopnarine, Geerat Vermeij, John W. Williams, Rosemary Gillespie, Justin Kitzes, Charles Marshall, Nicholas Matzke, David P. Mindell, Eloy Revilla, and Adam B. Smith. 2012. "Approaching a State Shift in Earth's Biosphere," *Nature* 486: 52–58. www.nature.com/nature/journal/v486/n7401/full/nature11018.html.

Baski, Soham and Chris Green. 2007. "Calculating Economy-Wide Energy Intensity Decline Rate: The Role of Sectoral Output and Energy Shares," *Energy Policy* 35: 6457–6466.

BCG and Swiss Re. Boston Consulting Group and Swiss Reinsurance Company. 2012. *From Silver to Gold: How Insurers Can Capitalize on Aging in China*,

April. www.bcg.com.cn/en/files/publications/reports_pdf/From_Silver_to_Gold_ Apr_2012_ENG_FINAL.pdf.

BEA. Bureau of Economic Analysis, the US Department of Commerce. 2013a. "GDP and the National Income and Product Account." www.bea.gov/iTable/ index_nipa.cfm.

BEA. 2013b. "Fixed Assets Tables." www.bea.gov/iTable/index_FA.cfm.

BGR. Federal Institute for Geosciences and Natural Resources, Germany. 2012. *Reserves, Resources and Availability of Energy Resources 2011*, Hannover, February. www.bgr.bund.de/EN/Themen/Energie/Produkte/annual_report_2011- summary_en.html.

Biello, David. 2011. "Using CO2 to Make Fuel: A Long Shot for Green Energy," *Yale Environment 360*, May 19. http://e360.yale.edu/feature/using_co2_to_ make_fuel_a_long_shot_for_green_energy/2405/.

Boyle, Godfrey. 2004. *Renewable Energy: Power for a Sustainable Future.* Oxford: Oxford University Press.

BP. 2013. *Statistical Review of World Energy.* www.bp.com/statisticalreview.

Campbell, Matt. 2008. "The Drivers of the Levelized Cost of Electricity for Utility-Scale Photovoltaics," SunPower Corporation. http://us.sunpowercorp.com/ power-plant/.

CASS. Research Group of the Chinese Academy of Social Sciences. 2002. "Zhong-guo Muqian Shehui Jieceng Jiegou Yanjiu Baogao (A Report on China's Current Structure of Social Strata)," in Ru Xin, Lu Xueyi, and Li Peilin (eds.), *Shehui Lan-pishu 2002: Zhongguo Shehui Xingshi Fenxi yu Yuce* (Social Blue Book 2002: Analyses and Predictions of China's Social Conditions), pp. 115–132. Beijing: Shehui Kexue Wenxian Chubanshe (Social Sciences Literature Press).

Chan, John. 2010. "Honda Rocked by Further Strikes in China," *The World Social-ist Web Site*, June 10. www.wsws.org/articles/2010/jun2010/hond-j10.shtml.

Cheng, Xiaonong. 2000. "Shi Shui Daozhi le Sulian Jieti (What Led to the Dis-integration of the Soviet Union)," *Shuwu* 2000(12). www.housebook.com. cn/2k12/3.htm.

Chernova, Yuliya. 2012. "The Economics of Installing Solar: Figuring Out Whether You Save Money Depends on A Lot of Factors—Especially Where You Live," *The Wall Street Journal*, The Journal Report: Energy, p.R6, September 17.

China Data Online. 2013a. "Indices of Gross Domestic Product of China," in National Statistics: National Accounts, The China Data Center at the University of Michigan. http://chinadataonline.org/.

China Data Online. 2013b. "Output of Major Industrial Products," in National Sta-tistics: Industry, The China Data Center at the University of Michigan. http:// chinadataonline.org/.

Deng, Xingpu. 2002. "20 Shiji Sanshi Niandai Da Weiji yu Sulian Gongyehua (The Great Depression of the 1930s and the Soviet Industrialization)," *Lishi Jiaoxue* 2002(7). www.cnki.com.cn/Article/CJFDTotal-LISI200207017.htm.

Dittmar, Michael. 2009a. *The Future of Nuclear Energy: Facts and Fiction*, Part II, "What Is Known about Secondary Uranium Resources?" www.theoildrum. com/node/5677.

Dittmar, Michael. 2009b. *The Future of Nuclear Energy: Facts and Fiction*, Part IV, "Energy from Breeder Reactors and from Fusion?" www.theoildrum.com/node/5929.

Economy, Elizabeth C. 2007. "The Great Leap Backward?" *Foreign Affairs* 86(5): 38–59, September/October.

EIA. US Energy Information Administration. 2012a. "Solar Thermal Collector Shipments by Type, Price, and Trade, 1974–2009," September 27. www.eia.gov/totalenergy/data/annual/showtext.cfm?t=ptb1006.

EIA. 2012b. "Photovoltaic Cell and Module Shipments by Type, Price, and Trade, 1982–2010," September 27. www.eia.gov/totalenergy/data/annual/showtext.cfm?t=ptb1008.

EIA. 2013a. "International Energy Statistics." www.eia.gov/countries/data.cfm.

EIA. 2013b. "Short-Term Energy Outlook," June. www.eia.gov/forecasts/steo/query/.

EIA. 2013c. *Technically Recoverable Shale Oil and Shale Gas Resources: An Assessment of 137 Shale Formations in 41 Countries Outside the United States.* www.eia.gov/analysis/studies/worldshalegas/.

EIA. 2013d. *Annual Energy Outlook 2013*, April. www.eia.gov/forecasts/aeo/.

EIA. 2013e. "Updated Capital Cost Estimates for Utility Scale Electricity Generating Plants," April. www.eia.gov/forecasts/capitalcost/pdf/updated_capcost.pdf.

Embleton, Richard. 2008. "Methane Hydrates: What Are They Thinking?" December 5. http://oilbeseeingyou.blogspot.com/2008/12/methane-hydrates-what-are-they-thinking.html.

EPI. Earth Policy Institute. 2012a. "Global Carbon Dioxide Emissions from Fossil Fuel Burning, 1751–2009." www.earth-policy.org/data_center/C23.

EPI. 2012b. "World Grain Production, Area, and Yield, 1950–2012." www.earth-policy.org/data_center/C24.

EPI. 2012c. "US Corn Production and Use for Feedgrain, Fuel Ethanol, and Exports, 1980–2012." www.earth-policy.org/data_center/C24.

EPI. 2012d. "Global Carbon Dioxide Emissions from Fossil Fuel Burning by Fuel Type, 1900–2009." www.earth-policy.org/data_center/C23.

EPI. 2012e. "Atmospheric Carbon Dioxide Concentration, 1000–2011." www.earth-policy.org/data_center/C23.

ERP. 2013. "Bond Yields and Interest Rates, 1941–2012," *Economic Report of the President (2013)*, Table B-73. www.gpo.gov/fdsys/pkg/ERP-2013/pdf/ERP-2013-table73.pdf.

European Environment Agency. 2012. "Atmospheric Greenhouse Gas Concentrations (CSI 013)," Assessment published January 2012. www.eea.europa.eu/data-and-maps/indicators/atmospheric-greenhouse-gas-concentrations-2/assessment.

Gaines, Linda and Paul Nelsen. 2009. "Lithium-Ion Batteries: Possible Materials Issues," Center for Transportation Research, Argonne National Laboratory, June. www.transportation.anl.gov/pdfs/B/583.PDF.

Global Phosphorous Network. 2012. "Facts and Figures." http://globalpnetwork.net/facts-figures?cachebust56159703125=9003357963.

Green, Chris, Soham Baski, and Maryam Dilmaghani. 2007. "Challenges to a Climate Stabilization Energy Future," *Energy Policy* 35: 616–626.

Hamilton, James. 2012. "Maugeri on Peak Oil," July 18. www.econbrowser.com/ archives/2012/07/maugeri_on_peak.html.

Hansen, James. 2010. *Storms of My Grandchildren: The Truth about the Coming Climate Catastrophe and Our Last Chance to Save Humanity*. New York: Bloomsbury.

Hart-Landsberg, Martin. 2011. "The Chinese Reform Experience: A Critical Assessment," *Review of Radical Political Economics* 43(1): 56–76.

Heinberg, Richard. 2003. *The Party's Over: Oil, War and the Fate of Industrial Societies*. Gabriola Island, BC: New Society Publishers.

Heinberg, Richard. 2006. *The Oil Depletion Protocol: A Plan to Avert Oil Wars, Terrorism and Economic Collapse*. Gabriola Island, BC: New Society Publishers.

Heinberg, Richard. 2009. *Blackout: Coal, Climate, and the Last Energy Crisis*. Gabriola Island, BC: New Society Publishers.

Heinberg, Richard. 2011. *The End of Growth: Adapting to Our New Economic Reality*. Gabriola Island, BC: New Society Publishers.

Hirsch, Robert L., Roger H. Bezdek, and Robert M. Wending. 2009. *The Impending World Energy Mess: What It Is and What It Means to You*. Burlington, Ontario: Apogee Prime.

Hubbert, M. King. 1982. "Techniques of Prediction as Applied to the Production of Oil and Gas in Oil and Gas Supply Modeling," in Saul I. Gass (ed.), *National Bureau of Standards Special Publication 631*, pp. 16–141. Washington, DC: National Bureau of Standards.

Huesemann, Michael H. 2003. "The Limits of Technological Solutions to Sustainable Development," *Clean Technology and Environmental Policy* 5: 21–34.

Hunt, Emery Kay. 2002. *History of Economic Thought: A Critical Perspective*. New York: M.E. Sharpe.

IEA. International Energy Statistics. 2012a. *Key World Energy Statistics*. www.iea. org/publications/freepublications/publication/name,26707,en.html.

IEA. 2012b. *Golden Rules for a Golden Age of Gas: World Energy Outlook Special Report on Unconventional Gas*. www.worldenergyoutlook.org/media/ weowebsite/2012/goldenrules/WEO2012_GoldenRulesReport.pdf.

IMF. International Monetary Fund. 2013. "World Economic Outlook Update," July 9. www.imf.org/external/pubs/ft/weo/2013/update/02/.

IPCC. Intergovernmental Panel on Climate Change. 2007. *A Report of Working Group III of the Intergovernmental Panel on Climate Change*, Chapter 3 (Issues Related to Mitigation in the Long-Term Context). www.ipcc.ch/pdf/assessment-report/ar4/wg3/ar4-wg3-chapter3.pdf.

IPCC. 2011. *Renewable Energy Sources and Climate Change Mitigation: Special Report of the Intergovernmental Panel on Climate Change*, edited by Ottmar Edenhoffer, Ramon Pichs Madruga, and Youba Sokona et al., Technical Support Unit Working Group III, Potsdam Institute for Climate Impact Research. Cambridge: Cambridge University Press. http://srren.ipcc-wg3.de/report.

Jia, Genliang. 1989. "Shilun Sulian Dongou Qishi Niandai de Jinkou Daidong Zengzhang Zhanlue (A Preliminary Analysis of the Import-Led Growth Strategy of the Soviet Union and Eastern Europe in the 1970s)," *Sulian Dongou Wenti* 1989(1). http://euroasia.cass.cn/news/59644.htm.

Keynes, John Maynard. 1964[1953]. *The General Theory of Employment, Interest, and Money*. New York: A Harvest Book, Harcourt Brace & Company.

Korpela, Seppo A. 2005. "Prediction of World Peak Oil Production," in Andrew McKillop with Sheila Newman (eds.), *The Final Energy Crisis*, pp. 11–28. London: Pluto Press.

Kuntsler, James Howard. 2012. *Too Much Magic: Wishful Thinking, Technology, and the Fate of the Nation*. New York: Atlantic Monthly Press.

Laherrere, Jean. 2008. "Energy, Greenhouse Gases and Environment." Universidade Fernando Pessoa, Porto, Portugal, October 6–8. http://aspofrance.viabloga.com/files/JL_Porto_long_2008.pdf.

Leeuwen, Jan Williem Storm van. 2007. *Nuclear Power—The Energy Balance*, Part D, October. www.stormsmith.nl/reports.html.

Leeuwen, Jan Williem Storm van. 2012. *Nuclear Power, Energy Security, and CO2 Emissions*, May. www.stormsmith.nl/reports.html.

Lenin, Vladimir I. 1996[1916]. *Imperialism: the Highest Stage of Capitalism*. London: Pluto Press.

Li, Minqi. 2009a. *The Rise of China and the Demise of the Capitalist World Economy*. London: Pluto Press.

Li, Minqi. 2009b. "Socialization of Risks without Socialization of Investment: the Minsky Paradox and the Structural Contradiction of Big Government Capitalism," The Political Economy Research Institute of University of Massachusetts Amherst, Working Paper 205. www.peri.umass.edu/fileadmin/pdf/working_papers/working_papers_201-250/WP205.pdf.

Li, Yuanhua. 2009. "21 Shiji Chuqi Zhongguo Shui Ziyuan Gongxu Maodun yu Duice (The Dilemma of Supply and Demand for China's Water Resources in the Early 21st Century and the Policy Implications)," Paper presented at the Third World Water Forum. www.cws.net.cn/waterforum/news/3.pdf.

Lightfoot, H. Douglas and Christopher Green. 2001. "Energy Intensity Decline Implications for Stabilization of Atmospheric CO2," Centre for Climate and Global Change Research Report 2001–7, McGill University. http://people.mcgill.ca/files/christopher.green/energyintensitydecline.pdf.

Lightfoot, H. Douglas and Christopher Green. 2002. "An Assessment of IPCC Working Group III Findings of the Potential Contribution of Renewable Energies to Atmospheric Carbon Dioxide Stabilization," Centre for Climate and Global Change Research Report 2002–5, McGill University. http://people.mcgill.ca/files/christopher.green/Report2002-5.pdf.

Lovelock, James. 2007. *The Revenge of Gaia: Earth's Climate Crisis and the Fate of Humanity*. New York: Basic Books.

Luo, Tianhao. 2010. "Zhongguo Weilai Laoli Quekou Jiang Chao Yi Yi (China's Future Labor Force Shortage Will Exceed 100 Million)," *Shidai Zhoubao* (Times Weekly), April 1. http://finance.ifeng.com/opinion/special/laolinghua/zjgc/20100401/1996946.shtm.

Maddison, Angus. 2010. "Statistics on World Population, GDP, and Per Capita GDP, 1–2008 AD." www.ggdc.net/MADDISON/oriindex.htm.

Marx, Karl. 1967[1894]. *Capital*, Volume 3. New York: International Publisher.

Marx, Karl and Friedrich Engels. 1972. "Manifesto of the Communist Party," in

Robert C. Tucker (ed.), *The Marx-Engels Reader*, pp. 469–500. New York: W.W. Norton & Company.

Maugeri, Leonardo. 2012. *Oil: The Next Revolution, The Unprecedented Upsurge of Oil Production Capacity and What It Means for the World*, Geopolitics of Energy Project, Harvard University John F. Kennedy School of Government, Discussion Paper #2012 10. http://belfercenter.ksg.harvard.edu/files/Oil-%20 The%20Next%20Revolution.pdf.

Meadows, Donella H., Dennis L. Meadows, Jorgen Randers, and William W. Behrens III. 1972. *The Limits to Growth*. New York: Universe Books.

Minsky, Hyman P. 2008[1986]. *Stabilizing an Unstable Economy*. New York: McGraw-Hill.

Mórrígan, Tariel. 2010. *Peak Energy, Climate Change, and the Collapse of Global Civilization: The Current Peak Oil Crisis*. Global Climate Change, Human Security and Democracy, Orfalea Center for Global and International Studies, University of California, Santa Barbara, October. www.global.ucsb.edu/climate-project/papers/index.html.

Müller-Steinhagen, Hans. 2008. "Solar Thermal Power Plants—On the Way to Commercial Market Introduction," Institute for Technical Thermal Dynamics, German Aerospace Centre. http://solarthermalworld.org/content/solar-thermal-power-plants-way-commercial-market-introduction-2008.

NASA. The US National Aeronautics and Space Administration. 2013. "Global Land–Ocean Temperature Index in 0.01 Degrees Celsius." http://data.giss.nasa.gov/gistemp/tabledata_v3/GLB.Ts+dSST.txt.

National Bureau of Statistics of China. 1985. *Zhongguo Tongji Nianjian (Statistical Yearbook of China)*. Beijing: Zhongguo Tongji Chubanshe (China Statistical Publisher).

National Bureau of Statistics of China. 2012 and various years. *Statistical Yearbook of China*. www.stats.gov.cn/tjsj/ndsj/.

National Bureau of Statistics of China. 2013. "2012 Nian Queguo Nongmingong Jiance Diaocha Baogao (2012 Report on the National Survey of Migrant Workers)." www.stats.gov.cn/tjfx/jdfx/t20130527_402899251.htm.

NEA. Nuclear Energy Agency, OECD. 2006. *Forty Years of Uranium Resources, Production and Demand in Perspective: "The Red Book Retrospective."* Paris: OECD (Organization for Economic Co-operation and Development).

NEA. 2012. *Uranium 2011: Resources, Production and Demand* (a joint project by the OECD Nuclear Agency and the International Atomic Energy Agency). Paris: OECD (Organization for Economic Co-operation and Development).

NOAA. The US National Oceanic and Atmospheric Administration. 2013. "Trends in Atmospheric Carbon Dioxide." www.esrl.noaa.gov/gmd/ccgg/trends/.

OPEC. Organization of the Petroleum Exporting Countries. 1999. *Annual Statistical Bulletin 1999*. www.opec.org/opec_web/en/publications/202.htm.

OPEC. 2012a. *Annual Statistical Bulletin 2012*. www.opec.org/opec_web/en/publications/202.htm.

OPEC. 2012b. *Annual Statistical Bulletin 2012*, Interactive ASB 2012, "Oil and Gas Data." www.opec.org/library/Annual%20Statistical%20Bulletin/interactive/current/FileZ/Main.htm.

Pollin, Robert and Gary Dymski. 1994. "The Costs and Benefits of Financial Instability: Big Government Capitalism and the Minsky Paradox," in Gary Dymski and Robert Pollin (eds.), *New Perspectives in Monetary Macroeconomics: Explorations in the Tradition of Hyman P. Minsky*, pp. 369–401. Ann Arbor: University of Michigan Press.

Rodionov, Kirill. 2012. "Russia May Share the Fate of the USSR," *EconoMonitor*, August 29. www.economonitor.com/blog/2012/08/russia-may-share-the-fate-of-the-ussr/.

Rutledge, David. 2007. "Hubbert's Peak, the Coal Question, and Climate Change," Excel Workbook. Originally posted at http://rutledge.caltech.edu.

Rutledge, David. 2011. "Estimating Long-Term World Coal Production with Logit and Probit Transforms," Excel Workbook. http://rutledge.caltech.edu.

Skrebowski, Chris. 2008. *The Oil Crunch: Securing the UK's Energy Future*, First Report of the UK Industry Task Force on Peak Oil and Energy Security. http://peakoil.solarcentury.com/wp-content/uploads/2008/10/oil-report-final.pdf.

Skrebowski, Chris. 2011. "A Brief Economic Explanation of Peak Oil," *Oil Depletion Analysis Centre Newsletter*, September 16. www.odac-info.org/newsletter/2011/09/16.

Smil, Vaclav. 2010a. *Energy Transitions: History, Requirements, Prospects*. Santa Barbara, California: Praeger.

Smil, Vaclav. 2010b. *Energy Myths and Realities*. Washington, DC: The AEI Press.

Spath, Pamela L. and Margaret K. Mann. 2000. *Life Cycle Assessment of A Natural Gas Combined-Cycle Power Generation System*. National Renewable Energy Laboratory, NREL/TP-570–27715. www.nrel.gov/docs/fy00osti/27715.pdf.

Spath, Pamela L., Margaret K. Mann, and Dawn R. Kerr. 1999. *Life Cycle Assessment of Coal-Fired Power Production*. National Renewable Energy Laboratory, NREL/TP-570–25119. http://efile.mpsc.state.mi.us/efile/docs/16077/0065.pdf.

Spratt, David, and Philip Sutton. 2008. *Climate Code Red: the Case for a Sustainability Emergency*. www.climatecodered.net.

Stavrianos, Leften Stavros. 1981. *Global Rift: The Third World Comes of Age*. New York: William Morrow and Company, Inc.

Trainer, Ted. 2007. *Renewable Energy Cannot Sustain A Consumer Society*. Dordrecht, Netherlands: Springer.

Trainer, Ted. 2011. "A Critique of the 2011 IPCC Report on Renewable Energy," August 2. http://socialsciences.arts.unsw.edu.au/tsw/IPCCREcrit.html.

Trainer, Ted. 2012. "The Limits to Solar Thermal Electricity," September 9. http://socialsciences.arts.unsw.edu.au/tsw/ST.htm.

Turner, Graham. 2008. "A Comparison of *The Limits to Growth* with Thirty Years of Reality," CSIRO Working Paper Series, June. www.csiro.au/files/files/plje.pdf.

USGS. US Geological Survey. 2000. *US Geological Survey World Petroleum Assessment 2000—Description and Results*, by USGS World Energy Assessment Team, US Geological Survey Digital Data Series DDS-60. http://pubs.usgs.gov/dds/dds-060/index.html#TOP.

USGS. 2012a. *Mineral Commodity Summaries 2012*. http://minerals.usgs.gov/minerals/pubs/mcs/.

USGS. 2012b. *Historical Statistics for Mineral and Material Commodities in the United States*. http://minerals.usgs.gov/ds/2005/140/.

Wallerstein, Immanuel. 1974. "The Rise and Future Demise of the World Capitalist System," *Comparative Studies in Society and History* 16(4): 387–415.

Wallerstein, Immanuel. 1979. *The Capitalist World-Economy: Essays by Immanuel Wallerstein*. Cambridge: Cambridge University Press.

Wang, Feng, 2011. "Jiaru Zhongguo Bu Tingzhi Jihua Shengyu, Jiu Mei Banfa Zouxiang Fuyu (China Will Not Achieve Prosperity unless It Abandons The One Child Policy)," *Guoji Xianqu Daobao* (*International Frontier Tribune*), January 4. http://finance.ifeng.com/news/special/laolinghua/20110104/3151835.shtml.

Wang, Junsheng, Lu Ruixian, and Xu Lei. 2010. "Xin Nengyuan: Quanqiu Weiji xia de Jiyu (Alternative Energies: Opportunities under the Global Crisis)," in Cui Minxuan (ed.), *Zhongguo Nengyuan Fazhan Baogao (2010)* (*China Energy Development Report 2010*), pp. 208–268. Beijing: Shehui Kexue Wenxian Chubanshe (Social Sciences Literature Press).

WEC. World Energy Council. 2010. *2010 Survey of Energy Resources*. London: World Energy Council (used by permission of World Energy Council, London, www.worldenergy.org).

Wen, Dale and Minqi Li. 2006. "China: Hyper-Development and Environmental Crisis," in Leo Panitch and Collin Leys (eds.), *Socialist Register 2007: Coming to Terms with Nature*, pp. 130–146. New York: Monthly Review Press.

Wikipedia. 2013. "Oil Megaprojects." http://en.wikipedia.org/wiki/Oil_megaprojects.

Wilburn, David R. 2011. "Wind Energy in the United States and Materials Required for the Land-Based Wind Turbine Industry from 2010 through 2030," US Geological Survey, Scientific Investigations Report 2011–5036. http://pubs.usgs.gov/sir/2011/5036/sir2011-5036.pdf.

WNA. World Nuclear Association. 2013a. "World Nuclear Power Reactors and Uranium Requirements." http://world-nuclear.org/info/reactors.html.

WNA. 2013b. "Uranium Production Figures, 2001–2011." www.world-nuclear.org/info/Facts-and-Figures/Uranium-production-figures/.

World Bank. 2013. *World Development Indicators*. http://databank.worldbank.org/data/views/variableSelection/selectvariables.aspx?source=world-development-indicators.

World Coal Association. 2012. "Uses of Coal: Coal and Steel." www.worldcoal.org/coal/uses-of-coal/coal-steel/.

WRG. 2030 Water Resources Group. 2009. *Charting Our Water Future: Economic Frameworks to Inform Decision-Making*. www.mckinsey.com/App_Media/Reports/Water/Charting_Our_Water_Future_Exec%20Summary_001.pdf.

WWF. World Wild Life Fund. 2010. *China Ecological Footprint Report 2010*. www.footprintnetwork.org/images/uploads/China_Ecological_Footprint_Report_2010.pdf.

WWF, ZSL, and GFN. World Wilde Life Fund, Zoological Society of London, and Global Footprint Network. 2012. *Living Planet Report 2012*. http://awsassets.panda.org/downloads/1_lpr_2012_online_full_size_single_pages_final_120516.pdf.

Ye, Liming, Jun Yang, Ann Verdoodt, Rachit Moussadek, and Eric Van Ransk. 2010. "China's Food Security Threatened by Soil Degradation and Biofuels Production," Paper presented at the 19th World Congress of Soil Science, "Soil Solutions for A Changing World," August 1–6, Brisbane, Australia. www.iuss. org/19th%20WCSS/Symposium/pdf/1237.pdf.

Zhao, Le and Gan Wenxiao. 2010. "Zhuazhu Lishi Jiyu—Woguo Shiyou Hangye Shixian Lishixing Zengzhang (Grasp the Historical Opportunity—Our Petroleum Industry Achieves Globalized Expansion)," in Cui Minxuan (ed.), *Zhongguo Nengyuan Fazhan Baogao (2010)* (*China Energy Development Report 2010*), pp. 72–121. Beijing: Shehui Kexue Wenxian Chubanshe (Social Sciences Literature Press).

Index

Page numbers in *italics* denote tables, those in **bold** denote figures.

Peak Oil, Climate Change, and the Limits to China's Economic Growth

Minqi Li

Routledge
Taylor & Francis Group

LONDON AND NEW YORK

First published 2014
by Routledge
2 Park Square, Milton Park, Abingdon, Oxfordshire OX14 4RN

and by Routledge
711 Third Avenue, New York, NY 10017, USA

First issued in paperback 2017

Routledge is an imprint of the Taylor & Francis Group, an informa business

© 2014 Minqi Li

British Library Cataloguing in Publication Data
A catalogue record for this book is available from the British
Library

Library of Congress Cataloging in Publication Data
Li, Minqi.
  Peak oil, climate change, and the limits to China's economic
growth/Minqi Li.
  pages cm
  1. Energy consumption–China. 2. Energy policy–China.
  3. Energy development–China. 4. Climatic changes–China.
  5. Petroleum reserves–China. 6. Economic development–
  Environmental aspects–China. I. Title.
  HD9502.C62L5245 2014
  333.8'2110951–dc23

                                                      2013031851

ISBN 13: 978-1-138-06596-3 (pbk)
ISBN 13: 978-0-415-63754-1 (hbk)

Typeset in Times New Roman
by Wearset Ltd, Boldon, Tyne and Wear

Contents

Figures